Very best wishes,

Harry Mead

A
PROSPECT OF THE
NORTH YORK MOORS

By

HARRY MEAD

With Photographs by Jill Mead

HUTTON PRESS
2000

Published by

The Hutton Press Ltd.,
130 Canada Drive, Cherry Burton,
Beverley, East Yorkshire HU17 7SB

Printed and bound by
The College Press
a division of the University of Hull

ISBN 1 902709 10 1

Moor sheep at Head House, Arnsgill, Snilesworth.

DEDICATION

For Helen, Stephen, and Jill,
trusting they will long enjoy
the Moors.

CONTENTS

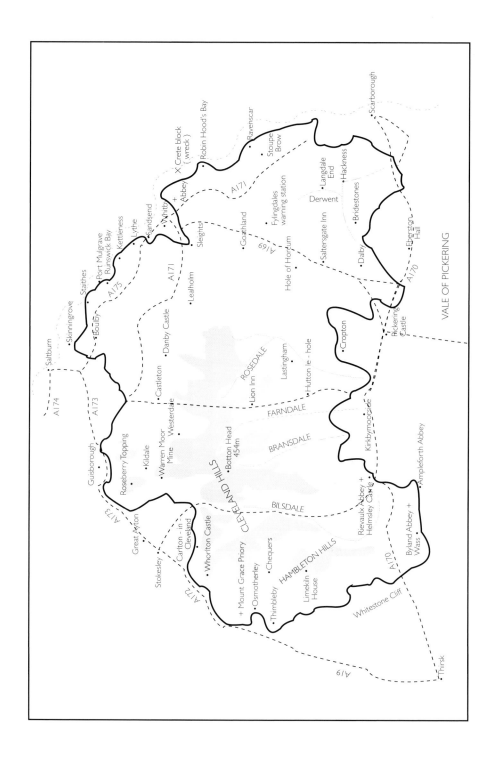

ACKNOWLEDGEMENTS

For permission to quote copyright material I am grateful to:

The Joseph Ford Trust, Some Reminiscences and Folk Lore of Danby Parish and District by Joseph Ford; Cassell publishers,Vol II of Sir Winston Churchill's History of the English Speaking Peoples; Mrs Mary Duck, Chronicles of Lealholm and Glaisdale by John Davison; A & C Black, publisher, and Prof J. C. Beaglehole, author, The Life of Capt James Cook; Penguin books, the North Riding volume of Nikolaus Pevsner's Buildings of England; Barry Harrison, author of an article on Whorlton in the 1978 Journal of the Teesside and Cleveland Local History Society; Robert Hale, publisher, Portrait of Yorkshire by Harry Scott; Mrs Jean Cowley, Cleveland Calendar and Snilesworth (Turker books), by her late husband Bill; Terry Fletcher, editor The Dalesman, for a quote from Bill Cowley's 1955 magazine article on the Lyke Wake Walk.

I regret that efforts to trace the copyright of a poem by the late Ronald C. Scriven, John Illingworth's Yorkshire's Ruined Castles , and drawings by the late Alec Wright proved unsuccessful.

I am also grateful to Dr Peter Phillips, of The Dower House, Cookham, for permission to reproduce the Laura Knight painting from his book The Staithes Group (Phillips and Sons). The photograph of Sydney Smith, and the example of his work, appear by kind permission of Pickering's Beck Isle Museum of Rural Life. My thanks also go to Whitby Literary and Philosophical Society for pictures relating to the Maharajah Duleep Singh, and Ryedale Folk Museum for permission to use a Raymond Hayes' photograph of The Lion Inn, kindly loaned by Fred Middleton, of Ainthorpe, son of the pictured landlord.

For the pictures of Bill Cowley, women wearing Staithes bonnets, and sheep in Swainby, I am indebted to, respectively, North News and Pictures, The Guardian (photographer Denis Thorpe), and the Evening Gazette, Middlesbrough.

Jim Muir, a stalwart of the Blackfaced Sheepbreeders' Association, patiently answered my questions on moorland sheep, and my thanks equally go to Wing Commander P. M. J. Angus, MBE, Commanding Officer of RAF Fylingdales, who allowed and arranged access to the Baker Stone within the boundary of the warning station.

7

My thanks to John Tindale, of Whitby, for material on Major Fairfax-Blakeborough, including a photo of him by John, are coupled with gratitude for his always-willing help over more than 30 years. Special thanks also go to Tom Burns, of Nunthorpe, for providing personal correspondence of A. J. Brown, which appears by very kind permission of A.J's family.

Early in her career, my photographer-daughter Jill gave perhaps greater priority than it deserved to taking pictures for 'Dad's book.' I trust readers will endorse my warmest appreciation*. Like me, they should also be especially grateful to my wife Shirley, whose encouragement during the drawn-out gestation of the book never flagged. Since she was the book's first reader, whose advice was almost always adopted, A Prospect of the North York Moors is truly as much hers as mine. Minus its mistakes of course.

*All contemporary photographs are by Jill Mead except the following by the author: Cropton's Nutholm Cottage, John Castillo's headstone, Whitestone Cliff, Wreckhills ironstone kiln, Chequers and its sign, Sandsend cement works, Commondale Shepherds' Stone, George Watson suicide stone and inscription, Bilsdale 'turve' stone, and Tyreman stone.

FOREWORD

Publication of my *Inside The North York Moors* marked the fulfilment of a long-held ambition to write a book about the wonderful part of Yorkshire I first grew to know and love through boyhood visits with my parents. I didn't anticipate writing a sequel. But the kind comments of readers, coupled with my regret at omissions from the book through lack of space, soon persuaded me to embark on this companion volume.

The outline was sketched within weeks of Inside appearing in 1978. But the demands of my work in daily journalism left little time for more than token progress. When the opportunity to retire early presented itself in 1992 I seized it with the chief aim of producing this book. I was strongly encouraged by my wife Shirley. Readers will judge whether my premature 'retirement' was worthwhile.

This book differs in emphasis from its predecessor. Although *Inside* contains several profiles of places and landmarks, such as Farndale, Roseberry Topping and the White Horse, many of its pieces scan widely, to illustrate topics like glaciation, the jet industry and moorland crosses.

Here, I modify that pattern. While some pieces again require a broad panorama, for instance to reveal a little-known network of foreshore tramways, and present a second look at the Moors' extraordinary heritage of engraved stones, most concentrate on particular features and personalities. Among these are several, such as Whitby's swing bridge, the Creteblock shipwreck, the Maharajah at Mulgrave and Lealholm's remarkable stonemason-poet John Castillo, that receive scant, if any, attention in most guidebooks.

Covering more well-worn ground, as in Staithes, on the Lyke Wake Walk, or at the region's abbeys, I hope my approach is fresh enough to justify the inclusion of the old favourites. With Whitby Abbey, for example, I explore the tyranny the abbey imposed on the town, stifling its growth as a port. And at Byland I highlight an extensive web of waterworks - an engineering feat arguably more fascinating than the floor tiling that usually takes the plaudits.

I also examine some contemporary matters, including the role of forestry and the complex task of maintaining the heather moors. And how much do even regular visitors know about the ubiquitous moorland sheep? How many years do the ewes spend on the moors? How often, and why, is the flock brought down each year? Who buys the wool and for what purpose? Ill-informed myself until I began writing this book, I have sought the answers.

But though the balance of the book is subtly different from Inside, I hope its overall variety is the same. A considerable bonus is the many pictures taken specially for the book by my daughter Jill, a professional photographer.

Added to the 55 pieces in Inside the 49 offered here make up more than a hundred cameos of the Moors. A region of extraordinary scenic diversity and wealth of history, its beauty can be appreciated for its own sake. But knowledge enriches enjoyment. This book by no means fills all the gaps left by its predecessor. And there is always more to discover. But if anyone's pleasure in visiting the Moors is enhanced through anything found in these pages, the book will serve its purpose.

The Old Bakehouse
Gt Broughton
October 2000

CHAPTER 1

A VIEW OF VILLAGES

Hutton-le-Hole

If one village had to serve for all in introducing a new visitor to the North York Moors, that flagship role would probably be filled by Hutton-le-Hole. Its hummocky sheep-cropped greens, cottages of sparkling limestone, and dancing beck spanned by neat, white-painted footbridges, combine into the perfect picture of a moorland village. It was not by chance that the founders of the North Yorkshire Moors Asssociation, a body of 'friends' of the national park and its immediate hinterland, selected Hutton for the association's inaugural meeting in 1984.

A visit to Hutton certainly brings little sense of descending into a 'hole'. The village is cradled by hills rather than entombed by them. In the Domesday Book it is recorded simply as Hoton - the 'ton', or town, near the 'howes', Bronze Age burial mounds up on Barmoor, to the north. In the thirteenth century it became Hoton under Heg . Of uncertain origin, the word *heg* could refer to one of the two north-facing hills, or nabs, at whose base Hutton rests. The winter shadow they cast over Hutton might explain how the name evolved into Hutton-in-the-Hole, which appeared in the seventeeth century. The fanciful le came with the Victorians - a bit of French polish similarly applied to Thornton- le -Dale and Appleton-le-Moors.

The open moor north of the Hutton rises steadily to the heart of the national park. As the Barmoor howes suggest, evidence of prehistoric settlement abounds. At Domesday, Hoton township supported eight peasant families.

But the village's main formative period was the seventeenth century when a ban on imported cloth led to Hutton, with its fast flowing beck and abundant supply of wool from the nearby moors, becoming a weaving centre. Most of today's cottages date from that period, before the Industrial Revolution took the weaving industry to the Pennines. The exceptional width of a staircase in Turnpool House, at the north end of Hutton, stems from the house's weaving days, when large bolts of cloth had to be carried from the upstairs weaving gallery. Run as a smallholding in the nineteenth century, Turnpool House again echoed to the clack of a handloom between the two world wars when it was occupied by a pair of craft weavers. Their 'fulling', or cleansing, of the cloth was achieved by treading on it in the village beck, which runs through the garden.

11

In Hutton's weaving heyday, the weavers and their families accounted for more than half the 200 or so population. They were mostly Quakers, of whom the best known was John Richardson. Away from his loom he travelled as a missionary, becoming famous in North America through riding 4,000 miles on a white horse. He preached to Indians and became a close friend of William Penn, founder of Pennsylvania.

Back home Richardson suffered some heartache. In 1733 his daughter Sarah, due to marry a Quaker from Stockton-on-Tees, eloped with a local lad. The pair were married in an Anglican church, a defection denounced by Hutton's Quakers as "unparalleled perfidy."

The Richardsons' former home, Quaker Cottage, is now a guesthouse on Hutton's east side. But the initials IR on its 1695 datestone are not those of a Richardson but a man named Robinson. He built the cottage as a traditional Viking-style longhouse - the last of its kind erected in Hutton - where the family and its animals were all accommodated under a single roof. John Richardson and his wife moved there after their marriage in 1705. In its 1930s incarnation as the Golden Teapot, a popular tearoom, it pioneered Hutton's tourist industry.

Adjoining Quaker Cottage, and also now a guesthouse, is Hammer and Hand House. Built of well-dressed sandstone, this sash-windowed Georgian building takes its curious name from a heraldic device on its exterior - a Phoenix and three hammers, with the motto By Hammer and Hand All Arts Do Stand. Put up by Emmanuel and Betty Strickland when they built the house in 1784, this is the crest of the Blacksmiths Company of London. While running Hammer and Hand as an alehouse, whose cellar trap door is still visible, the Stricklands also owned the forge next door.

Today the forge is the The Crown Inn, Hutton's only pub. Largely rebuilt in the 1940s it too once had some curious heraldry. In the 1970s, a local woodwork teacher donated a series of gilded wooden shields. Hung in the bar these celebrated imaginary local bodies such as the Hutton Polo Club, whose emblem was a mint, and motto Vincere Non Possum - Victory Is Not Possible. Many visitors took the shields seriously, and Crown regulars gleefully played up the joke. Sadly, the shields have disappeared.

Real history in plenty awaits the visitor in the neighbouring Ryedale Folk Museum. A major attraction of the Moors, the museum was founded in 1963 by local man Bert Frank, in a cottage bequeathed to him for the purpose by two sisters of his late friend Wilf Crosland. Happily Bert (1913-96), lived just long enough to see his creation named Britain's Museum of The Year in 1995.

A farmer-turned-travelling-shop driver, with a passion for local history, Bert opened the museum with his own collection of local 'bygones' and antiquities collected by Wilf. By the time he retired in 1979 the museum had expanded to occupy most of its present two-and-a-half acre (1.01ha) site. Attracting around 50,000 visitors a year it is the showcase for the social history of the Moors. Among a number of once-threatened vernacular buildings re-erected there are a thatched moorland cottage, a horse mill, and an Elizabethan manor house. The museum stages craft displays, and each September hosts the 'World Merrills Championship', in which locals (mainly) demonstrate their

Hutton history - the heraldic device of the former Hammer & Hand Inn.

Osmotherley: an inland Whitby? The roofscape in this Alec Wright drawing suggests so.

expertise in this ancient peg board game, a combination of draughts, chess and noughts and crosses. In 1995 the locals were stunned when a posse of Merrills' Grand Masters from Switzerland, where the game is taken as seriously as chess, arrived and literally swept the board. Despite desperate brushing up of their skills by the locals, the Swiss notched up their hat-trick of victories in the 1997 tournament.

Probably the museum's rarest treasure is a medieval glass furnace, the best preserved of its kind in Britain. Removed from Rosedale, where it was unearthed in 1966, this was originally built by French Hugenot glassmakers in about 1570. Producing green bottle-glass, it was one of at least two glass furnaces in the district, the other being on Yoadwath Bank, in nearby Douthwaite Dale. But the immigrant glassworkers seem to have remained a separate community. When the wife of one of them died in 1593 her full name was apparently unknown, for she was recorded in the parish register simply as 'wife of Amabie, the glassman.'

The registers suggest that the glassmakers left early in the seventeenth century, just as the weavers arrived. The brevity of their stay is attributed to a retired admiral who lived in Douthwaite Hall. Arguing that wood-fired furnaces, like those at Hutton, deprived the nation of timber for ships he successfully petitioned James I to ban wood for glass making. He is said to have had a financial stake in the alternative use of coal, from which he ultimately made a fortune.

If the Hugenot glassmakers made little impact on Hutton the same can't be said of the ironstone miners of nearby Rosedale. During that valley's ironstone Klondyke of the 1860s, Hutton became an overspill village. In 1870 its 500 lodging miners outnumbered locals by two to one. A favourite pastime was bare knuckle fighting, in which they were often challenged by Crown landlord Tom Proud - 'Boxing Tom' as he became known.

The miners' children swamped the village school. Built in 1845, just eleven years before mining began, it was too small by 1875, when it was replaced by a larger school. Tucked away by stepping stones across from the folk museum, the original school, a charming little Gothic building, has since served as a reading room, billiards' room, gift shop, and pottery. Today it is a cottage.

In 1939, thirteen years after the Rosedale mines closed, stone from the locomotive shed was used to build Hutton's village hall. A less tangible link with the mining era is a story of a Sinnington miller who retired to Hutton. Unable to sleep without the familiar sound of rushing water he engaged two miners to create a waterfall by dynamiting the beck. The explosion shattered windows in nearby homes, including the miller's.

Though the miller's waterfall silted up long ago, his home, on Hutton's west side, is still there. Now named Brookside, it began life in 1698 as the Quaker Meeting House. Converted to a house in 1849, its ground floor was originally stables for worshippers' horses.

Hutton's trim appearance owes much to its unpaid greenkeepers - the village's wandering moor sheep. In 1980 a complicated restructuring of local grazing rights, designed to prevent overgrazing of the moors, threatened the survival of the 'Hutton' flock, which was to be reduced from 400 to just sixteen.

As the flock was owned and tended by a woman, 69-year-old Miss Rose Farrow, the newspapers were soon full of stories about a real-life Bo-Peep losing her sheep. The crisis was averted by allowing grazing rights to pooled, with flockowners able to take up rights unexercised by other villagers. So Hutton's greens remained immaculate, thanks to a classic British compromise. (But see Maintaining the Moors, pages 194-5)

The village lies within the ancient manor of Spaunton, owned by the same family for the last two centuries. When the present lord of the manor, George Winn-Darley, inherited the 7,500-acre estate in 1986, he spent two days observing the traditional custom of walking its boundaries.

Local rights on the moors are administered by a Manor Court, or Court Leet, which sits at Manor Farm, Spaunton, each October. Like its counterpart at Danby it exercises its authority through twelve local jurors. At the court's annual sitting it imposes fines, in reality small annual fees, for permitted 'encroachments' on common land. In 1986, for example, the then maximum annual 'fine' of £1.99 was levied on the owners of Jasmine Cottage, Hutton-le-Hole, who had been allowed to create a vehicle access. A similar sum, since slightly increased, was paid by Ryedale Museum for its trestle sign on the green.

In Victorian days geese, hens, ducks, horses and donkeys foraged on the green. With the beck serving as an open sewer (the location of that pretty 1845 school was determined by the discharge of its five-seater latrine into the beck) the village had no pretensions to 'beauty'. Up to the Second World War gipsies camped on the now inviolate greens.

But by then the world was discovering Hutton and its charms. In his 1931 book *Puppets in Yorkshire*, the travelling showman Walter Wilkinson hails a view of the village in terms most people would endorse today:

> To round the crest of the hill was to look down suddenly on the roofs
> of the village, to see the cottages scattered oddly about the
> green...Obviously Hutton was not a real earthly village but a dream-
> come-true sort of place, a rural Utopia suspended between heaven and
> earth, remote from time and all the blasted vulgarity of modern life.

Hutton fiercely defends that 'Utopia'. In 1967 a county council scheme for culverting the watersplashes at each end of the village raised fears of a juggernaut route being thrust through the village. But the scheme, which included protective kerbing of the greens and bankside retaining walls, all in sandstone, proved a model of restraint and sensitivity.

In 1977 a further row erupted over yellow no-parking lines. Hutton was granted a special dispensation, the first in Yorkshire, for the lines to be painted at only half the standard width and in a muted colour.

But Hutton's social character had changed completely. By the late 1960s one in six of its 74 dwellings was a holiday cottage or second home, and only 13 children lived in the village. Built for 100 pupils, the 1875 school was educating just ten scholars when it closed in 1972. Today it is the Merrills Gift Shop. The Methodist chapel folded in 1967, and the loss soon after of the village shop and post office was only partially remedied by the opening in November 1999 of a post office on two half days a week in the Barn Hotel. Meanwhile the former garage and filling station had switched to selling garden furniture. In 1982 a resident wrote to the Malton Gazette and Herald : 'The weekly grocery van stopped a year ago, the butcher now comes once a week instead of twice, milk is delivered only three times a week...We are still fortunate to have a daily paper delivered.'

Only about six Hutton homes are now occupied by people born in the village. Most of the 150 or so residents, who include an ever increasing proportion of incomers, insist that social life is vigorous. But public transport is minimal, and tourist pressures, acute on Bank Holidays and peak summer Sundays, have brought complaints about visitors staring into windows. In 1987 the national park authority felt impelled to introduce a plan restricting commercial development to the core of the village.

In 1918 Hutton's schoolmaster, J. M. Curtis, composed a song whose chorus goes:

> *Then Hurrah hurrah for Hutton-le-Hole,*
> *Which we love with all our heart and soul.*
> *Set like a gem in a casket of hills,*
> *With the moorlands far stretching above,*
> *Moorlands with bracken, and heather and rills,*
> *'Tis the village we all of us love.*

Though those sentiments still hold true, it's clear that even a 'dream-come-true sort of place' is not without problems.

Osmotherley

In the 1909 edition of his charming book Rambles in Cleveland, Stockton printer Michael Heavisides declared:

> To the jaded and overtaxed businessman, the hardworking artisan, the fatigued housewife, and children run down with scholastic duties - if you desire to recuperate your powers, I know of no better place than the quiet and old world village of Osmotherley.

Some 60 years later, that view was enthusiastically echoed by Alec Wright, the noted Cleveland artist and historian:

> Of all the villages adjacent to the Tees, Osmotherley has long been the favourite. Particularly because of its nearness to Stockton it has been esteemed by the South Durham businessman, who planned his retirement to the green pasture of his dreams.

Since then, the upgrading of the nearby A19 to virtual motorway standard has brought Osmotherley within reach of many more get-away-from-it-all homeseekers. Some of the results are unfortunate. The first buildings to greet walkers entering Osmotherley on the Cleveland Way are large modern suburban homes. More of the same line the Cleveland Way's exit from the village up Rueberry Lane. How did the national park planners come to approve these unsympathetic intrusions?

Happily, Osmotherley's centre retains the sturdy moorland character that draws both visitors and commuters. Clustered around a sloping junction are three pubs, several shops, including a Post Office and a chip shop, and terrace cottages with partly-cobbled frontages. The atmosphere is more of a small market town than a village. So it is no surprise to learn that 'Ossy', as the village is known locally, once had a weekly market, and annual fairs for sheep and cattle.

From a couple of vantage points, Ossy's huddle of red-roofs, overtopped by the square tower of St Peter's church, is reminiscent of Whitby. But though the sea is far away, the moors are much closer. The village is hoisted on a shared shoulder of the Cleveland Hills and Hambleton Hills, which meet at this point. With the Clevelands striding away eastwards, and the Hambletons swinging south, this strategic position helps explain Osmotherley's former commercial importance.

The name stems from a Norseman, Asmund, who made and settled in a *leah,* or clearing. But legend has it that an infant Saxon prince, Oswy, was buried there after being tragically drowned. His grieving mother soon followed him into his grave. Hence: Os-by-his-mother-lay! A likely tale.

The village has been an extraordinary focus of religious fervour. Tireman Close, a byway off West End, is named after an early Osmotherley Quaker, Cuthbert Tireman. In 1671 his possessions were confiscated as punishment for allowing his house to be used for a Quaker meeting. Ten years earlier, James Dunning, another local Quaker, died in York gaol, where he had been imprisoned for refusing to pay tithes to the parish church.

In 1723 successors of these pioneers built a meeting house, which still stands in Tireman Close. Overlooking a small Quaker burial ground, it is used for worship about once a month. Part is rented to deserving groups for weekend breaks or holidays.

The Methodist founder John Wesley visited Osmotherley sixteen times. Up the flagged and cobbled passageway that brings the Cleveland Way into the heart of Osmotherley is the terrace-cottage-like chapel built by Wesley's followers in 1754. Inside is the stool on which Wesley, a small man, stood when preaching in the chapel. In 1864 the Methodists moved to a larger chapel in the main street, but in 1977 they returned to their original home, since when the 1864 chapel has become a house.

Oddly, Wesley's first address in Osmotherley, in 1745, was delivered on Roman Catholic ground - the home of an expelled Franciscan priest. Having married his housekeeper eight years earlier, the priest defied the church's attempts to evict him and his wife, who were still living in the three-storey Old Hall when Wesley arrived.

Just up the street from the Methodist chapel, the hall had been bought for the Franciscans by a Lancashire benefactor in 1650. A chapel added later remains the local Roman Catholic place of worship today. Like the Old Hall itself, it has undergone many changes, but its exposed roof timbers are original. Wesley was invited to the Old Hall by the ex-priest, who remained there until three years before his death in 1777. It is thought that strong local sympathy for the former friar and his wife helped Wesley gain his large following in Osmotherley.

A short distance out of the village, on a grass terrace beyond the head of Rueberry Lane, stands a Roman Catholic shrine of national importance - the Lady Chapel. Licensed for Mass in 1397 it pre-dates nearby Mount Grace Priory, founded a year later. The chapel almost certainly existed even before it was formally licensed. Indeed, its presence might have been a factor in the founding of Mount Grace, whose original endowment included the chapel. The monks might have worshipped there while the priory was being built.

Afterwards, it became a monk's hermitage or retreat. The last monk to live there, Thomas Parkinson, of Thirsk, occupied it through a grant of money from Catherine of Aragon, first wife of Henry VIII. She is honoured in Osmotherley with the Queen Catherine Inn, believed to be the only one of that name in Britain.

Anticipating Henry's suppression of the abbeys, a shrewd Mount Grace prior leased the Lady Chapel to a lay landowner. This not only saved it from destruction but turned it into a place of pilgrimage. Though it decayed to a roofless shell, it attracted so many pilgrims that in 1614 the Archbishop of York ordered an inquiry 'to sift out the cause and purpose of their going there.' In a swoop on the chapel, seventeen people at prayer were arrested.

But the faithful kept coming and in 1642 a nun noted 'Catholics praying hours together' in the chapel. Soon afterwards, Sir Thomas Gascoigne, founder of the Bar Convent in York, offered an endowment to found a nunnery at the chapel, which he described as 'a place of devotion, much frequented.' The authorities viewed this as part of a Cromwellian plot to kill Charles I. Though Sir Thomas extricated himself, two of his associates, a nephew and a nuns' chaplain, went to the gallows.

In 1942 the then scanty remains of the chapel were bought by the Middlesbrough Roman Catholic Diocese. Unearthing many of the original stones, some marked with crosses by pilgrims, they rebuilt the chapel, which was rededicated in 1960 by the Archbishop of Westminster. Mass and Evening Prayer are celebrated there each Saturday afternoon, and on a Sunday in mid-August a procession from Mount Grace to the chapel marks the Feast of Assumption - Mary's ascent to heaven.

The crown of a recast bell from Mount Grace stands in Osmotherley's parish church. Successor to an Anglo-Saxon church on the same site, the present building dates largely from the 15th century, though its main doorway is Norman its interior largely Victorian. As in many churches, pews have recently been removed from a side aisle to create space for social occasions. A kitchen is concealed behind the organ chamber. Apart from making fuller use of the church, these changes have an advantage explained to me on one visit by a church helper: 'We save the hire charge on the village hall.'

A touching memorial tablet is to a vicar and four of his children, all of whom died of a fever between 2 March and 10 March, 1840. Scoured into the walls of the porch are deep grooves. Not the result of arrow sharpening, as is sometimes supposed, these were made by weavers sharpening their shuttles.

Centred on two mills powered by the local Cod Beck, whose name, incidentally stems from the Celtic word *coed*, meaning woody, weaving was an even bigger industry here than at Hutton-le-Hole. In the mid nineteenth century, 300 people worked at Cote Ghyll Mill, now the Youth Hostel, weaving imported flax into webbing, sailcloth and canvas sheets. On 8 August, 1857, the mill dam burst. A workman raised the alarm just in time to enable his workmates to flee before water cascaded through the mill, sweeping away heavy machinery. The mill closed in 1915, and some Osmotherley folk remember it as a cinema and dance hall, before it became the 80-bed youth hostel in 1980.

The village's other mill, the Walk Mill, off the Thimbleby road, operated as a bleach mill. On its 60-acre bleaching ground, linen from Cote Ghyll and other mills was stretched out for between four and five weeks. Much of it was made up into garments at a large mill at Brompton, near Northallerton. In 1759, the badly-treated workers there staged a strike, perhaps the first labour revolt, preceding the Tolpuddle Martyrs by 75 years. The trouble spread to Osmotherley, whose bleachmill-master was kidnapped at the ford on the Thimbleby road and briefly held captive in the moors. The Walk Mill closed in 1940, when it was turned into a house.

Just down the bank from Osmotherley, beyond parkland of Thimbleby Hall, is 'Ossy' 's sister settlement, the hamlet of Thimbleby. Consisting of a handful of unspoilt cottages and a couple of farmhouses it is a particularly timeless place. Shared with Osmotherley and classically located by the gates to the hall, its cricket field has a large oak tree within its boundary.

But Thimbleby's best-known feature is, or rather was, the Hanging Stone. Jutting from the hillside, this large sandstone rock was once the object of a popular short walk from Osmotherley. But forests have enclosed it, and few now follow the thin track to the stone, off the path to Over Silton. Even fewer mount the stone, following in the footsteps of the thousands who wore a foothold on the stone as they stepped across the narrow gap from the hillside. It seems a pity that the stone can't be opened to view once more, perhaps a co-operative venture between the parish council, Forest Enterprise and the national park.

Meanwhile there is yet more to discover back in Osmotherley. Engraved on a cottage in South End, with the date 1821 and initials ET, the outline of a clog identifies the former premises of one of several clogmakers, who kept the millworkers stoutly shod. Many no doubt shopped at Thompson's general store which, as letters painted on an internal beam reveal, was Established 1786 . The shop has been in the Thompson family ever since, and the present incumbent, Miss Grace Thompson, presides over a veritable Edwardian time-capsule. Articles are stacked on the floor and counter, and even Miss Thompson isn't too sure what fills the range of tiny drawers along the back wall.

Clamped to the shop's front wall is a fragment of the shaft of Osmotherley's medieval market cross. This was saved from destruction by

An Osmotherly institution - Thompson's shop has been in the family since 1786.

But long gone is the clog-maker denoted by this sign.

Grace's grandfather when a new cross was erected in 1874. Standing at the crossroads, this shares a little cobbled island with a chunky stone table on stumpy stone legs. Known as the 'barter table' this was a permanent market stall from which dairy produce, chiefly butter and cheese, was sold. Surviving when the market folded in 1823, it last served something like its original purpose when a travelling fishmonger used it before the First World War. John Wesley is also believed to have preached from the table before the Methodist chapel was built.

Call of nature or not, no visit to Osmotherley is complete without popping into the public toilets. Lovingly cared for by local housewife Ann Cation since they opened in 1965, these boast cut flowers, carpets, climbing plants and fragrant soap, all tokens of absolute cleanliness. Re-emerging ladies have been seen grabbing their male partners and escorting them in with the words: 'You've got to see this.' But the Gents is just as spotless and welcoming. On my last visit, the appreciative notes always pinned up included one that read: 'Scotland has nothing like this.' Another declared: 'What a memory to take back to Australia.' A third urged: 'Come to Arizona and show us what clean is.' And a Canadian visitor, an official in the Toronto Department of Buildings and Inspections, had left his business card, on which he had written: 'Passed Inspection.' There are many worse ways of earning international fame.

Goathland

Goathland's two bus shelters are gated against the village's wandering sheep. What better symbol could there be of a traditional moorland village?

But wait. Goathland isn't a 'traditional moorland village.' Until the late nineteenth century it was scarcely a village at all, merely a few cottages by the church. When the Whitby-Pickering Railway arrived in 1836 Goathland didn't merit a station, simply a halt named Bank Top. Even when the present station opened in 1865 it was initially named Goathland Mill - a mile or so from the church.

But the alighting passengers liked what they found - a green sheep-cropped oasis in heather moor, girdled by delightful little dales, with glowing woods and enchanting waterfalls. The invigorating air completed the Victorian ideal of moorland, which here could be enjoyed without too much exertion.

Along the broad common between mill and church hotels sprang up to cater for the new visitors. Large villas filled the gaps, and Goathland soon assumed the appearance of a miniature inland spa. Beneath a very recent veneer of day-tripping, that remains its essential character.

And yet Goathland's roots go deep. As Godeland it is noted in a charter issued by Henry I in 1117. Though it is most probably derived from a Norse settler, the name could literally mean 'God's land.' For Henry's charter conferred Royal approval on an existing small community of monks. Some historians believe its purpose was to save or protect the monks from eviction. In return for the king's blessing they were required to 'lodge and entertain the poor' and pray for the soul of Henry's mother, Queen Matilda, wife of William the Conqueror.

The monks' cell was probably near the present Abbot's House farmhouse, which overlooks Eller Beck about a mile east of the church. A later charter from Henry granted the monks the land on which the church itself stands. There they erected a thatched chapel, soon adopted by Whitby Abbey.

On the abbey's suppression in 1539 the chapel survived as Goathland's parish church. It fulfilled this role for almost 300 years, until it was demolished in 1821. But its successor, built only a generation or so before Goathland's railway-induced expansion, lasted only 75 years. During its replacement by the present church in 1896 a thick stone slab was found in the churchyard. Roughly engraved with five crosses, the traditional symbols of the wounds of Christ, this was almost certainly the altar of the monastic chapel, and it might even have been in the original cell. Given a place of honour near the altar of the new church, where it still stands, the slab had probably been cast aside in 1570, when churches were ordered to replace altars with moveable communion tables.

With its broad, squat tower, the present church is a fine example of the work of the noted York architect Walter Brierley (1861-1926). Celebrated as the 'Lutyens of the North,' he followed the Arts and Crafts tradition, engaging the best local craftsmen to work with good quality vernacular materials - here sandstone and oak. Like most of Brierley's buildings, Goathland church sits comfortably in its surroundings.

Much of its oak furnishing is by Kilburn's Robert Thompson, whose famous mouse trademark adorns the altar, vestry doorway and about ten other pieces. But the lovely little pulpit isn't Thompson's. Together with the elegant brass chandelier it was saved from the 1821 chapel, which stood about 25 yards south-west of the present church.

Commemorated by a tablet in the church is William Smith (1822-1914). A founder of the Blackfaced Sheepbreeders' Association, Smith was seldom seen without his sheepdog. During church services it lay patiently under its master's pew. Smith's home, Hunt House, Wheeldale, has been a sheep farm since at least 1301, when a 'Thomas de Hontehouse' paid grazing rent to the Duchy of Lancaster, which still owns much land in the district.

Perhaps Smith and his dog were among the worshippers one Sunday early this century when a violent thunderstorm erupted. The parish clerk called to a member of the congregation: 'Ah saay, John, wilt tha cum an' clerk a bit whahl ah gan an' git t'meer an' fooal in.'

Another church story centres on the local practice of 'crying' - announcing details of strayed animals during morning service. It is said that a farmer who had lost a cow dozed off during the sermon but awoke when the marriage banns were being read. Assuming his cow was being 'cried' he called out: 'She's brown and white, wi' spots on her belly.'

Shaded by the churchyard yews, a table-top tomb bears the inscribed terms of a bequest. This bound the eldest son of John Cockerill, who died in 1715, to give 10s (50p) worth of bread to the Goathland poor each Christmas. Elsewhere, an elaborately-carved headstone tells how the vicar, George McLane, 'went his rounds in the bitter winter of 1963, dying on parochial duty on 4th March that year.' During the Second World War, the 6ft 2in tall McLane displayed more stamina than any other member of the local Home Guard in manoeuvres among the heather. How sad that he collapsed and died, aged 60, in a blizzard near Goathland station.

Opposite the church, the ivy-clad Mallyan Spout Hotel, another comfortable-looking Brierley building, is the crowning feature of Goathland's Victorian growth. Built as a hotel in 1893, it took over the licence of the Cross Pipes Inn, now the private house at the junction by the church.

In the 1920s, the Mallyan's owner, Mr Pullman, dammed up Moss Slack, a glacial overflow channel, to create a skating pond for his guests. Now called The Tarn, this lies a short way up the moorland track rising from a pinfold near Cross Pipes House. Apparent prehistoric earthworks by this path are a good deal less ancient - the bunkers and greens of Goathland's former golf course. Another early tourist feature, five of its original six holes were within the village, and the course rules required golfers at the second, or 'Church', hole, to take special care not to hit the church clock. The more alarming danger to pedestrians and motorists led to the closure of the course in 1921. And although a new six-hole course was laid out on the adjoining Moss Rigg, in 1948 this too was abandoned. But in 1991 members of Whitby Golf Club, dressed in Victorian golfing outfits, marked the centenary of the Goathland course, the first in the district, by playing a brave, if erratic, round over the Moss Rigg links.

Still going strong are Goathland's Plough Stots. Described by the *Whitby Gazette* as long ago as 1891 as 'these funny and interesting people,' they claim to be Britain's oldest established longsword dancers. Apart from a brief break early this century the group has been performing since medieval times. A stot is a young bullock, formerly the main plough-drawing animal. This underscores the origin of the dances as fertility rites, handed down from the Vikings. The clash of swords was believed to drive away evil spirits.

Originally the Stots danced on Plough Monday, the first Monday after Twelfth Night, when ploughboys returned to the land. Their performance at various points in and around the village culminated in a mammoth village feast, with dancing on the green. In Victorian times they practised a kind of 'trick or treat'. Touring the village, they would sweep the paths of those who gave money to the church, but threaten to plough up the common in front of the homes of those who refused. Perhaps this explains why they folded around the turn of the century.

Re-formed in 1923, without the unpopular ploughing-up custom, the Stots today give their main village performance on the Saturday after Twelfth Night. At Morning Service the next day they carry a replica plough into the church sanctuary, for a Blessing of the Plough ceremony. Popular at folk festivals, the Stots can usually turn out three or four teams, each of eight dancers. Until the advent of the National Curriculum in 1993, longsword dancing was even taught at Goathland primary school. The Stots still offer tuition in their headquarters, the village's former Reading Room, which also houses a display of their costumes and memorabilia.

Another Goathland rarity is an independent fire brigade. Formed in 1964 on the initiative of Goathland Women's Institute, this came into being after a blaze in a carpenter's shop highlighted anxiety about the 20-minute journey to

Goathland for the firefighters from Whitby. Initially, Goathland's eight unpaid volunteers operated with a hand-cart that carried a few lengths of hose, two stirrup pumps and three buckets. Later, Bill Lightwing's grocery van doubled as fire tender, a role now taken by a converted Land Rover.

But despite these Will Hay overtones, the brigade is an efficient, well-trained unit. With moorland fires in particular, the 'holding' operation it is able to carry out until the main brigade arrives has proved invaluable, saving acres of precious heather. In recognition of its contribution, the county fire service announced plans in 1996 to bring the unit within the county network, with improved equipment and paid part-time firemen.

Strangely, Goathland's earliest social links were not with Whitby. The parish was an outpost of Pickering, where Goathland's dead were buried. The corpses were carried over Simon Howe and then probably along the old Roman Road at Wheeldale, which linked Malton with the coast. When snow blocked this route, burials took place on Chapel Green, the common near the church. Goathland didn't get its own burial ground until 1635.

Stone trods through the village identify other routes. The main one went down to Beck Hole and on to the former market village of Egton, where sections of the trod survive on the bank from Egton Bridge. The road to Whitby went from Goathland church to Abbot's House and then through Darnholme - very different from today's route via the railway station.

The railway itself originally reached Goathland via the mile-long Beck Hole Incline, now a popular path. The bypassing of the incline in 1865 was the catalyst for building the railway station.

Meanwhile other industries had come and gone. In the eighteenth century coal was worked near the now tranquil Darnholme, a green hollow with stepping stones, a couple of cottages and a lovely house. Packhorses transported the coal to the Pickering district, from which they returned with lime. Ironstone has also been worked. In medieval times it was dug from simple pits that are now depressions in the ground near the Tarn. In the fourteenth century ore was smelted in a furnace in Wheeldale Gill, now an exhibit in Whitby Museum. More spectacularly, in 1858 ironworks employing 180 men sprang up near the now delectable hamlet of Beck Hole. Brambles now obscure the scanty remains of the short-lived venture, which folded in 1864.

Seven years later, large-scale quarrying of roadstone was started on Sil Howe. Exploiting the easternmost outcrop of a volcanic dyke that crosses Britain to the Isle of Mull - incidentally creating Teesdale's High Force - this has left mounds of waste near the railway station. A crushing plant there was fed by a mile-and-a-half tramway from the mine, which closed in 1950. In 1979 a plan to open the vast underground caverns as a tourist attraction was turned down by the national park authority.

Goathland folk prefer the district's natural attractions. Notable among them are its waterfalls - nine within five miles of the village. All but one are known as a foss - e.g. Thomason Foss and Falling Foss. And the only exception, Mallyan Spout, was formerly Mallin Foss! Like the more common force, foss stems from the Scandinavian word for waterfall - *voss* .

Reached by a path alongside the Mallyan hotel, Mallyan Spout, the best known waterfall, is often a disappointing trickle. The most impressive view of it is from a few yards upstream. Those who venture further discover the most Lake District-like scenery in the North York Moors - a mile-long gorge with oak-clad crags overhanging a stream littered with huge tumbled boulders. From near its far end, at the Egton Bridge road, a track leads to Nelly Ayre Foss, a small but powerful waterfall, which has scoured deep potholes in the boulders.

Very similar is Thomason Foss, a short walk from Beck Hole. But my favourite in Goathland is Water Ark Foss. Seen to best advantage when nearby trees are bare or just coming into leaf, the fall is the centrepiece of a sunny little ampitheatre crossed by the Moors Railway. Fitted with a couple of seats, this is easily reached by a path off the road between Goathland and Beck Hole, to which the path continues. The simple walk can be completed by returning by either Darnholme, the railway incline, or West Beck. Typical of the rich walking possibilities of the district, this varied choice illustrates why the Victorians loved Goathland. The other Fosses, by the way, are Keld Scar, Mill Foss, Mill Scar, Walker Mill Foss and - most distant but most beautiful - Falling Foss at Littlebeck.

In recent years Goathland has become famous as the setting of ITV's Heartbeat drama series, about a 1960s village bobby. While the former Goathland Stores now trades as Aidensfield Stores, displays about Heartbeat are the biggest draw at the recently-opened Goathland Exhibition Centre, at Church Farm.

The half-million or so Heartbeat tourists have brought problems, notably traffic congestion and damage to the common and verges by careless parking. In 1996 a resident made the telling comment: 'People used to come here to get away from the hustle and bustle. Now it all comes here instead.' The hope must be that this will pass. Meanwhile, what unites those Goathland residents who welcome the Heartbeat visitors with others who resent them is the comment that the village must have been a backwater before television put it on the map.

As any Goathlander who hears this tartly points out, the village has always been popular. Of course. There wouldn't have been a Goathland for the makers of Heartbeat to discover if the Victorians hadn't found it a century earlier.

Lealholm

Of the string of attractive villages along the Esk Valley, Lealholm is the most instantly inviting. Set in a bend of the Esk, with a riverside green and pub, a broad anglers' pool overlooked by a handsome stone bridge, and an unusual wealth of specimen trees, it tempts many people out for a drive to stop and look around. Beyond cottages opposite the green, some soon find a set of stepping stones. These are the key to a simple ten-minute circuit of the village. It is extraordinary how much of interest awaits discovery on this short stroll. For richness of history, in a setting of intimacy and charm, Lealholm is hard to beat.

Hutton with its 'greenkeepers' - the local sheep. The foreground building is the original school.

A Goathland tragedy...the Sydney Porrit stone (See Stories in Stone - 2).

Perversely, the feature most often mentioned in guidebooks can't be visited or even seen. Out of sight a short way up river from the stepping stones, Crunkly Gill, a spectacular legacy of the Ice Age, lacks public access. But this was not always so. Early this century the gill, formed when the Esk, dammed by a glacier thrusting into Eskdale from the North Sea, carved a passage to the coast as the ice began to melt, was laid out as a natural rock garden and opened to the public. Behind the venture was the then owner of the Lealholm estate, Sir Francis Ley (pronounced Lee), a Nottingham lace manufacturer, and his wife Alison. Their brainchild brought thousands of people, by train and 'charabanc', to view what was hailed as a Wonder of the North: admission 4d ($1^1/_2$p), or 1s (5p) for four. Interspered with viewpoints, a network of zig-zag hand-railed paths led visitors through the almost mile-long gorge, where the boulder-strewn Esk surges between thickly-wooded cliffs up to 200ft (61m) high.

But on July 23, 1930, a huge flood swept away the Leys' ambitious handiwork, since when the gill has remained wild, secluded and secret.

The devastation caused by the flood supports a theory that the gill's earliest-recorded name - Crumbeclive in Domesday Book - meant Crumblecliff. But some say it means 'the coombe or gorge in the cliff'. Either way, in pre-Conquest days the gill, the district's strongest landscape feature, gave its name to a mid-Eskdale estate, or Manor.

At the Conquest, Crumbeclive Manor, together with adjoining land in upper Eskdale, was gifted by the Conqueror to Robert de Brus, who built a castle at what became Castleton. The original manor house of Crumbeclive was thus abandoned - and later disappeared. It probably stood at Wild Slack Farm, on the edge of the gill. Ancient mullions are embedded in the internal walls of the present farm, and in the 1870s fragments of architectural features, like part of a large stone newel post, were found in the farm's field walls.

Locally, 'Lealholm' is still pronounced 'Leelum'. That literally harks back to the Domesday Book, in which the village is recorded as ' Lelum' - old English for 'a place of twigs and branches'. But despite its antiquity it has never been a parish in its own right. For centuries attached to Danby, which was also part of Crumbeclive Manor, it has been linked to Glaisdale since 1741. This explains why its oldest place of worship is not the church but the Methodist Chapel.

Simple and dignified, with attractive Georgian windows, the chapel beckons directly beyond the stepping stones. Among its stonemason-builders in 1839 was Lealholm's own celebrity - John Castillo, the 'Bard of the Dales' (see Chapter 4). Unmistakable among the faces he carved at the corners of the roof is a young Queen Victoria, wearing a crown that recalls her coronation two years' earlier. An evangelical Methodist, Castillo no doubt preached in the chapel. From well after his time, however, are two engraved floodmarkers by the chapel door. The highest records the 1930 flood, when the river rose eighteen feet six inches (five-and-half metres) above normal.

The narrow lane beside the chapel was once a highway. Unable to use the village bridge, which was only wide enough for packhorses until 1755, carts crossed the river by one or other of two fords. The first was immediately upstream from the bridge, the second by the stepping stones. Either way, many of the carts were bound for Lealholm Mill, between the chapel and village centre. Recorded as far back as 1336 this was unusual in being powered directly by the small beck it straddles. For more than four centuries, the lack of a controllable mill race race caused the mill to stand idle during drought or flood. But an enterprising eighteenth-century miller, Tom Watson, overcame this major handicap by digging a half-mile mill race from the foot of Crunkly Gill to the mill. The bold task took him three years, during which he also rebuilt the mill. His silted up race can still be seen where it passes under the Danby road, at the foot of the hill beyond the chapel.

A private footgate at the same spot marks the former public entrance to Crunkly Gill. Close by, in a tiny roadside Quaker burial ground, stands a single gravestone. Inscribed TW, December 18, 1725, it is almost certainly that of miller Watson, who donated the land. In return, he was made an exception to then current Quaker practice of not erecting gravestones. What of the mill itself? Grinding its last corn in 1940, it subsequently became a community hall before being converted into a house in the 1970s. It too bears Esk floodmarkers - 1903, 1914, and 1930.

In 1763, a second mill was built to take advantage of Watson's mill race. Erected between the corn mill and the river, this produced wrapping paper, in a range of colours. Like the output of a similar mill at Ellerburn, near Thornton-le-Dale, most of the paper was shipped from Whitby to other parts of Britain. The mill closed in 1850 and during its demolition in 1935 a huge quantity of buttons was found. These had been stripped from the old clothes that were the mill's raw material.

A short cartway that loops behind houses opposite the old corn mill creates an interesting corner of Lealholm. In John Castillo's day the tall roadside building was the Bamford Inn, whose long-time landlady, Mrs Moon, is celebrated in one of his poems. He lived in a cottage at the back. Now part of the larger house called Poet's Cottage, it was at the opposite end from where a modern sculpted head of Castillo, installed by the present owner, Hilda Rees, about 20 years ago, juts from the wall.

Occupying the former paddock behind Castillo's cottage and an adjoining garden, the 'Poet's Cottage Shrub Nursery', started and run by Mrs Rees, is an unexpected - and deservedly popular - feature just off Lealholm's tiny yet bustling centre. A garage, Post Office, and well-stocked general store form the hub. Stone steps up the sheep-grazed bank facing the shop lead to the church, on a knoll above the village. More steps head for the nearby railway station. Within hailing distance of all these and each other are the pub and a primary school. Very few villages, especially those as small as Lealholm (pop about 250), still boast this full set of village parts, all in full working order. Long may they remain so.

Despite its ecclesiastic subservience to Danby and Glaisdale, Lealholm has been a distinct community for far longer than those neighbours. Not until the railway arrived in 1865 did villages emerge at Danby and Glaisdale, previously a scattering of farms. But Lealholm has been a focal point from its Crumbeclive days. In the striking words of a local man quoted by the late John Davison in his book The Chronicles of Lealholm and Glaisdale : 'Lealholm was the metropolis.'

In one small way the opening of the Esk Valley railway confirmed this. For eight years, until the Middlesbrough-Whitby coastal railway was completed, the fish catches from Staithes and Runswick Bay were despatched from Lealholm station.

On summer evenings, the thwack of bat on ball, drifting from Lealholm's cricket field, behind the mill, sometimes mingles with the resounding clang of iron on iron. No, it's not a blacksmith working late. A quoits' match is in progress. Puzzling to visitors at other times, the purpose of box-like covers on the green is now revealed: they protect the clay ends of the two quoits' pitches.

Like most other Eskdale villages, Lealholm competes in the long-established Danby and District Quoits League. And though quoits, a rarity until recently, has staged a comeback throughout the North-East, it still has no more picturesque setting than the villages of Eskdale, its traditional stronghold.

Played by the bridge, the games bring a chance to appreciate a particularly lovely image of Castillo's - 'the ancient bridge, where still the swallow comes and dips her wings.' Inquests on games - quoits and cricket - take place in the nearby Board Inn. Built as Lealholm Bridge House in 1742 this was a pub by 1759, when its occupant was described as an innkeeper.

For many years it was the venue for the annual meeting and dinner of the Society for the Prosecution of Felons at Lealholm. Formed by 40 farmers in 1822, this provided a central fund to meet the cost of prosecuting suspected criminals, mainly sheep stealers. The cost otherwise fell on the victim of the crime, with the result that many offenders went scot free.

Together with many counterparts throughout rural Britain, the Lealholm SPF dispels the myth of the Victorian countryside as a blissful Arcadia. Hordes of vagrants, poor people for whom society made no proper provision, wandered from parish to parish, begging and/or stealing to survive. The founding Deed of the Lealholm SPF notes the 'divers Burglaries, Housebreakings, Larcenies and Felonies that have been lately committed within the township and village.' And though the crime rate fell following the Poor Law of 1832, this was simply because vagrants and other poor people were swept into the workhouse.

In Lealholm, however, law and order at Lealholm took a downturn for a local reason. The building of the Esk Valley railway, closely followed by the opening of ironworks at Glaisdale in 1866, fuelled conflict between the immigrant workers and local country folk. Lealholm's constable, blacksmith William Readman, had his head pushed through a window of The Board three times.

Peace seems to have returned by 1894 when the annual meeting of Lealholm's 'Felons', as the members of the SPF are known, acknowledged that 'these advanced times of legislation have almost nullified the Society's once useful purpose, so that it is now beginning to look like an antiquated relic.' Yet it survives today - with a waiting list for membership, restricted to 45! No longer harrying criminals, the society is cherished as a link with history and contributor to community life. It still holds an annual dinner, whose centrepiece is a reading of the minutes of the AGM of a century earlier - an imaginative way of remembering the society's founding purpose.

Lealholm stepping stones - key to a simple walk round the village.

Not a fountain. Bearing the insignia of Lealholm benefactor Sir Francis Ley this handsome alcove housed a public water tap.

The dinner now takes place in the former meeting room of another Lealholm co-operative - the Loyal Order of Ancient Shepherds Friendly Society. Founded in 1860 the now defunct society invested contributions by shepherds to fund a small retirement pension. In colourful regalia and headed by a brass band members paraded proudly to an annual service in Lealholm church. A grandiose tablet still identifies the society's HQ, 'Shepherds' Hall', now a thriving restaurant and tearoom. It is one of few places that still serves a traditional Yorkshire ham-and-egg tea.

Assumed by most visitors to be obsolete drinking fountains, three handsome stone alcoves - near the chapel, the mill, and a on the common below the church - housed the taps of the village's first piped water supply. Another innovation of Sir Francis Ley, this was inaugurated in 1904 with bunting, a band, and - to quote the *Whitby Gazette* - 'a sumptuous luncheon'.

Sir Francis's elegant insignia adorns not only the water alcoves but a number of 'model' cottages. Lealholm owes much to Sir Francis and Lady Ley, the latter of whom planted the village's ornamental trees - beech, hornbeam, oak, maple, and a row of sycamores. The Leys also also gave the land for the church, where they are commemorated in stained glass.

Built in 1902, the church was a 'chapel of ease' - literally a church to ease pressure on the parish church, in this case Glaisdale. It is among a number of churches in the Moors designed by a notable church architect Temple Moore. Perfectly suiting it surroundings it demonstrates Temple Moore's gift for catching the *genius loci,* the spirit of place. How different, but equally appropriate, are the powerful churches he designed in Middlesbrough, and his sumptuous St Wilfred's, at Harrogate. His other moorland churches are Carlton, near Stokesley, its namesake near Helmsley, and East Moors, Bransdale.

In 1931 the church gained a Roman Catholic neighbour. Buried there is Major John Fairfax-Blakeborough, the legendary authority on moorland life and folklore.

On 27 April, 1979, Lealholm narrowly escaped major disaster. Engaged on a low-flying exercise from RAF Alconbury, Lincolnshire, a US Phantom jet bomber crashed on the northern hillside overlooking the village. Striking the ground west of the bank out of the village towards Whitby, it skidded for half a mile, crossing the road and destroying four stone walls before coming to rest in front of the far end of the row of houses known as Lealholmside. From the front window of his home, Crosby House, half way up the bank, retired postman Jack Perry saw the plane veer sharply away from the village at the last moment. Convinced that the pilot had saved the village, where 55 children were in the school, villagers set up a stone memorial to the plane's two US crewmen, both killed in the crash. This stands at the Lealholmside road end.

In September 1869, natural disaster struck when lightning set fire to a thatched cottage at Shaw End, on the Rosedale road. Though the unmarried couple living there, John Watson and Jane Agar, perished, their six-month-old old son, asleep under sacks in his outhouse-bedroom, survived. His rescuer, Robert Hicks, raised the infant as his own son, reportedly with happy results.

Until it closed in 1959, a sandstone quarry at Shaw End was among the last to be worked regularly in the North York Moors. Between 1906 and 1909 it supplied stone for Lord Dugdale's Crathorne Hall, near Yarm, one of the last stately homes built in Britain, now a hotel. Lealholm's cricket roller is also said to have been hewn in the quarry, from which it was rolled to the village, a steep downhill journey, with brakepower provided by villagers, including children, pulling on long ropes. Perhaps Lealholm is fortunate not to be famous for the great Cricket Roller Tragedy

Cropton

When Nicholas Cheeseman got married, he built a neat cottage for himself and his bride. Over its lintel he engraved his initials, the date 1695, and the legend: Memento Mori - Remember You Must Die.

What did Mrs Cheeseman think of this? With what probable foreboding, perhaps even alarm, did she cross the threshold of her new home on her wedding night? And what sort of man was her husband? Was he the grim puritan his inscription suggests, or a jester with a with a highly-developed, if ghoulish, sense of humour. Either way, owners of Cheeseman's cottage, in Cropton, near Pickering, keep faith with his sombre message by painting the stone doorframe of his cottage black.

Fortunately, this funereal touch doesn't dispel the generally cheerful air that pervades Cropton. An open, sunny village, it crowns a headland of the Tabular Hills, the tilted plateau that slopes up gently from the Vale of Pickering and then dips sharply to the main moors. Most of its cottages, including Cheeseman's, are set in long gardens that line the single, wide street. With little through traffic disturbing the tranquil atmosphere, Cropton is an agreeable place in which to wander on a fine summer's day.

The sleepy feeling has a long pedigree. Take Cropton castle. If a prize were to be awarded for the Yorkshire Castle with the Least Eventful History, Cropton would win it comfortably. Today no more than a twenty-foot-high (six-metre) mound, grazed by sheep and cows in a field down a short lane opposite Cheeseman's cottage, it has little to tell other than a record of changing ownership.

Most accounts say it was built by a French knight, Robert de Stuteville, on land given by William II in the late eleventh century. These sources say that when Robert was captured in a battle in France in 1106, Henry I reclaimed the castle for the Crown and promptly handed it to one of his favourites, Turgis Brundos. But local opinion is that Brundos built the castle.

No matter. By the end of the 12th century it was back with the Stutevilles. Henry II is thought to have rewarded William de Stuteville with it in gratitude for William's brave leadership of Royal troops against the Scots in the bloody Battle of the Standard, near Northallerton, in 1138.

A powerful dynasty, the Stutevilles were already established in a castle at Kirbymoorside, of which only the moat and fishpond survive today. At Cropton they installed a steward, who is believed to have lived in a hall within the castle's three-acre bailey or outer enclosure. A moat, still discernible, separated this from the keep-crowned castle mound.

In about 1290 the hall was replaced by a half-timbered house, east of the moat. A few grass-covered foundations of this house, abandoned in the fifteenth century, also survive.

The castle itself was a ruin by the mid fourteenth century, and only a much-later postscript enlivens this dull tale. In 1668 stone from the castle was used to build Beck House, a substantial farmhouse by the road to Lastingham. Then or shortly after an owner engraved on its wall an inscription even more bizarre than Cheeseman's: He who comes to steal plums, look above and see who comes. Beware. Accompanying this is a now very vague figure thought by some to symbolise God - or the Devil! This is perhaps the most intriguing inscription in the national park.

In the sixteenth and seventeenth centuries coal was mined in the now-afforested Spiers Wood, north of Cropton. There and in the neighbouring moorland area, so many coal pits once existed that the the Blacksmith's Arms, at Hartoft, Rosedale, was for a time named The Pick and Shovel. The coal fuelled local lime burning, which was a considerable industry. In a quarry off the road between Cropton and Wrelton is a bank of kilns that were in use until about 1950. Much earlier, packhorses carried lime to the northern part of the moors, and sections of one of their flagged routes survive near the foot of Cropton Bank.

Shading a small green at the bank top, where the village street branches off the busier Rosedale-Pickering road, is a huge horse-chestnut tree. Each Easter Monday and August Bank Holiday villagers set up tables there, from which they sell home-made produce in aid of the parish church. In the days before most homes had a phone, a red rag used to be tied to the nearby signpost to alert the local doctor, on his twice weekly round from Pickering, that a villager required a visit. The patient's name was left at a nearby house.

Up the street, another odd piece of medical history is recalled by a mullion-windowed cottage fronting a neat square of grass. In the eighteenth century it was a small private asylum. A public notice of 1762 trumpeted its success in treating 'the distempers due to melancholy and disturbed humours.' The proprietor, a Dr Stephenson, was said to be 'famous for these cures.' Perhaps he was, for W. Gordon Home, in his book Pickering: The Evolution of an English Town (1903) notes that Stephenson 'possessed the prescription for a very remarkable medicine which was supposed to have a most beneficial effect upon his partially demented patients.' The prescription for this cure was last heard of in the possession of a Lastingham resident in 1915. Is Lastingham exceptionally free of the 'distempers due to melancholy and disturbed humours'? If so, the credit probably belongs to Dr Stephenson.

Back in Cropton, its Old Manor House, also on the main street, is the successor to the half-timbered hall at the castle. Rebuilt in Victorian times, it is associated with the neighbouring Court House, where a now defunct manor court was held.

In common with other villages along the limestone escarpment, Cropton lacked running water. Resolved in some places, such as Carlton, near Helmsley, by an ingenious system of watercourses from the high moors, this was overcome at Cropton by sinking a well to the colossal depth of 216ft (66m). Water was drawn from it until 1899, when squire John Gill laid on a piped supply. In 1988 machinery from the well was restored and set up at the capped well head in the main street. Meanwhile, Squire Gill's system had been replaced by a mains supply. But a pair of fluted cast-iron columns that housed Gill's public taps still survive - one on the green, the other up the street.

Despite - or perhaps because of - the difficulty in obtaining water, Cropton folk were never loathe to share it. In medieval days a chalice of fresh water was always kept at Cropton Cross, the stump of which stands in the churchyard. Welcomed by travellers who had toiled up the steep escarpment after crossing the moors, this refreshment inspired a rhyme:

On Cropton Cross there is a cup
And in that cup there is a sup.
Take that cup and drink that sup,
And set that cup on Cropton Cross.

In the same lane that leads to the castle, the church is a somewhat austere affair. When it was built, in 1844, the custom by which worshippers could buy places in particular pews had not long been abandoned. I remember a faded board just inside the door which announced: *All the seats are for the free use of parishioners according to law.* But on my last visit this interesting relic seemed to have been removed.

A stained-glass window commemorates 16-year-old James Reckitt. A member of the family synonymous with Reckitt's Blue, that cube that helped whiten Britain's weekly wash, he died of pneumonia in 1925. The Reckitts came each summer from their main home at Hull to Keldy Castle, a battlemented shooting lodge built for them in 1870 on the moor north of Cropton. Eventually absorbed into Cropton Forest, whose first trees were planted in 1928, the domestic part of the castle was demolished by the Forestry Commission in 1950. But since 1975 its outbuildings have been the hub of a self-catering holiday complex, with 58 Swiss-style log cabins.

Though such tourist developments find an ideal home in the 11,375-acre (4.514ha) Cropton forest, the largest in the Moors, the presence of two other former shooting lodges in the same district - Sutherland Lodge, now an outdoor centre, and Elleron Lodge, still a private home on the edge of the forest - testifies to the quality of the heather moors surrendered to the forest.

But Cropton also shares in some of the finest deciduous woods in the national park. Clothing the steep valley of the river Seven, the woods that link Cropton and Sinnington are particularly attractive in late spring, when they are carpeted with anemones, violets, wood sorrel, primroses and the early purple orchid. Best begun at Sinnington, the walk through them, mostly on a terrace path above the glittering river, is among the most beautiful in the national park.

Vengeance is theirs. Villagers assemble to demolish the Lastingham cottage of Cropton murderer Robert Charter. A contemporary report notes that they 'set to work with a will.'

Hidden charm. Deep in woods, Cropton's Nutholm cottage was the unlikely birthplace of Whitby whaling skippers William Scoresby Senior and Junior.

35

Cropton's New Inn, where they brew superb beer, in a brewhouse open to the public, makes a perfect midway stop, before the walk is completed either via Appleton-le-Moors or on an alternative, higher-level path through the woods.

Among the New Inn's ales is Scoresby Stout. This honours Cropton's most famous sons, the whaling skippers William Scoresby Senior and Junior. Their birthplace, a single-storey whitewashed cottage called Nutholm, is passed on the walk between Cropton and Sinnington. Deep in the woods, with the river rippling at its rear and a meadow out front, the cottage seems an unlikely starting point for careers in whaling, with which the younger Scoresby combined distinguished scientific research. And it was in sad and poignant circumstances that it all began.

Bullied at school, where he was slow and backward, Scoresby Senior (1760-1829) was also treated cruelly when he started work on a local farm. So he decided to try a seafaring life. Carrying his infant son in his arms, he walked with his wife to Whitby. Amazingly, he became Europe's most daring and successful whaler, venturing further into the Arctic than any previous sailor. The achievements of his son (1789-1857) included drawing the first accurate maps of Greenland and the first depictions of the structure of a snowflake. As a founder of the British Association for the Advancement of Science, Scoresby Junior met the President of the USA in the White House - a long journey from Nutholm. But at the age of 34 Scoresby gave up science to become a parish priest, serving in poor parts of Liverpool and Bradford.

Much less lustrous is Cropton's Robert Charter. A labourer on Joe Wood's farm in Cropton Lane in 1872 he murdered Wood and his nine-year-old son Joseph. The motive was probably theft, for Wood was known to keep a large amount of cash in his house. But the crime wasn't immediately recognised, for the victims simply disappeared.

They were last seen on 17 May. Three days later Charter posted a letter in Liverpool purporting to show they had emigrated. Signed Joseph Wood and sent to one of Wood's relatives, it said: 'Dear Cousin, I write these few lines to let you know that I am going to take the water foreign.' Although Wood's brother declared the handwriting false, the police didn't search the farm. And when finally drawn there by a ghastly smell two months later they accepted Wood's explanation that the smell came from bad tinned meat.

Only after Wood's brother entered the farmhouse and discovered items that the missing farmer might have been expected to take abroad, like his pocket watch, was a thorough search made. From a shallow grave were recovered the amputated remains of an adult. Some of Wood's clothing was dragged from a pond, and a pair of boy's boots was found in the boiler house.

The suspicion has always been that Charter boiled down the lad's body and fed it to the pigs. But he somehow escaped the gallows. After serving a long prison sentence he died in Malton workhouse. In 1885, when it was decided to build a school at Lastingham on land occupied by Charter's cottage, locals turned out in force to tear down the cottage.

More homely Cropton history is represented by Moses Morley and Jim Gray. Cropton's joiner early this century, Moses patented a pioneering washing machine, now exhibited in Pickering's Beck Isle Museum. Jim, village shopkeeper and a Methodist lay preacher between the world wars, was very proud of his exceptionally large head. He carried prints of an X-ray photograph of it, which he sold to anyone who was interested. Customers at the shop could also buy a replica of his specially-made outsize cap. Cropton has never lacked characters.

Seemingly-bashful in this 1938 drawing, shopkeeper Jim Gray sold X-ray pictures of his large head.

CHAPTER 2

AROUND THE ABBEYS

Rievaulx

Extolling the beauty of Rievaulx Abbey, Walter Daniel, a monk in the late twelfth century, hailed its setting as 'a second paradise of wooded delight.' He continued:

> High hills surround the valley, encircling it like a crown. These are clothed by trees of various sorts...From the loftiest rocks the waters wind and tumble down...They give out a gentle murmur of soft sound and join together in the sweet notes of a delicious melody...

More prosaicly, present-day visitors say: 'The monks certainly knew how to pick a beautiful spot.'

But Rievaulx's setting wasn't a 'paradise' when a dozen French monks from Clairveaux, the premier Cistercian abbey, arrived in 1132. As Daniel himself remarked, it was then 'a place of horror and waste solitude.' Swamp and scrub dominated the Rye valley, from which the abbey takes its name. It was by clearing and draining the land that the monks, or rather their labouring lay brothers, gradually transformed the valley, together with neighbouring Bilsdale, into the green and lovely places of today.

The first roads through the valleys were also the work of the monks. Replacing routes over the drier moor tops these included the bridleways that still run along both sides of Bilsdale. The road up Newgate Bank evolved as a link between Bilsdale's monastic tracks and Helmsley, whose growth as a town probably began with trade generated by the abbey.

It was Helmsley's Norman overlord, Walter Espec, a towering black-bearded figure, who donated the original two square miles of land for the abbey, the first Cistercian settlement in the North and only the third - following Waverley, Surrey, and Tintern, Monmouthshire - in Britain. Espec's gift, which also included land for the founding of Kirkham Abbey, is often said to have been prompted by the death of his son in a riding accident. But since his son's name is absent from a list of people in Rievaulx's charter for whose eternal spiritual wellbeing the monks were required to pray, this is doubtful.

If lacking its eventual beauty, the new abbey's setting, below hanging woods in a narrow part of the valley, would be as sheltered then as now. But the site was so constricted that the church had to be aligned North-South instead of East-West. Contrary to former opinion the monks didn't divert the Rye to gain more level land. Formerly regarded as the original course of the river, shallow channels north and south of the abbey were created as canals, along which stone was barged for building the abbey. This makes them the first known industrial waterways in Britain.

The first abbot, William, had been secretary to St Bernard, head of the Cistercian Order, established at Citeaux, near Dijon, in 1098. The Cistercians aimed for the simplicity and humility which they believed the longer-established Benedictines had abandoned. Spurning silk, they wore white linen robes as a sign of purity. Their crosses were wood, their candlesticks iron. The only precious metal in their abbey was the silver of their chalice. Bedspreads, underwear, and even combs were banned as luxuries. To create maximum time for prayer and study, they devised the lay-brother system - teams of worker half-monks. Obliged to attend some religious services, they chiefly served the abbey in return for their keep.

Each Cistercian abbey was intended to be self-sufficient within a compact area. But Rievaulx grew with astonishing speed. Within 30 years it housed 140 monks and 500 lay brothers - 'so that the church swarmed with them like a hive with bees,' as one old account vividly put it. Only by expanding its estate could the abbey support such a huge community. By 1170 it controlled 50 square miles and had fisheries at Scarborough and Teesmouth and ironstone mines in Bilsdale and near Wakefield. A bloomery to smelt the iron stood near the confluence of the south canal with the Rye, and a larger iron furnace, virtually a full-scale blast furnace, operated near Laskill in Bilsdale. The first blast furnace in the North, mass-producing iron bars and other items for sale, this gives Rievaulx abbey more industrial claim to fame.

Larger than Fountains Abbey, Rievaulx was England's premier Cistercian abbey, whose abbot headed the Order in England. The best known abbot, Aelred (1147-67), became a monk in remarkable circumstances. A courtier of King David of Scotland, he made an impromptu visit to then fledgling Rievaulx Abbey in 1134 after completing some royal business with the Archbishop of York. Riding away the next day, he was so affected by the lovely view of the abbey from the hillside that he turned his horse around and presented himself for admission as a monk.

A phrase of Aelred's written at Rievaulx - 'everywhere peace, everywhere serenity, and a marvellous freedom from the tumult of the world' - is often used to express the spirit of the North York Moors, which it does. But careful reading of the full passage suggests that Aelred was explaining the atmosphere of a Cistercian community rather than describing a particular place.

Despite its extensive commercial interests the abbey was often in debt. In the thirteenth century the Crown, at that time still sympathetic to monastic aims, baled it out three times to stave off bankruptcy. But the founding ideals had largely been abandoned, and much of the abbey's debt was due to a lavish rebuilding and enlargement of the original church in 1230.

It was similar extravagance throughout the Order that led the Cistercians into sheep farming, which offered quick profit through wool. Rievaulx's 14,000 breeding ewes spent the summer on the Bilsdale moors and the winter on the Wolds and in the Vale of Mowbray. The abbey's woolhouse is believed to have been at Laskill Bridge, near the foot of Newgate Bank, where the foundations of pillars of a large hall, 80ft by 21ft, have been found at the present day Laskill Farm. Associated with it was a guesthouse, where wool merchants, mostly from Italy, were accommodated. One hopes they weren't disturbed by the roar of the blastfurnace. Edward II also almost certainly spent a night there in 1323. Financial accounts of a royal hunting trip in the Moors record him staying at 'Glascowollehouse' - almost certainly a courtier's attempt at 'Laskill woolhouse,' as pronounced by the Bilsdale woolmaster.

Spreading out from 'home' farms at Griff, near Rievaulx, and Stiltons, near Helmsley, the abbey's rural economy embraced corn, cattle and even vineyards as well as sheep. But the decimation of sheep flocks by disease in 1276 struck the abbey a severe financial blow. And when the human community was ravaged by the Black Death of 1349-50, the abbey went into a decline from which it never recovered. By 1379 only eighteen lay brothers were employed, and at the Dissolution in 1538 the once great abbey housed only 23 monks. Parts of the building had been pulled down, and the lay brothers' dormitory had been turned into a grain store.

But except for Fountains, the Rievaulx ruins are today the most extensive of any Cistercian abbey in Britain. Their greatest glory is the church chancel, which stands to its full height of about 90ft. With its soaring arches, cluster-columns and double tier of lancet windows, this was the no-expense-spared successor, in Early English style, to the plain chancel of the original Norman church. More than twice as big as its forerunner, it was grafted on to the Norman nave, of which only fragments - bits of walls and the bases of the massive pillars - now survive.

Combining lightness with strength, the Early English style supplanted Norman during the building of the abbey. The two styles appear not only side by side but intermingled. In the transept, for instance, round-headed Norman windows were replaced by the pointed Gothic kind, but the Norman doorway, linking the south transept to the vestry, was left unchanged. Much of the abbey's domestic and working quarters is also unaltered Norman, but the large refectory, a substantial feature of the ruins, is Early English on a Norman base.

Numerous small features help to bring the place alive. A doorway from the church to the night stairs evokes the monks in their white habit passing to and from their nocturnal services. In two rooms with giant fireplaces, the only ones provided for comfort, one can picture the monks warming themselves. A well-preserved niche in the cloister held their books. Its plain style suggests it dates from the very foundation of the abbey. The refectory shows recesses where the monks washed their hands, and part of a pulpit from which mealtime readings were given. The chapter house contains a shrine to the first abbot and an empty coffin that was probably Aeldred's.

A symbol of the abbey's ultimate decadence is the abbot's lodgings. These enfold the original infirmary, moved elsewhere when an abbot decided he needed bigger and more impressive quarters. Incorporating a carving of the Anunciation, his ornate new doorway signals the luxury that no doubt lay within.

Like other monastic Orders, the Cistercians interpreted 'Christianity' in their own way. Ruthlessly evicting tenants on gifted land, they also refused hospitality to strangers. Nor did they have any mission to educate. The lay brothers, often the evicted yeomen who could find no other work, were even forbidden to possess books.

But the Rievaulx monks seem to have treated retired servants well. When an annual allowance of four cartloads of firewood was made to one dependant, the abbey register carefully noted: 'Be it known that a cartload is what can be drawn by eight oxen.'

In 1536 the penultimate Rievaulx abbot was executed - hanged, drawn and quartered - for taking part in the Pilgrimage of Grace, an attempt to halt the suppression of the abbeys. No doubt realising the game was up, his successor, the last abbot, threw caution to the winds. At least once a year he led a party of about eight monks who hunted and hawked around Skiplam, near Helmsley.

Three centuries after the Dissolution, Thomas Duncombe, of Helmsley, created his famous terrace on the hillside above the abbey to gain exquisite views of the ruins. Less formal and more intimate, the view of them from a path across Ashberry Hill, on the other side of the river Rye, is also worth seeing. The inspiration for paintings by Turner, Cotman, and Girton the ruins impressed Dorothy Wordsworth, who visited them with brother William during their journey to the home of William's future wife, Mary Hutchinson, at Brompton, near Scarborough, in 1802. 'I could have stayed in this solemn, quiet spot till evening without a thought of moving, but William was waiting for me,' wrote Dorothy - ever the willing slave to her brother.

In the nineteenth century Helmsley vicar the Rev Charles Gray commissioned a plan by Sir Gilbert Scott, architect of the Albert Memorial and St Pancras railway hotel, for rebuilding the abbey. Though this came to nothing, an annual service of evensong inaugurated by Gray still takes place each July.

At most other times the peace of the abbey church is disturbed only by the soft cooing of pigeons, who share the abundant nesting sites with house martins. No longer shaved like a lawn by English Heritage, the grassy banksides have become host to drifts of wild flowers.

An addendum to the Rievaulx story leads us to York Minster. In the early 1920s an excavation at the west end of the abbey nave uncovered ingots of lead stamped with Henry VIII's Tudor rose and a crown. Obviously made with lead stripped from the abbey roof at the Dissolution in 1538, which would have been melted on a fire of the abbey's oak furnishings, these had apparently been stacked and awaiting collection when a large section of wall fell on them, after which they were forgotten. In 1923 they were again melted down and used to re-lead the Minister's famous Five Sisters window, admired by hundreds every day.

Whitby

Each year brings a worldwide reminder of Whitby Abbey. It was there in 664 that the method of calculating Easter was fixed - a profound mystery ever since.

How did this immortal moment come about?

At the close of the Dark Ages that followed the collapse of the Roman Empire, Christianity was brought back to England from two sources - Rome and Ireland. Each had its own method of setting the date of Easter. To resolve the confusion that thus arose, King Oswy of Northumbria, a province that stretched from the Firth of Forth to the Humber, convened a Synod at Whitby abbey.

Supported by the Whitby abbess Hilda, the Irish, or Celtic, camp was represented by the Bishop of Lindisfarne, with Bishop Wilfred, of Ripon, speaking up for the 'Romans.' He won the debate by pointing out that since St Peter, who was entrusted by Christ with the keys of heaven, belonged to the Roman line of the church, the Roman method of setting Easter must be correct. Oswy, a Christian convert, pronounced himself in favour of this 'lest when I come to the gates of heaven there be none to open them to me, being at a variance with him who is acknowledged to hold the keys.' Applause greeted this statement, and the Roman system was adopted. Like the Celtic it is based on phases of the moon, but worked out differently.

At that time, incidentally, Whitby was known by its original Saxon name of Streonshalh, pronounced Strenshall. A mere six years old, its abbey had been selected for the prestigious Synod because Hilda had already led it to the forefront of British monasteries. A Northumbrian princess-turned-nun she founded Whitby's Benedictine abbey on a wild clifftop donated by Oswy in gratitude for victory in a battle. Like an existing abbey at Hartlepool, where Hilda had been abbess for seven years, the new community consisted of both monks and nuns.

Each occupied an individual cell, a system later abandoned by the Benedictines but adopted by the Carthusians. The sexes were separated, and though the monks and nuns worshipped together, they were kept apart by a wall down the centre of the abbey church.

Faithful to their spartan lifestyle the Whitby community became renowned for Christian learning and scholarship. Six monks trained by Hilda became Bishops. The earliest biography of Pope Gregory (c540-604), who sent St Augustine from Rome to Britain in 597, was written at Whitby. Bede's history of early Christianity, published within 50 years of Hilda's death, states that 'kings and princes' sought Hilda's advice. When King Oswy died his grieving widow requested that he be buried at Whitby Abbey, which she then entered as a nun.

The many legends about Hilda suggest an extraordinary personality. The ammonite fossils in the local cliffs are said to have been serpents that infested the site of the abbey when Hilda arrived. She turned them into stone. The village of Hinderwell takes its name from Hilda's Well. Still a feature of the churchyard, this is fed by a spring reputedly created by Hilda during a pilgrimage. Feeling thirsty, she struck the dry ground with her staff, and water burst forth.

On the night of Hilda's death, aged 66 in 680, a nun at Hackness Abbey, a daughter house of Whitby Abbey, is said to have seen Hilda's soul ascend to heaven. As described by Bede, the soul - its form alas unspecified - was borne aloft by 'attending angels' as 'a light from above diffused all around'. Bede also tells how the sleeping nun who witnessed this vision 'suddenly heard in the air the well-known sound of the bell by which they were wont to be summoned to prayers.' The earliest reference to the use of a church bell in Britain, this could be the origin of the tolling of a bell at funerals.

Hilda's abbey was destroyed by invading Danes in 867. Nothing of it is visible today, and it has little in common, spiritually as well as architecturally, with the successor whose dramatic ruins now occupy the headland.

This second Whitby Abbey exercised tyrannical rule over the neighbourhood. Throughout most of its history it was in conflict with the town, which it regarded as a potential threat to its power. Under the abbey's unyielding thumb Whitby's population remained static at about 750 for almost four centuries. Only when the abbey was dissolved in 1539 did the town begin significantly to grow. Only then did it gain a proper harbour, the key to its future shipbuilding and maritime trade, initially in alum but later whaling and coal.

The one link between the two abbeys is that it was probably Hilda's enduring fame that led a Norman Benedictine monk, Reinfrid, to found the post-Conquest abbey in 1078. While serving as a soldier with the Conqueror, he came across the forlorn remains of Hilda's abbey. Under Reinfrid, reputedly a man of great humility and patience, the new abbey probably re-established the spirit of Hilda. But within a few years Reinfrid was ousted by Stephen, an ambitious, quarrelsome monk, who changed the abbey's character completely.

Stephen wrote: 'Being thus elected abbot, and seeing the place to be in its infancy and possessed of no worldly revenues, I wished, by the divine assistance, to restore it to its former glory.' Clearly, 'glory' was to be measured in riches. Soon clashing with the Percy family, which had donated the land for the abbey, Stephen moved briefly to Lastingham and then to York, where he founded St Mary's abbey. Meanwhile the pious Reinfrid, still a monk at Whitby, died tragically. He was struck by a wooden beam when he stopped to help some men building a bridge over the river Derwent near Hackness. A contemporary account of his funeral speaks of his 'little body' - a phrase that suggests affection for Whitby Abbey's founder.

But the abbey was now firmly set on its worldly course. It soon controlled most of a coastal strip ten miles north and south of the abbey and five miles inland - Whitby Strand. Owning many houses in York it also possessed land as far away as Lincolnshire. In his History of Whitby (1817) George Young - admittedly probably biased as a Presbyterian minister - explains how properties were acquired:

> The life of the early monks was one of poverty, retirement and devotion, and to contribute to the support of persons so heavenly was regarded as meritorious. Long after they had begun to degenerate, this favourable view of their character continued to prevail. Every person

who had property, and wished to be thought pious, was ready to bestow his benefaction. Most of the property granted to the monks was designed to secure their prayers for the souls of the donors, and in those days of rapine and bloodshed it was no wonder that sinners, laden with guilt should adopt this method of appeasing their conscience and escaping future woe.

The monks were also willing to buy land whose owner needed to settle a debt or maybe even finance a military expedition, perhaps to the Crusades. Donors were required to swear oaths and sign documents that made the gifts watertight for all time. Trouble often arose when people expecting an inheritance found it had been gifted to the abbey.

Sometimes entire communities lost land that way. One day in 1381 the villagers of Ugglebarnby, on Whitby Strand, awoke to discover they could no longer graze their animals in the common fields. Their historic right of pasturage had been extinguished in a deal between the abbey and the Lord of the Manor. In an attempt to recover their birthright and source of livelihood, the villagers occupied the 'stolen' fields - but to no avail.

Road tolls levied by the abbey meant that Whitby people had to pay to enter their own town. Fishermen also had to pay tithes on catches and even for use of the beach to dry nets. The abbey established a right to all 'wreck of the sea', strayed cattle and any lost or forfeited goods. And though a tolerant abbot of 1189 granted the town a charter as a free borough, which was confirmed by Richard I, eleven years later a new abbot managed to have the charter rescinded on the ground that his predecessor had lacked the power to grant it. Whitby once again fell under the abbey's yoke.

In 1279 the nationwide abuses of the monastic system led to the Statute of Mortmain, which banned further acquisitions without the approval of the King. Another new law outlawed the Sunday markets operated by many abbeys, including Whitby. But a clause that permitted the sale of 'necessary victual' enabled the abbeys to get round this ban.

At its zenith, about 1230, Whitby Abbey housed about 40 monks. Abbey registers reveal much spending on entertainment, provided by minstrels, strolling players etc. The monks also hunted, with the abbot controlling his own extensive deer park. Its entrance was at Park Gate Farm, Fylingthorpe. About a mile south of there, near Demesne Farm, part of the park's boundary wall survives.

The abbey displayed some care for the local community. Today's Youth Hostel occupies the site of an almery, where food was given to the poor. And the abbey also ran a leper hospital.

The pre-Conquest, or Saxon, abbey stood immediately north of the present ruins, close to today's cliff edge. Excavations in the 1920s failed to find any trace of the original buildings, almost certainly of wood. The scanty remains of later stone buildings were considered too slight to be worth displaying.

The first church of the post-Conquest abbey has also vanished, but its foundations are exposed in the later abbey church, which replaced it in the 13th century. Half way along the nave of the second church, narrow lancets give way to wider traceried windows. Experts believe the lancet-windowed section was probably always big enough for the abbey, and the extension with more elaborate windows was added solely for prestige - further evidence of the abbey's worldliness. An oddity is an inscription on a pillar stating that it was rebuilt by L. Smelt in 1790 - some say for a bet.

Exposed to the savage winds that often sweep the bare clifftop, the abbey church is perhaps the most spectacularly-situated ancient monument in Britain. Until June 25, 1830 the church still retained its massive central tower, reminiscent of York Minster's. Its sudden collapse that day was witnessed by a small boy, who rushed home to tell his father. He got his ears boxed for telling such a tall story.

On December 16, 1914 it was the turn of the abbey's west end to suffer. Bits were knocked off when German warships pounded the town. The infamous raid gives Whitby, together with Hartlepool and Scarborough, which were also attacked, the distinction of being the first places in Britain to experience world war.

Very little of the rest of the monastery survives because, immediately after the Dissolution, Whitby's Sir Francis Cholmley pillaged the stone for his fine mansion, Abbey House, now a holiday centre, near the abbey. Between 1672 and 1682 another Cholmley added a sumptuous banqueting hall. But an eighteenth century gale whipped off its roof. It has remained a ruin until now, when it is about to become a new Visitor Centre for the abbey.

The re-siting of a car park that has covered the site of the Saxon abbey will also pave the way for a new dig there. Archaeologists hope the latest conservation techniques will make it possible to put the abbey's fragile foundations on permanent display. Visitors will then have the satisfaction of a tangible link, slight but highly significant, with the abbey before it lost its founding ideals.

Mount Grace Priory

The monks of Mount Grace Priory had something very remarkable to be grateful for. Not until the middle of the twentieth century did most people in live in such comfort as these medieval Carthusians.

Each monk occupied a well-constructed two-storey stone house, with study, workroom, bedroom, and living room with open fire. Water was on tap, sewage was efficiently flushed away, and the monk could take exercise, and tend plants, in his own private walled garden.

The theory behind the excellent living conditions was that if bodily comforts were met, the monks could concentrate exclusively on matters of the spirit. But - who knows? - perhaps a high degree of physical comfort was necessary to draw men to a rigorous regime of fasting and near-absolute solitude and silence. For that was what was demanded of Carthusian monks, whose ruined priory at Mount Grace is the best of its kind in England.

The strictest and most severe of the monastic orders, the Carthusian system was based on the tradition of the hermit monk, who symbolised Christ in the wilderness. Committed to what they called 'the lonely blessedness and the blessed loneliness', the Carthusians would probably have preferred each monk to have been totally isolated, like a hermit. They adopted monasteries mainly for safety and administrative convenience. Only nine were established in England. Within them, each monk dwelt alone - that well-appointed house officially his cell. With part of the bedroom furnished as an oratory, or chapel, the cell was virtually a mini-monastery, in which the monk prayed, meditated, copied or translated manuscripts, and did physical work, mainly weaving or carpentry. Twice a day a meagre meal was brought by a lay brother. It was passed to the monk through a right-angled hatch, which denied server and receiver sight of each other. Built into the doorway of each cell, these hatches are a distinctive feature of Mount Grace.

The Carthusian system also required a strikingly different abbey to those of the better known Benedictine and Carthusian orders. Unlike the impressive centrepiece of a conventional abbey, the Carthusian abbey-church was small - more like a parish church. Nor was there any dormitory. But the cloister, around which the cells were grouped, was exceptionally large. With fifteen cells along three of its sides, and the fourth lined by the prior's cell, sacrist's cell and chapter house, the Mount Grace cloister is the largest in England.

Nine more cells are fitted in elsewhere. The full effect is to make Mount Grace easily the most architecturally-memorable of all British abbeys. Once seen it can never be confused with any other abbey, many of which are remembered mainly for their settings.

Not that Mount Grace, tucked at the foot of the Cleveland Hills, near Osmotherley, lacks beauty. Against its rich backdrop of oak woods, it looks especially lovely in a summer sunset. And though the A19 thunders only a few hundred yards away, peace and tranquility still reign among the ruins.

Founded by twelve monks in 1398, on land gifted by Thomas de Holand, Earl Marshall to Richard II, Mount Grace was the last medieval monastery to be set up in Yorkshire. Just two years after its inception Holand was beheaded for plotting to regain the throne for Richard, his uncle, who was deposed in 1399.

The founder's death left some legal uncertainties over Mount Grace. Arguing that Holand's treachery gave him the right to land, the disgruntled ex-tenant passed it to Gisborough Priory. In the long wrangle that followed, the Mount Grace monks twice petitioned the Crown before their right to the land was confirmed in 1439. But Gisborough Priory, an Augustinian house, continued to press its claim. In 1508 the Mount Grace community, perhaps tired of the friction, agree to pay an annual rent to Gisborough as a condition for keeping their priory.

But the ownership challenge didn't deter the Carthusians from developing Mount Grace to their customary high standards. As Dr Glyn Coppack, English Heritage's principal inspector of ancient monuments, noted during a visit in 1993: 'Their plumbing and sanitation was the best in the Middle Ages. It was not only superior to that of other monastic orders, but to the plumbing in most Bishops' palaces and Royal palaces.'

The Mount Grace monks tapped three springs. One was fed to a water tower in the cloister, from where it was piped to the cells. Another was harnessed to flush the drains, which passed under each cell's lavatory, usually at the bottom of the garden. The third spring supplied the abbey's guesthouse. And though the latter is now on private land, visitors can still see the other two, protected by reconstructed spring houses.

Collectively, the ruined cells still contain all their key features: tap-recesses, drains, lavatories, fireplaces, the serving hatches, the walled garden, and a small covered area where the monk could exercise in bad weather. One cell has been has been carefully reconstructed and furnished, and its garden planted with herbs of the period.

The monks attended church three times a day - five fewer than in most monastic regimes. But they spoke to each other only at a Chapter meeting each Sunday. A communal Sunday meal was eaten in a silence broken only by Bible readings. The washbasin, or *laver*, in which the monks washed their hands before this meal can still be seen. Its water came from the central tower.

The land enclosed by the cloister was the graveyard. When a monk died his body, with the face covered by his reversed cowl, was lowered into the grave on a plain board. The grave was marked by a wooden cross without name or dates. One wonders whether this austere procedure was maintained when Thomas Beaufort, a son of John of Gaunt, was buried at Mount Grace in 1427. He requested burial there in the hope of eternal salvation.

Modern Carthusian monasteries, including one at Parkminster, Sussex, still follow a regime similar to Mount Grace. Among Mount Grace visitors who have found it not to their taste was the late Harry Scott, founder and first editor of *The Dalesman*. In his book *Portrait of Yorkshire* he comments:

Always when I have visited Mount Grace I have been unable to rid myself of the thought of the unnatural peace which must have rested upon this place, where men lived and spoke not and tortured themselves - how ingenious and horrible those hatches are - to save their souls in complete retreat from the world.

Like the Cistercians, the Carthusians had no mission to spread Christianity or help the poor. An early Carthusian, Guiges du Pin, observed that it was 'not for the temporal cure of other folk's bodies but for the welfare of our souls that we took refuge in the retirement of this desert.'

But of all the monastic orders, only the Carthusian remained true to its founding ideals. When Henry VIII tore down the monasteries, the Carthusians alone still enjoyed public respect.

Three of the nine Carthusian priors went to the gallows rather than take Henry VIII's handsome pension. And though the Mount Grace prior wasn't among these martyrs, two Mount Grace monks were imprisoned for refusing to swear the oath of allegiance to Henry. Meanwhile - and with what irony - the monks' piety had swelled the priory's coffers. For people were still keen to give land and money in return for perpetual prayers - the bargain long-since discredited at most abbeys. On its dissolution in 1536 Mount Grace had a final annual income of £325 - £50 more than Rievaulx. Nineteen monks and six lay brothers were there at the end.

In 1654 the abbey's ruined guesthouse was converted into a handsome Jacobean mansion by Thomas Lascelles. In 1898 Sir Lowthian Bell, a Teesside ironfounder, extended this sympathetically, furnishing it in Arts and Crafts style. Worth seeing for its own sake, the house now contains an excellent exhibition on Mount Grace.

Byland

Anglers fishing in a couple of trout lakes near Oldstead probably don't realise they are re-creating the history of Byland Abbey. For the lakes, excavated from a boggy glacial channel by local man Peter Bradley in 1970s, incidentally restored part of an extensive network of abbey fishponds and other waterworks. Re-shaping the landscape over a wide area, particularly with a necklace of lakes that virtually encircled the abbey, these represented an outstanding triumph of monastic civil engineering.

The ambitious waterworks solved the severe drawbacks of the abbey's site at the foot of the Hambleton Hills. Not drained by any stream, it was even more of a swamp than the Rye valley, tamed by the monks of Rievaulx. The absence of fresh water also denied the monks their own fish, a staple of their diet. Though the abbey established fisheries at Teesmouth and on the Swale, these were respectively two days' and one day's packhorse journey away.

To bring running water to the abbey the monks diverted the headwaters of two nearby streams - Holbeck and Thorpe Beck. Holbeck was harnessed to flush drains, provide drinking water, and drive corn mills - the first at Low Pasture House, just below the abbey, and a successor within the abbey precinct. Beyond Low Pasture, the diverted Holbeck joined Thorpe Beck. The monks dug a new channel for the combined stream. Today known as Long Beck it carried the surface water from the abbey site. By chance or design it also fed a new fishpond at Newburgh Priory.

The Newburgh pond, a popular feature by the road just outside Coxwold, is the most obvious evidence of the Byland waterworks. But a short way east of the pond, where a bridge crosses the byway known as the Colley Bridge Road, the embanked artificial channel which conducts Long Beck to the pond can also be seen. Nearer to Byland Abbey, the captured section of Holbeck, which rises in Ducken Dale behind Wass village, runs parallel with the road between the village and the abbey. At the sharp right bend, its original bed, now dry, turns eastwards, away from the abbey. Within half a mile or so it collects water from springs and small gutters, thus making a new start.

The skilful civil engineering didn't stop there. The Holbeck supply to the abbey was boosted by water from the glacial channel, between the abbey and Oldstead. This was brought by a cut, which passes under the Oldstead road just west of the abbey's ruined gatehouse.

North of the road at the same spot is the large embankment of a fishpond dam. Once carrying a cart track used by the monks as access to the moors, it impounded the lowest of a string of ponds in the mile-and-half glacial channel.

During the excavation of his trout lakes, Peter Bradley found lead weights and a paved area - the latter perhaps a monastic mooring point, or the floor of a storage hut.

Three more ponds almost lapped the abbey walls on its north, south and west sides. But the largest pond was more than a mile away. Half a mile long and a quarter of a mile wide, and up to about 30ft (9.1m) deep, it covered most of the triangle of land between Scencliffe Grange, Oldstead Grange and Fox Folly Farm. Partly tree-covered, its substantial earth dam can be seen from a footpath running east of Fox Folly.

Summing up this considerable endeavour in 1197, a new Byland abbot, Philip, observed:

> They [the monks] began manfully to root out the woods, and by long and wide ditches draw off the abundance of water from the marshes; and when dry land appeared, they prepared themselves an ample, fitting and worthy site in the eastern part of that land.

The monks' readiness to tackle this mammoth task surely testifies to the strength of their faith. Especially since they had been sorely tried through other reasons. Originally sent out in 1134 as a mission from Furness Abbey in Lancashire they spent four years at Calder, in Cumbria. Plagued by marauding Scots they sought re-admission to Furness but were turned away because their leader, Gerald, refused to give up his rank as abbot. Crossing the Pennines, they took temporary refuge with a hermit monk at Hood Hill, near Sutton Bank.

In 1143 a gift of land from Roger de Mowbray enabled the monks to move to Byland, near Helmsley. But their new abbey was so close to the established Rievaulx Abbey that the two communities could hear each other's bells. As a monastic chronicler put it, this clash was 'not fitting and could by no means be endured.' So in 1147 the 'Byland' monks moved yet again. For 30 years their abbey was at 'Stocking', believed to be where Oldstead Hall now stands. Built when they were offered a larger, albeit boggy, site, its successor, today's abbey, was therefore the community's fifth home in little over forty years.

In its last two moves, the community retained the name 'Byland'. The exact site of the probably-wooden abbey at Byland, about five miles from the present abbey, is unknown, though some authorities believe it was Tylas Farm. To make way for it a peasant community was evicted - one of about sixty that suffered this fate at the hands of Yorkshire monasteries. But the Byland monks, originally members of the Savigny order, which merged with the Cistercians in 1147, resettled the displaced Bylanders, in what is now Old Byland village.

At Wass, their final destination, the 'Byland' monks were keen to make up for lost time. Completed within twenty years, their abbey church was the largest Cistercian church built up to that time. It remains the largest ever built in a single go.

A key difference from earlier Cistercian abbey churches, including Rievaulx's, was the freestanding altar, with an aisle at the rear. Byland's carved stonework was also of exceptional quality. Widely copied after its probable

49

introduction here, a waterleaf design on the pillars, best seen in the chapter house, is now synonymous with Byland. The abbey's musum contains many other finely-carved stones, as well as lead weights from the fish ponds.

Dominating the ruins is the great half-circle of the abbey's broken west window. Though Nikolaus Pevsner calls it 'eloquent' it always looks forlorn and desolate to me. Pieced together in the museum, the tracery of the 26-ft (7.9m) wide window closely resembles that of the inner part of York Minister's Rose Window, which was probably modelled on the Byland window. Very faintly discernible on the inside of the abbey's west front is the pattern of the window's centrepiece. Engraved by the mason as a guide when assembling the window, this would afterwards have been covered with limewash.

Though scanty, the rest of the ruins hold plenty of interest. Running between the cloister and the lay brothers' range is the Lay Brothers' Lane - a passage with 35 niche seats, in which the lay brothers, abbey workers who had taken religious vows, assembled for their twice-daily attendance at church. The monks attended seven times.

Tiered benches identify the chapter house, where the abbot's seat, with the socket of his lectern, is in the centre of the east wall.

The church itself is famous for its extensive tiling. But also worth noting is the proximity of the kitchen, dining room and dormitory to the church and cloister. A deliberate feature of Cistercian design this kept the monks close to the sacred heart of the abbey even when not worshipping. To maintain this spiritual contact it was deemed acceptable for the monks to hang washing in the cloister, where they also had their hair cut.

Built for 40 monks and 100 lay brothers, the abbey probably housed double that number at its peak. In 1231 demand for admission was so great that a limit of 80 was set, and all recruitment of lay brothers was halted until the number fell below 160.

The abbey's most dramatic moment came in 1322. Edward II was dining at Byland during a hunting trip when marauding Scots were reported on the nearby moors. After defeating the King in a battle or skirmish at Scotch Corner, on the hill above Oldstead, on 14 October, the Scots pillaged both Byland Abbey and Rievaulx Abbey. Edward is thought lucky to have evaded capture.

Ravaged by the Black Death of 1348-50, the abbey housed only eleven monks and three lay brothers in 1383. As elsewhere, the lay brother system collapsed, to be replaced by tenancies and paid labour. At the abbey's suppression in 1538, 26 monks took the King's pension - £6 for the rank and file, £50 for the abbot.

Ampleforth

When Henry VIII's men stripped Byland Abbey after its suppression in 1538 they left behind its most holy object: the high altar. In 1820 this sacred relic, a large sandstone slab, was removed by the local landowner. Twenty years later he gave it to the monks of nearby Ampleforth Abbey. And there it rests today - the most revered treasure of the abbey church.

An uneventful rural scene? Apparently. But this low bank near Fox Folly Farm was a feature of Byland abbey's extensive waterworks.

A monk goes about his duties at Ampleforth. His community stems directly from Westminster Abbey.

Founded in 1802 and now England's largest religious house, Ampleforth Abbey might not seem particularly old. But it can claim an antiquity founded on more than that cherished link with Byland. Its pedigree stems from Westminster Abbey. Indeed, in a very real sense Ampleforth Abbey IS Westminster Abbey. For its Benedictine monks are direct successors of those who founded Westminster in 1170. Ampleforth is thus Westminster's spiritual heir.

The crucial figure in this remarkable story is a monk named Sigebert Buckley. In 1607 he became the last survivor of the monks occupying Westminster Abbey when it was suppressed - for the second and final time - in 1560. On 21 November he enrolled two other monks to form a new 'Westminster' community. Lacking an abbey they kept alive the spirit of the original Westminster Abbey through study and prayer.

In 1613 one of Fr Buckley's colleagues entered a monastery for English monks at Dieulouard, in Northern France. The presence of this 'Westminster' monk led to the community being formally recognised as Westminster's successor.

The Dieulouard monastery was one of several set up in France by English monks exiled through the persecution of Roman Catholics. But when England declared war on France in 1793, the French authorities closed these monasteries and imprisoned their monks.

A number of 'Westminster' monks escaped. Soon joined by others formally freed, they returned to England in 1794. After eight nomadic years they settled at Ampleforth through the invitation of the local Roman Catholic priest, Father Anselm Bolton, chaplain to the Fairfax family, of nearby Gilling Castle. In 1786, Fr Bolton had been the last man prosecuted in England for practising as a Roman Catholic priest. The dismissal of the charge signalled the end of the persecution of Catholics.

Fr. Bolton accommodated the Westminster monks in the spacious Georgian house built for him by his patron, Anne Fairfax. This historic cradle of Ampleforth Abbey survived until 1985, when it was deemed unsafe and demolished. Its site is marked by an inscribed tablet in the floor of the building that replaced it in 1988.

The first abbey church has also passed into history. Designed by York-born Joseph Hansom (1803-82), inventor of the eponymous cab, it lasted precisely 100 years - 1857 to 1957. But the present church, built in phases between 1924 and 1961, is a worthy successor. Its architect was Sir Giles Gilbert Scott, grandson of the Victorian Sir Gilbert Scott, who drew up the plans for rebuilding Rievaulx Abbey.

Best known for Liverpool's Anglican Cathedral, Sir Giles also designed the traditional red telephone box. Some might say there is a hint of the phone-box's domed roof in the ceilings of the nave and central tower of Ampleforth's abbey church. Their style is certainly very unlike the Gothic exterior. In fact Scott cleverly designed the church to look Gothic, or Early English, on the outside, but Romanesque, befitting its Roman Catholic role, inside. Despite some impressive statuary and a flourish of organ-blown trumpets high above the main altar, the predominant impression, conveyed mainly by the plain, rendered walls, is of a calm, cool simplicity.

In the south transept the Westminster connection is honoured with a tablet that incorporates a tile from the crypt of Westminster Abbey. Flanking this are the arms of Westminster and Ampleforth and a quote, in Latin, from Isiah: *Look to the rock from which you were hewn*. Most appropriately, the side chapel by the sanctuary contains the Byland altar and another precious Byland relic - a small alabaster carving of the Holy Trinity.

Including two crypts, linked by a series of chapels, the church is heavily infested by mice. The famous rodent trademark of 'Mousey' Thompson (1876-1955), the Kilburn woodcarver and furniture maker, appears on oak pews, prayer desks and benches. Thompson was largely unknown when Father Paul Nevill, headmaster of Ampleforth College from 1924-54, entrusted him with furnishing the church, his first major commission. He went on to do much more work at the college, whose library, with oak tables, chairs and reading desks, and Tudor-arched study alcoves, is regarded as his masterpiece. Father Nevill is also believed to have urged Thompson to adopt a trademark - genesis of the mouse.

The school library serves as abbey chapter house. This dual role underlines the historic unity of abbey and school. Even before they settled at Ampleforth, the abbey's founding monks ran a school, to prepare boys for monastic service or the priesthood. Today that aim has broadened to provide a wide education founded on strong Christian ethics.

About 650 pupils now attend the College, England's leading Roman Catholic public school. Demolition of the original monastic house created the chance to give the union of school and abbey a clear physical form. Known as the Central Building, the replacement of the monastic house is a concourse common to both school and abbey. Determindedly modern it nevertheless fits well with its neo-Gothic and neo-Tudor neighbours. As Fr Felix Stephens, the abbey's director of development, observed when the building was officially opened: 'By linking the monastery with the school we have joined the spiritual and the secular, the old and the new.'

Some 30 or so of the 70 resident monks teach in the school, where they form around a third of the staff. Other monks are engaged in theologicial studies or pastoral work. Several are in training, and some are retired.

The monks also direct work on the abbey's 1,000-acre agricultural estate. Until sold in 2000 because of plummeting milk prices, its centrepiece was a 190-strong dairy herd, whose milk provided pintas for the abbey and the public, and went into an Abbey brand of yoghurt. The estate still boasts England's most northerly commercial apple orchard. Apples can be bought there, 'farmgate' style, from August to spring, and pre-booked parties can also tour the orchard, where 58 varieties grow on 2,500 trees.

Ampleforth Abbey gives visitors to the North York Moors a rare chance to discover something of the spirit and atmosphere of a modern monastic community. The church is always open, of course, and visitors are also welcome to the ground floor of the Central Building, which has a bookshop and fine view over the grounds.

Unlike the medieval Cistercians, who shunned contact with the outside world in the belief it would sully their sanctity, the Benedictines have always fostered links with the community. Opened in 1975, Ampleforth College's indoor sports' centre is well used by local individuals and clubs, and a newer hall has become a regular venue for concerts and other arts events in the annual Ryedale Festival. About 3,000 people a year also benefit through a hostel run for groups of young people and a guest house for adults seeking spiritual refreshment.

In 1955 Ampleforth Abbey set up a satellite community, including school, in St Louis, USA, which is now an abbey in its own right. And while a similar 'daughter' abbey is currently being established in Zimbabwe, Ampleforth maintains an extensive mission in Britain. Almost a third of its 100 or so monks live and work away. While serving as Archbishop of Westminster, leader of the Roman Catholic Church in England and Wales, the late Cardinal Basil Hume remained firmly an Ampleforth monk. Many others are parish priests, some in inner-cities.

During the Second World War several Ampleforth monks were military chaplains, and one today combines the roles of parish priest and chaplain at RAF Spadeadam, the Cumbrian rocket-testing range. The life of an Ampleforth monk is by no means as cloistered as it might seem.

CHAPTER 3
AT THE CASTLES

Helmsley

On two of the three approaches to Helmsley - and on the third when trees shed their leaves - the shattered keep of the castle forms a strong landmark. Particularly impressive is the view from the east at dusk, when the keep's dark silhouette rises above the shadowed cottages. With the pinnacled church tower also catching the last of the dying light the town presents a very English scene. It suggests the market-town hospitality and comfort that does indeed await the traveller in Helmsley, the unofficial 'capital' of the North York Moors.

But hospitality and comfort were far from the mind of Robert de Ros, lord of Helmsley, when he began building the castle in about 1190. Defence was his purpose - and he wanted the best.

At that time, square castle towers were just beginning to give way to round ones. Though more awkward to construct, these were less vulnerable to undermining, and deflected missiles more effectively. But Ros wasn't entirely convinced about the innovation. So while most of the towers of his castle, including the pair guarding the main (north) gate, were D-shaped (i. e. a half-circle jutting from the wall) others, including the south gateway, today's visitor entrance, were square.

Built in hybrid form, with square walls inside the castle but a round one protruding out, the largest tower was, and is, the keep. And with this Ros took a lead in castle-building. As every schoolchild knows, or used to, a keep was traditionally in the centre of the castle, where it formed the last and strongest of a series of defences. But castle-builders gradually preferred all-round strength. From the late thirteenth century this produced great keepless castles such as Conway and Harlech, where every tower is equally strong. By placing his keep in the outer wall, Ros anticipated this change. Among Yorkshire's sixteen or so principal castles, only Richmond, whose keep bestrides the gateway, and Scarborough, where it guards the castle approach, also pioneered this trend.

Positioned to repel attack from the most likely quarter - the open level land to the east - Helmsley's keep is just one of several features that make Helmsley castle a masterpiece of design. In his classic book *Yorkshire's Ruined Castles*, John Illingworth notes:

Nowhere else in the county can we see such unity of plan, such an interlocking of defensive details, to produce, on a site of no great natural strength, a fortress of the very first class...

Proof of this came when the castle withstood an assault by King John, and again when it held out for three months in a Civil war seige...But more of those dramas in a moment.

The son of a sister of Walter Espec, benefactor of Rievaulx Abbey, Robert de Ros inherited the Helmsley estate in 1186. His new castle probably replaced a wooden one. Because the chosen site, a small limestone bluff, was overlooked by a slope rising to the west there was little point in creating a conventional castle mound. Instead Ros dug two immense ditches, which encircled the castle and embraced two outer wards.

Formidable barriers in their own right, these ditches, the inner one of which was hewn through rock to a depth of 32ft (9.7m), were never moats. But the rampart between them could be reached swiftly by the garrison from either gateway. Later, access was also provided from the barbicans - defensive extensions to the gateways. As troops could also emerge at several points on the berm, the platform of land at the foot of the walls, the castle's defenders could make sudden, unexpected appearances almost anywhere. Attackers could never be sure of not facing a counter attack from any quarter. Combined with the castle's all round physical strength, this flexibility made Helmsley as near impregnable as any castle of its era.

But all this was still untested when an angry King John led his troops against the castle in 1216. Still smarting from having been forced to sign Magna Carta the previous year, he was determined to regain absolute power. Helmsley was in his sights because Robert de Ros was among the 25 barons elected to make sure the King observed Magna Carta. John's failure to take the castle was followed the same year by the better-known loss of his baggage and jewels in the Wash - to say nothing of his death from dysentry.

The Ros dynasty ruled at Helmsley for 350 years - from about 1154 to 1508. Robert, the castle's builder, also began laying out the town, for which he obtained a charter as a borough at the end of the twelfth century. His son William built the castle's barbicans, one of which survives. A later William (1285-1316) claimed the Scottish throne. To strengthen his castle against the new seige weapon, a giant sling called a trebuchet, he raised the keep to its present height of 100ft (30.4m). The junction of his brown sandstone with the original limestone is still visible.

William's son, the third lord, entertained Edward III at the castle in 1334. The 7th lord, yet another William (1393-1414), showed a common touch: in his will he left a lifetime annuity of twopence a day to the castle gateman. No doubt the estate could afford this sum, as William had been England's Lord Treasurer. The penultimate Ros, Thomas, was executed after fighting on the losing Lancastrian side in a Wars-of-the-Roses battle at Hexham in 1464. His tomb, with an effigy of a knight in armour, is in Helmsley church.

The epoch of castles was almost over when Helmsley was beseiged in the Civil War of 1644. Defending the castle for the Royalist Duke of Buckingham, who was occupied elsewhere, 25-year-old Sir Jordan Crosland resisted a Parliamentary force of 700 soldiers and 300 horsemen for three months. During that time the castle was relentlessly pounded with heavy cannon, probably from across the river Rye at the southern end of the town.

In one skirmish, the commander of the Parliamentary troops, York's Sir Thomas Fairfax, a formidable soldier, nicknamed 'Black Tom' from his black beard and swarthy features, was shot in the shoulder and forced to retire.

The castle's defenders surrendered only on highly-honourable terms. Kept at the British Museum, the surrender document states that the garrison 'shall march out with the armes, horses, and all the rest of their goodes...and be safely conveyed to the garrison at Scarborough [a Royal Castle] without aine molestacon.'

A further provision was that 'the castle...be absolutely demolished and no garrison hereafter be kepte there by either party.' The keep's appearance today is the direct result of that agreement, by which the eastern half was blasted away with gunpowder.

Besides unravelling the masterly layout, today's visitor can pick out telling details of the defences: steps to the inner ditch, portcullis grooves, the chain pit of one of the four drawbridges, and the slot holes for its retaining bars. Novel botanical interest comes when the tiny pink flowers of *Erinus alpinus*, the alpine fairy foxglove, grace the castle walls in June. A native of South Africa, its seeds were sown here, and at Middleham Castle, by botanist Sir Walter Acheson in the 1930s.

But what chiefly intrigues visitors is a range of well-preserved Tudor domestic buildings. Despite their fine plaster ceilings, handsome fireplaces and oak panelling, these are not, as many assume, the castle's original great hall. Its scanty remains are nearby. This Tudor range was converted from mundane domestic castle buildings between 1563 and 1587 into an elegant house for Edward Manners, third Duke of Buckingham. His coat of arms, impaling that of his wife, is incorporated in a plaster freize in a large room that was probably their solar, or parlour. This manor house within the castle remained the home of Helmsley's squires until 1713, when Sir Charles Duncombe, who had lived there since 1689, moved to his new mansion of Duncombe Park. Perhaps it is appropriate, therefore, that the Duncombe Park grounds offer probably the best overview of the castle and its complex and daunting earthworks. One realises why they proved too much for King John and the fearless 'Black Tom'.

Pickering

In 1323 Edward II ordered extensive improvements to Pickering Castle. An entry in the castle's records for 10 August states that a new outer ward was to have 'a stone wall and a gate with a drawbridge.' Within the gate, a 'new chamber' was to be built.

Various existing buildings were to be re-roofed, and there was also to be a new postern, or rear gateway. To complete the project, John de Kilvington, described as 'keeper of the castle', was ordered 'to thoroughly point, both within and without, the walls of the castle and tower, and to clean out and enlarge the castle ditch. All this to be done...as the King has enjoined him by word of mouth.'

Three centuries later, a survey commissioned by Oliver Cromwell, in 1651, painted a more depressing picture. Immediately inside the gate stood 'a ruynous howse...ready to fall.' This was almost certainly Edward II's 'new chamber.' In addition, towers had been stripped of their wood, lead and iron. The bridge linking the castle's inner and outer wards was 'decayed', and a complete range of buildings was 'now ruyned and fallen to the ground.' The neglect had reached the castle's heart, for the survey observed: 'In the midst of the whole castle standeth a mount...on which there is a spatious, ruyned and old decayed building, being nothing but ruyned walls.'

The glory had thus departed from one of the great royal castles of the North. Between 1100 and 1400, nearly every British monarch stayed at Pickering castle. Apart from York, Pickering has more royal associations than any other Yorkshire town. Even today, its castle and much neighbouring countryside are part of the Duchy of Lancaster, a Crown estate. The connection brought the present Queen on a tour of the district in 1975. The centrepiece was a visit to Pickering castle, where a red carpet was laid on the latest successor to that 'decayed' inner bridge. As the Queen, accompanied by Prince Philip, stepped on to it, the Royal standard was unfurled from the castle keep and the band of the Green Howards struck up the national anthem. In the inner ward the Queen met 76 Duchy tenant farmers and their wives. Like most of her medieval ancestors, the Queen then dined at the castle - though in a marquee rather than a medieval hall. Her two-hour stay was the first visit by an English monarch for almost 600 years.

William the Conqueror is believed to have founded the castle, in which he also probably stayed. For when he parcelled-out Yorkshire to his friends, he kept a large tract of land around Pickering, mainly hunting forest, for himself. This is the probable origin of the Crown ownership.

But documented royal visits begin with Henry I, who issued a charter while staying at Pickering in 1122. He also gave the royal hunting forest the resounding title the Honour and Forest of Pickering. Administered from the castle and covering 150 squares miles, this stretched from Rosedale's river Seven in the west to the river Derwent, near Scarborough, in the east. Its northern boundary was the moorland watershed between Rosedale and Eskdale and its southern the rivers Derwent and Rye where they cross the Vale of Pickering.

The earliest record of work on the castle is in the royal accounts of Henry II (1154-89). Unfaithful to his wife, Eleanor of Aquitane, Henry entertained his mistress, Rosamund de Clifford, at Pickering Castle. Known as 'Fair Rosamund', she became a popular figure in the town. Eleanor murdered her by tricking her into drinking poison. But Pickering folk always thought fondly of Rosamund, and when a new tower was built at the castle in the fourteenth century it was named after her. Rosamund's illegitimate son by Henry became the 31st Archbishop of York.

King John visited the castle several times. In February 1201, he too signed a charter there - for the nuns of nearby Wykeham priory. In 1210 he is said to have lost ten shillings (50p) to the Earl of Salisbury in a game of backgammon at the castle. The game would be played in what is now called the Old Hall, fragments of which survive.

It was Henry III who forged Pickering's Lancastrian connection. In 1267 he gave the Pickering lands to his son, Edmund Crouchback, whom he also created Earl of Lancaster. In the complex power struggles of medieval England, ownership of the estate swung back and forth between the Crown and the House of Lancaster for 146 years. But since 1413, when the Duke of Lancaster was enthroned as Henry V, the property has been in the continuous ownership of the Crown.

Though not a monarch, Edmund Crouchback's son, the second Earl of Lancaster, lived like one at Pickering castle. In 1314 he spent £400 on a New Hall for his wife, Countess Alice. Welcomed for the work it provided the project required '400 cartloads of stone...152 planks for doors and windows...1,000 broad-headed nails, 20,000 tacks, 22 hinges for the doors, 28 hinges for the windows'. The castle accounts that record this also reveal that eighty planks sawn from oaks felled in the forest were used to make a gangway between the countess's chamber and the adjoining chapel. To stop draughts, crannies in the castle's slate roof were tightly sealed with moss. In 1321 the Earl was executed following his defeat by Edward II at the Battle of Boroughbridge.

In August 1323 Edward II spent three weeks at the castle. The accounts note payments of 10s (50p) each to 'Agnes, wife of Roger de Mar, porter of the Queen' chamber,' and 'John...who followed the king the whole day when he hunted the stag.' But most fascinating was a transaction that took place 'on Blakey Moor' on 23 August. The royal accounts state:

> Paid to Sir Roger de Felton, Knight of the King's Chamber, for his ransom at the time when he was taken by the Scots at Rievaulx in company with the Earl of Richmond, in October 1322 - a gift by the hands of John Harsike, who delivered the money to Sir Roger in the King's presence. £100.

What this reveals is that the king, up on Blakey Moor - the one near Saltersgate, not Farndale - witnessed the handing over of cash from the royal purse. This followed the king's defeat by Scottish marauders, who surprised him while he was dining at Byland abbey in October 1322. Though the king escaped, Sir Roger de Felton, one of his commanders, was captured. He was released on payment of £100 from his own pocket. And now the king was paying him back, though the reimbursement was euphemistically described as a 'gift'. What lustre this bestows on Blakey.

It was to Pickering Castle that Edward, mounted on a grey charger, fled after the Battle of Byland. Eight years later Edward III, yet another monarch to visit Pickering, lost a hound in the hunting forest. He rewarded its finder with 6s 8d (34p). The dog was evidently a great favourite, for during this same stay at Pickering Edward donated only a little more than double that reward - 12s 6d (58p) - to provide food for 100 poor people.

After Edward III's reign (1327-77) royal visits to Pickering petered out, probably because the hunting forest was in decline. But Henry Bolingbroke, the future Henry IV, spent two days at the castle on his return from exile in July 1399, to wrest the crown from Richard II. According to local tradition, Richard himself was imprisoned briefly in the castle later that year before being taken to Pontefract Castle, where he was murdered.

But for all its royal associations, Pickering castle was never much of a fortress. While Helmsley castle was strong despite an imperfect site, Pickering was weak despite its strong position - on a rocky headland overlooking the town. Jutting from the wall, its keep-topped mound was highly vulnerable. Even when this defect was remedied by extending the wall to create an outer ward in the fourteenth century, the new defences were badly flawed. The main gateway lacked a tower, and others were built in then obsolete rectangular form, easier to undermine than round towers.

And yet Pickering castle illustrates better than any other in Yorkshire the evolution of a castle from the early 'mount-and-bailey' Norman type - i.e one consisting of keep on a earth mound, with an enclosure defended by a ditch and stockade - into a fully-fledged medieval fortress.

No-one knows exactly when Pickering's 70ft (21.3m) mound was raised, though it was almost certainly soon after the Norman Conquest. In view from the castle, a similar mound 600 yards (548.6m) west could be the site of an earlier castle, perhaps built by William the Conqueror.

As at most early Norman castles, Pickering's first 'keep' was merely a fortified enclosure on top of the mound. Until the late twelfth century its only defence was a wooden palisade. The small outer ward was also defended only by stakes. Duchy tenants were required to give free labour to maintain this stockade. In the thirteenth century a cash payment was substituted for this tithe. Though stone walls replaced the stakes in the fourteenth century, the Duchy continued to levy a charge for their maintenance until early in the nineteenth century - by which time the castle had been a ruin for almost 200 years.

Despite its weakness the castle withstood a siege in 1261, when it was held by its steward for the king. But the special element in its history is that Honour and Forest of Pickering. In the castle's old hall is the recessed seat where the king's steward presided over a court that administered the forest law. Most of its business related to poaching or the illegal taking of wood - usually for building.

The king's court was certainly not in awe of that other power base - the church. The abbot of Rievaulx was once summonsed for failing to repair a bridge. The indictment reveals that the inconvenience to travellers mattered less than the fact that their detour caused 'annoyance to the Lord's deer and treading down of their pasturage.' The Prior of Bridlington was similarly brought to book for erecting a sheepfold - 'injuring thereby the Lord's deer'. The Abbot of Whitby was once fined three shillings (30p) for removing a 'green oak' at

Goathland. But of course there was no penalty for the official felling of 30 oaks in six days in 1267 to provide fuel for the apartment of the first Earl of Lancaster and his wife.

In 1314, 1,300 deer roamed the forest. An audacious poaching offence took place in 1334. Poachers, of whom there were many, are belived to have been held while awaiting trial in the castle's Coleman Tower. The prison proper was the Mill Tower. In 1347 former forest bailiff Hugh de Neville was imprisoned there after he and companions erected the head of a poached hart 'in sight of the Earl of Lancaster.' Hugh had lost his job because he had falsely arrested a certain Robert the Dyer and, as the court record says, had 'bound his hands as if he were a felon, and took from him a horse, harness, and other goods and chattels...' Evidently an unpopular figure, Hugh was later seized during a church service by another ex bailiff, who held him 'in the depth of the gaol in iron fetters for seven weeks...'

Few castles exceed Pickering in such well-documented human history, bringing the place to life.

Danby

Strikingly in view from the valley road and railway half a mile below, the massive north wall of Danby Castle gazes sternly over the green fields of Eskdale. But on the south side - what a different picture. A charming garden, with cottage flowers and informal lawns among old holly and apple trees, provides the pleasing foreground to an historic but very-much-lived-in house.

Enter the wide gateway alongside the garden, and you might be greeted by calves peering from a stone barn. Kittens could be playing in the paved yard of what is now clearly seen to be a farmhouse. Beyond a ruined stone archway in the yard stands a forlorn complex of ruins. High in one wall is a magnificent Tudor fireplace, which once warmed a long-vanished upper chamber.

Set on a steep hillside where Eskdale's tributary valley of Little Fryup heads for the high moors, Danby Castle intriguingly combines the roles of ancient monument and working farm. And it is also a Court of Law. For in the lord of the manor's former parlour, the Danby Court Leet sits each October. A rare survival of a manor court it administers the common rights on the 14,000-acre Danby Estate, owned by Lord Downe, of Wykeham, near Scarborough. Usually a solicitor, the court's presiding officer, or steward, conducts the court from a high-backed seventeenth-century judge's oak seat. But justice is dispensed by thirteen local jurymen.

Traditionally, old properties on the estate have certain rights attached to them - such as the right to cut peat, or graze sheep. The court swears in new owners of rights and also considers requests for 'infringements' on the common land - perhaps to create a parking space, erect a telegraph pole, or make a path to a cottage. Applicants permitted to make these encroachments must pay an annual 'fine', in reality a nominal fee, for the privilege.

Danby Castle...farm and fortress. The field gate indicates the former main gateway.

Seat of justice. The oak judge's bench in Danby Castle's historic 'jury room.'

Binding on the lord of manor as well as the so-called 'freeholders', these arrangements go back a very long time. A deed drawn up when the Danby estate was purchased by an ancestor of the present Viscount Downe in 1656 forbids him and his heirs, together with the freeholders and their heirs, to 'enclose, take-up, or improve any part of the commons or wastes of Danby.' An exception, now never exercised, was the right to take timber to repair buildings.

The castle's current guise as a farmhouse makes it hard to realise that a future Queen of England, Catherine Parr, sixth and last wife of Henry VIII, lived there. Before marrying Henry in 1543, she had two previous husbands. Her second husband, Danby's Lord Latimer, died the year before she married Henry. Legend has it that the King once visited Catherine at the castle, sheltering during a storm at a farm known ever since as Stormy Hall. But the name stems from a Norse personal name, Esturmi, and historians doubt whether Henry ever set foot in Eskdale.

Described by Sir Winston Churchill in his A History of the English Speaking Peoples as 'a serious little widow from the Lake District', Kendal-born Catherine was keenly interested in theology. As an eighteenth-century writer put it, she was 'a great favourer of the Gospel, and would earnestly argue for it, speaking more than her husband would willingly bear.' Evenings at Danby with Catherine can't have been much fun. How different was another much-wedded woman often associated with Danby Castle. Married three times, divorced and widowed once, and bearing a son to each of two lovers, Lucia de Thweng set pulses racing right across the North York Moors. Alas, we know nothing of her physical appearance. But looks were probably not her main attraction.

Born in 1279 at Kilton Castle, near Saltburn, Lucia became heiress to a number of estates, including Danby, when she only nine months old. Made a ward of Edward I, she was virtually auctioned off by the King to the highest bidder. This turned out to be William Latimer, a former Sheriff of Yorkshire and governor of the Royal castles of York and Pickering. With Lucia also came custody of the Danby estate and the right - officially the 'responsibility' - to arrange Lucia's marriage. Latimer paired her with his seventeen-year-old son, also William, whom Lucia married in 1296.

A reluctant bride, Lucia left William within a year for her cousin and childhood sweetheart Marmaduke Thweng, of Kilton Castle. She soon bore him a son. But on the death of Marmaduke in the Battle of Stirling in 1297 she returned to William Latimer.

Latimer later legitimised Lucia's son by Marmaduke as his own. But meanwhile, during Latimer's absence fighting in Scotland, Lucia had an affair with Peter de Mauley, of Mulgrave Castle, near Whitby.

In 1304 she vanished. Convinced she had been abducted, Edward I ordered a search for her, with authority to 'carry her back.' But Lucia had gone willingly to live with Nicholas Meynell, of Whorlton Castle, near Swainby. Though Lucia bore Nicholas a son, the pair never married. Divorced by Latimer in 1312 she left Meynell at about the same time and had two further husbands - a Sir Robert Everingham and Bartholomew Fanacourt, a French servant of the Latimers. What a gripping film, or TV series, all this would make.

Alas, Danby Castle wouldn't feature in it. For while many guidebooks say the castle was built by the Latimers around 1300, when Lucia's amorous adventures were in full swing, experts now believe it wasn't built until either the late fourteenth century or early fifteenth century. By then, not only was Lucia dead (1346), but the castle had passed by marriage to the Nevilles of Raby, Teesdale. Lucia's supposed 'abduction' was actually from Latimer's East Yorkshire manor house at Kirkburton, near Driffield.

Built by Robert de Brus when he was given most of Eskdale by William the Conqueror, the first castle in the district was at Castleton. Only a few earthworks survive, near the top of the hill between the railway station and the village.

The Nevilles replaced the original castle with a new one at Danby in a period when comfort and convenience were beginning to take precedence over defence in castle design. Like Castle Bolton, with which it is roughly contemporary, Danby castle was more a large fortified house than a traditional castle. Lacking outer defences, such as ditches or a moat, it was intended to repel occasional raids by Scottish borderers rather than figure in full-scale medieval war.

The main reason the castle was formerly believed to have been built about 1300 is the presence in the north wall of a form of royal arms abandoned after 1339. But experts now believe these arms, together with others of the Latimer and Ros families, were moved from an older building - probably the castle at Castleton. The obscure location of the arms supports a theory that the castle was built when, or soon after, it was acquired by the Nevilles in 1380. For the will of the last Lord Latimer required the Danby Nevilles to adopt the Latimer arms. This probably didn't please them, so they placed them where they would be mainly unseen.

Again like Castle Bolton, Danby Castle was built round a courtyard. But its corner towers, set at the unusual angle of 45 degrees to the main wall, gave it a peculiar butterfly shape. Distinguished by its broad chimney stack, the south-east tower now forms the main part of the farmhouse. Its ground floor is the living room, with bedrooms above. A nineteenth century extension to the tower is the farm kitchen.

The famous courtroom occupies most of the upper storey of the main range. Adjoining it is the 'jury room', a small chamber where the court jurors meet during the year to discuss court business. Formerly part of the castle's parlour it still has its original oak panelling.

Built into an angle between the courtroom and the tower is a turret whose spiral staircase leads to the castle's chapel. Though disused this still has a fine hammerbeam roof.

This entire range is believed to have been renovated and heightened in the sixteenth century, when the chimney stack was probably built. By then, the Nevilles obviously considered it safe to display their own arms, which are mounted on this frontage, facing the road.

Now just a cart track from the farmyard to a field, the castle's original gateway was between the north wall and a tower now reduced to just a garden wall. Chutes in the north wall show that all the main apartments had their own

Farm and fortress...this Alec Wright drawing illustrates the dual role of Danby Castle.

Whorlton Castle...witnessed match-making for Mary Queen of Scots.

lavatory - a considerable refinement. Directly beneath the lord's quarters there still survives a barrel-vaulted wine cellar, located to give the family access without entering the general part of the castle. A huge ground-floor fireplace identifies the kitchen, adjoining which are the remains of a bakehouse and a bacon-curing room. Part of the great hall also survives.

An excellent overview is obtained from a track heading up the moor directly opposite the castle. Group visits can be arranged through the Wykeham estate office, near Scarborough. Subject to the needs of the tenant farmer and agreement with the estate, guided walks may be introduced from the nearby National Park Centre. A redundant horse-mill at the castle has been tentatively suggested as a possible place where display boards could inform visitors about the castle, the court and the 165-acre farm - where David Smith currently raises heifers for beef, and calves that join dairy herds run by other members of his family. Danby Castle certainly deserves a firmer place on the Moors map.

Whorlton - Castle and Church

Climb a short hill out of Swainby, along a lane past the church, and you come upon a ruined gatehouse and a few grassy earthworks. Listen hard. Is there not the faint sound of singing - a pair of sweet female voices, followed by applause?

During his well-chronicled hunting trip in the North York Moors in 1323 Edward II arrived at Whorlton Castle on September 1. His treasurer's accounts record a payment of four shillings (20p) to 'Alice the red-haired and Alice de Whorlton', who sang Simon de Montfort and other songs 'before the King.'

The stillness and silence of ruined Whorlton Castle today, in a setting of tranquil, pastoral farmland, gives the imagination full rein to bring back this appealing cameo of Merrie England. Crowning a low spur of the Cleveland Hills, the privately-owned castle has none of the trappings of tourism - car park, pay booth, neat lawns etc. Nothing disturbs an atmosphere accurately described by Nikolaus Pevsner as 'eerie'. Here and close by the aura of the past is tangible. Which is unsurprising since Whorlton consists, in Pevsner's equally telling words, of 'a castle in ruins, a church in ruins, and hardly anything else.'

Though only half a mile from Swainby, a popular village just off the A172, the castle seems profoundly lost and lonely. And yet it once embraced its own village. Established within the earthworks in the twelfth century this was a *burgus*, a village that enjoyed the protection of a castle. In return for its security, the villagers, or burgers, paid tolls on goods to the local lord, at whose mill they were also obliged to grind their corn. Though it was not uncommon for small castles to contain a burgus - a name derived from the Scandinavian verb *bergen*, to shelter - Whorlton is Yorkshire's best example.

Local historians believe there may have been earlier dual forts and civil settlements on this strategic spur, commanding routes into and out of the hills and along their northern foot. The Romans were certainly in the district, for in 1810 a farmer ploughing the slopes of Whorl Hill, the 700ft (152.3m) conical outlier that gives Whorlton its name, unearthed a leather bag containing a hoard of

Roman coins and silver. Now in the British Museum the coins were dated from the mid fourth century to the reign of the Honorious, the Emperor under whose rule (408-423) the Romans left Britain. Several pieces of Roman pottery have also been found in the church graveyard, most recently when it was extended in 1977. So a Roman villa probably stood at Whorlton. With what despair would its occupants bury their money and cherished possessions, including a beautiful silver dish, in the open fields?

Little is known of the probable founder of the castle, Robert de Meynell, whose grandfather received Whorlton after the Conquest. First real light on the family's racy story comes in 1290 when Sir Nicholas Meynell, a friend of Edward I, accused his wife, Christian, of attempting to poison him. Cleared at a hearing before the Archbishop of York, Christian successfully sued her husband for alimony.

The son of this pair, also Sir Nicholas, lived at the castle with the notorious Lucia de Thweng, the heiress bedded by a string of Yorkshire noblemen. Her divorce from William Latimer, of Kirkburton, Driffield, after she had eloped with Meynell, sparked a protracted wrangle about her personal estate, which included several Cleveland manors. To prevent these passing to her children by Latimer, rather than her illegitimate son by Meynell, Lucia transferred them in trust to a sympathetic local clergyman. Latimer retaliated by bribing a retired soldier to swear he had been hired by Meynell to murder him. But the soldier retracted his evidence, and Latimer's plot to besmirch Meynell, and thus exclude him and his family from the inheritance, failed.

It was Lucia's illegitimate son, yet another Sir Nicholas Meynell, who entertained Edward II at Whorlton. The king's payments to the singing Alices, one of whom was Meynell's wife, were not the only ones made during the visit. Among others were several to servants who 'set nets to take roe-deer in Whorlton Park.'

Curiously, the Meynells at that time didn't technically own Whorlton Park. For in 1217 a wardship tangle culminated in custody of the estate being granted to the Archbishop of Canterbury. The Meynells retained full control in return for a not-too-onerous duty: at the consecration of each Archbishop, the head of the Meynell family was to act as *pantler*, the official who hands the communion cup to the primate!

Yet another dispute over ownership culminated in the manor's takeover in 1541 by Henry VIII - who promptly gave it to his friend the Earl of Lennox. In a letter written at Whorlton twenty years later, to Mary Queen of Scots, the Countess pressed the credentials of her son, Lord Darnley, for marriage to the nineteen-year-old Queen. Her audacity paid off, and in 1603 the son of Mary and Darnley ascended to the throne as James I of England, James VI of Scotland - the first of the Stuart kings. Alas, however, Mary had been executed and Darnley murdered - events that doubtless reverberated at Whorlton.

The Lennox castle was very different from the Norman original, which had been replaced in the late fourteenth century by a fortified house. Entered by the present gatehouse, this was built by Lord Philip D'Arcy, whose father inherited the estate by marrying a Meynell. To create enough space for his house D'Arcy sliced off the top half of the castle mound. This produced a level site of threequarters of an acre, on which D'Arcy erected a house, stables and other buildings.

Now owned by Lord Ingleby, of Snilesworth, the castle is freely open to visitors. With its seven-and-a-half-foot (2.2m) thick walls, which stand to a height of 28ft (8.5m), the gatehouse is an impressive building. Surviving internal features include guard chambers, fireplaces, part of a spiral staircase, drawbridge chain slits, and portcullis slots. Shields on the exterior wall are the arms of the Meynells, D'Arcys and Greys, all linked by marriage. A higher shield shows the arms of the Meynells impaling those of D'Arcy. At the back, steps lead down to vaults and chambers built into the hillside. In Victorian days these served as cattle stalls.

Pockmarks on the gatehouse show where the castle was hit by cannon and musket fire in a Civil War seige. Though the then owner, Lord Bruce, held the castle for Charles I, the damage persuaded his son, the first Earl of Ailesbury, to rebuild the entire house apart from the gatehouse. The point where the pitched roof of the new manor house abutted the western wall of the gatehouse is still clear.

This house eventually became a tenanted farmhouse, which was abandoned in the nineteenth century. In 1876 most of its stone, including the foundations, was used to build a new church at Swainby. No record, not even a ground plan, was made of the historic manor house.

The building of the new church reflected the growth of Swainby and decline of Whorlton. Local tradition says the village vanished with the Black Death of 1483. But Barry Harrison, a leading Cleveland historian, believes otherwise. In the journal of the Teesside and Cleveland Local History Society in 1978, he observed:

> The village itself did not disappear; there were three farms and four or five cottages at Whorlton as late as the eighteenth century, and it is unlikely that there had ever been more. The disappearance of two of the farms and the cottages was the result of estate improvements by the Ailesbury family in the late eighteenth and early nineteenth centuries.

Before the new church was built, Swainby folk trekked up the hill to Whorlton's old church, a short way beyond the castle. Approached through a sombre avenue of churchyard yews the half-ruined building, with three Norman arches flanking a roofless nave, is more melancholy - and intriguing - than the castle.

Built in the early thirteenth century it gained its square tower, still intact, two centuries later. A peephole in a locked door gives a view into the chancel, also intact. Here stands a major church monument - an oak effigy of a knight under an elaborate stone canopy. It commemorates either the first Sir Nicholas Meynell or his son, who became Sheriff of Yorkshire. Beautifully-carved, the effigy is believed to be the work of the same fourteenth century craftsman - name alas unknown - who carved the monument in Westminster Abbey to Edmund

Plantagenet, a son of Edward I. The stone canopy was erected a century after the effigy was installed, some say as a memorial to Lord D'Arcy, who built the castle gatehouse.

Outside, a buttress of the south wall has a rare 'mass dial'. A primitive form of weekly calendar this consists of seven holes - six in row, with the slightly-larger seventh above. Each day the priest placed a stick in one of the holes, reserving the larger hole for Sunday. His illiterate flock had no excuse for not attending Sunday Mass.

The church fell into decay long before it was formally abandoned. A mid-Victorian account tells of a large branch of ivy overhanging the altar. But the ruins was consolidated in 1891 - the date engraved on a buttress. Though now redundant, the church still hosts services four or five times a year, the main one being an open-air service in summer. In 1995-6 villagers and other well-wishers provided £12,000 towards a £40,000 programme of repairs funded mainly by English Heritage.

In 1988, the national park authority, noting what it called 'the renewed local interest in the history of the castle, church, and associated settlement pattern', launched discussions on the future of Whorlton. Some kind of management plan was expected. In 1993 the castle was adopted, with the owner's permission, by a medieval re-enactment society. It members spoke of transforming Whorlton into a 'living history exhibition,' a mock medieval village where visitors would 'watch battles and take part in ancient crafts like weaving and pottery.'

Thankfully nothing has come of this. For it is through Whorlton's profound silence, stillness and, yes, strangeness, that its haunting atmosphere is felt.

CHAPTER 4
MEN OF THE MOORS

Major Fairfax-Blakeborough

Many visitors to Westerdale village still ask: 'Where did Major Fairfax-Blakeborough live?' They are surprised to learn he didn't live there and was very rarely seen in the village. Low House, the major's former 'Westerdale' home, is about two miles away, on the far side of the valley. Narrowly within Westerdale parish, it is more closely linked with nearby Castleton.

But the keen public interest in the major more than 20 years after his death testifies to his legendary status. An authority on racing, rural folklore and Yorkshire dialect; a saviour of the Cleveland Bay; author of well over 100 books; and newspaper columnist extraordinary. These were the varied, yet often interlinked, roles that secured his fame.

Of course there was also the major's robust individualism. He always wrote to friends with a quill pen. Inquiries about his routine at Low House were met with the reply: 'I dress each evening for dinner...in pyjamas and a dressing gown.' In fact after dinner the major worked at his desk until two or three o'clock in the morning. He never took a full day off from the end of the First World War, 1918, to his death on New Year's Day, 1976 - just 14 days before his 93rd birthday.

Christened John but always known as Jack, or Fairfax, the major was the remarkable son of a remarkable father - Richard Fairfax-Blakeborough. Born in Ripon, the multi-talented Richard became best known as an authority on Yorkshire folklore. Published by Oxford University Press in 1898 his *Yorkshire Wit, Character and Folklore* remains a standard work. He also wrote plays, and as a young man won cups for boxing and rowing. Later he made furniture and became a skilled bookbinder. In the 1890s he invented a photographic plate that went into commercial production. And in the early days of the telephone he rigged up a battery-powered instrument, a forerunner of today's cordless, in his home at Guisborough. Of him, son Jack, born at Guisborough on 15 January, 1883, said: 'I have not the tithe of the brain and ability of my father. He was a genius in every way except making money.'

Richard travelled extensively in rural Yorkshire, recording traditions and dialect. That is how Jack, who often accompanied his father, gained his interest in country life.

At home in Westerdale - Major John Fairfax-Blakeborough, master of moorland lore.

'Miles from anywhere on a wolf-infested moor'? Not exactly. Low House, Major Fairfax-Blakeborough's former home, sits conveniently by a moorland road.

Lifted as an infant on to a hunter by Jack Walton, a noted Cleveland trainer, Jack developed a particular passion for horses. Between the wars, this led him into the role of secretary of the Cleveland Bay Society. An outstanding draught horse, the Bay was facing extinction at that time. In countless articles and talks Jack tirelessly promoted the breed, especially stressing its record in siring top-class hunters. Ultimately recognised in his election as president of the society, his efforts helped raise the number of breeding stallions from just four in the 1920s to more than 60 forty years later.

Jack hadn't seemed destined for such rural endeavour when he left school. But three miserable months in a Teesside stockbroker's office convinced him he was no more suited than his father to the world of finance. Entering journalism with the *Evening Gazette*, Middlesbrough, he took the bold step of leaving at 20, to become a freelance specialising in country life and sports.

Renting the sixteenth-century Old Hall, at Battersby, near Great Ayton, Jack managed to keep a couple of horses, on which he hunted with the Bilsdale, Farndale and Cleveland packs. To gain working experience with horses he became assistant to a racehorse trainer at Hambleton House, Sutton Bank. Moving to larger stables at Middleham, he accepted an invitation by Sir Loftus Bates, manager of several racecourses in Yorkshire, Northumberland and Scotland, to become his assistant at race meetings.

The First World War (1914-18) interrupted this progress. Enlisting on the second day, Jack served in the 15th Hussars, a cavalry regiment, with which he rose to the rank of major and won the Military Cross. Appropriately, he spent the final year of the war in charge of the regiment's 1,000 horses.

Afterwards, the major became a racing judge. He often recalled his first meeting, at Sedgefield: 'About twenty horses were in a tight finish. When the result went up, someone shouted "He isn't fit to judge the donkey races on Redcar sands." ' But for almost 50 years he was a valued judge on courses from Lincolnshire to Perth. On his retirement in 1962, when he was Britain's oldest licensed turf official, the Jockey Club presented him with a silver model racehorse and cheque for £700.

His short stint as the first judge at Middlesbrough's greyhound stadium proved less distinguished. In his words:

The patrons of greyhound racing were not quite as restrained as turf crowds. Not infrequently my dog decisions were greeted with calls like:

'Put your b_____ specs on,' or 'Give a f_____ fair decision.' I said goodbye to the dogs...

In 1929 the major married Doris _ 'the best winner I ever backed' - daughter of a Northumberland lawyer and his wife. After spending their early married life at Norton-on-Tees, they moved in 1945 to Low House. Dated 1673 on a lintel, it stands by a little-used road at the foot of a bracken-clad slope just off Castleton Rigg. A friend of the major who visited the couple soon after they moved in wrote: 'Fairfax has gone to live twenty miles from anywhere, in a tumble down cottage on a wolf-infested moor, where they have nine months of winter and three of bad weather.'

Quoting this some years later the major revealed a less-than-charitable view of visitors to the Moors:

> We do not need sympathy, nor are the libels merited. True, the gales may be stronger, the snow deeper and more frequent, and the frosts more severe...But except for midnight motor rallies and frequent invasions of litter-lout plant-uprooting, turf-sod digging vandals we live amid the peace that passeth all understanding.

But he is still fondly remembered for the weekly newspaper column he wrote from 1907 to his death. A miscellany of country lore, this was first published in the *Whitby Gazette*, which decorated it with a charming line-drawing of rabbits in a harvest field. Minus that adornment it was soon adopted by the *Darlington and Stockton Times*, followed by a score or more of other northern papers.

Typical column subjects were the habits of rats ('awd rattens'), the incidence of cream-coloured moles ('mowdiwarps'), and the folklore of the rowan tree. Most popular were dialect conversation pieces centred on a fictional villager named Lizzie Leckonby, who was often mildly at odds with her neighbour, Mary Thompson. The major's very last column contained this typical example:

> It's been public house talk that old Lizzie Leckonby, after scrufflin' through the collection of Christmas cards at Betty's shop, asked: 'Have you none wi "We're nut senin' cards this year" printed on 'em.' It is also village talk that Mary Thompson and Lizzie have had frequent arguments as to which received the greater number of greetings. 'I coonted each one t'posstman handed ti my next door nybor, so I know who got t'most cards,' said Mary. 'Of course I'se so well respected.'
>
> This last remark infuriated old Lizzie, who said: 'I knew she was winder-peeping ivvery mornin' when t'posstman cem, but she missed coontin' yan morning when he cem wi' a big batch of cards. As for being well respected, I'm glad ti knaw that I evn't t'reppitation and carackter of being a nosey-parker scannell-monger wi' a bitter tongue, like a certain party that ah'll nut soil mi tongue by namin'.

A staunch Anglican, Lizzie sometimes summed up her little differences with Mary, a Methodist, by reference to their religious faiths: 'She's chech and ahm chapil.'

The major also had a deep fund of dialect stories. Fond of whisky, he loved to tell about a Farndale farmer who went to Castleton for a meeting of the Blackfaced Sheepbreeders' Association. Entering a meeting of the local Temperance Society by mistake he turned to go. The chairman called out: 'Would you like to testify brother, before you depart?' The farmer replied: 'Aye, mebbee ah will. Mi father lived ti be 91. Whisky was hauf a croon a bottle. He drank a bottle ivvery day - and he looked a lot livelier than any of you fellas three days after he died.'

On his retirement from hunting, in 1969, aged 86, the major wrote in his column:

> I parted with my last scarlet coat, all my white breeches and other impedimenta to a young Nimrod in his teens. May he have many good days with hounds, on good horses, in company with good sportsmen.

The sale of the major's horses five years earlier prompted him to reflect later: 'One of the things I miss most is the welcoming whinnies of the horses. That is one of the great deprivations of growing old.'

In a *Dalesman* article reviewing changes in his lifetime, the major mentioned several memories common among his generation - horses ploughing, the man with a red flag in front of early motor cars etc. Far more interesting was this recollection:

> I remember when most of the older country folk still firmly believed in the power of witches, their spells and curses, and the dire results of human beings and farm stock being 'looked on' by the evil eye. Country people still had a deep-rooted fear of ghosts, and clung to a thousand superstitions.

Giving an example, he said that two veteran Bilsdale huntsmen, Bobby Dowson and Nicholas Spink, were convinced the death of a foxhound was due to its having caught a lame hare, which they believed was a local witch, Peg Humphrey, credited with being able to turn herself into any animal.

Unsure himself how many books he had written, the major certainly produced more than a hundred. They included 50 hunt histories and a four-volume Northern Turf History. Particularly sought-after today are his memoir of Canon John Kyle, the hunting, pub-owning parson of Carlton, near Stokesley, and a Dictionary of Yorkshire Dialect, compiled with Sir Arthur Pease.

Before the Second World War the major also wrote thirteen novels. Mysteries with a racing theme, they were reprinted in paperback and sold in Woolworths for sixpence (2p) a copy.

At Low House the major worked in a book-lined study converted from a cowshed. Routinely, he wrote from 10am to 12.10pm. He then usually walked the quarter of a mile to a nearby crossroads, where he posted his mail in a postbox that is still there. Lunch and tea were each followed by another two-hour writing spell, with that longer burst into the small hours after dinner.

On his 90th birthday the major was profiled on TV and in *The Times*, *The Guardian* and other newspapers. Awarded the OBE in 1975, he continued writing virtually up to his death, his last column appearing posthumously on January 3, 1976. A devout Roman Catholic, he was buried at the RC church at Lealholm, where he had attended morning Mass on every Sunday but one - in the severe winter of 1947 - during his 31 years on that 'wolf-infested moor.'

Besides his books and former homes, other reminders of the Major include a beech tree he planted in 1973 at Potto Grange, near Hutton Rudby, home of

Canon Kyle's daughter, and an oak planted in his presence the following year at Battersby by Viscount Ingleby. A plaque with the latter salutes 'a lifetime's writings on Yorkshire lore, horses and sport.' The late Bill Cowley often urged that a 'Fairfax-Blakeborough Memorial Room' should be established in a Cleveland library as a tribute to the major and his father. But this idea has yet to be acted upon.

Bill Cowley - and the Lyke Wake Walk

On 1 October 1955, fourteen people set off across the North York Moors on what their leader, Bill Cowley, later described as 'my most infamous escapade.' More than 170,000 people have so far followed in his adventurous steps.

Now paved in parts, the broad track beaten out by this legion of walkers makes it difficult to realise that when Bill and his companions embarked on their 42-mile trek there was no path to ease their steps for most of the way. Even in places where a well-used path might have been expected, like the short climb up Cringle Moor from the road at Carlton Bank, or to Botton Head, highest point of the Moors, from Clay Bank, only a single-file track led through the dense heather. The transformation of the entire route into what Bill himself dubbed 'an elephant track' is largely due to the success of Bill's brainchild: the Lyke Wake Walk.

Its popularity has brought criticism. But this is undeserved. As a leading article in *The Guardian*, welcoming the walk soon after its inception, noted: 'Most mountain districts evolve in time a 'classic' long distance walk. The Three Peaks in the Yorkshire Dales, the Welsh 3,000's, Marsden to Edale in the Peak District...' Bill's concept of a traverse of the North York Moors, keeping as closely as possible to the highest ground, created a worthy addition to those and other 'classic' treks. Since the very reason the North York Moors were designated a national park is because they contain England's largest expanse of heather moor, it is fitting to have a walk that pays homage to it. Though there are now other challenge walks in the Moors that surpass the LWW in toughness or variety, the LWW remains the most inspired. Elephant track or not, it is the one walk above all others that most moorland addicts feel obliged to get under their belt at sometime.

The idea came to Bill while he was gazing up to the whaleback crest of Black Hambleton from a smallholding he ran at Over Silton after the Second World War. In an article in published in *The Dalesman* in August, 1955, he wrote:

> You can get up to the 'tops' above Swainby and walk due east on heather all the way, except for crossing one main road at the head of Bilsdale, and one or two minor ones...And if you did that in September you would kick up a cloud of pollen from the purple heather at every step for 40 miles...You might never meet a soul for the two or three days it would take you. I challenge anyone, Three Peaks champion or no, to do it in one.

Of the thirteen people who responded, ten - seven men and three women - were from York Mountaineering Club. With Bill at its head, the group set off at noon

A prehistoric settlement? No? Pictured in 1993, Bill Cowley stands amid the gateposts of Snilesworth's vanished Stebbinthwaite Farm, sometimes known as High Cote.

POLICE NOTICE

FIRES now Burning on the MOORS
in the
GLAISDALE and WHEELDALE Areas
present
Serious Hazards to Walkers and the
Public are strongly advised to
KEEP AWAY.

LYKE WAKE WALK

THIS WARNING particularly applies to
Persons intending to undertake
THE LYKE WAKE WALK,
large sections of which
are INACCESSIBLE.

NORTH YORKSHIRE POLICE — JULY, 1976.

A bleak moment for the Lyke Wake Walk - closed in 1976 because of moor fires.

on 1 October from Beacon Hill, Osmotherley. Bill dubbed the expedition 'a mini Everest of our own making.' At 3 a.m. the next morning, as he led the struggling party over the boggy Loose Howe, between Rosedale and Glaisdale, into his mind came the words of Cleveland's ancient Lyke Wake Dirge. Formerly sung at funerals, and well-known enough to appear in the *Oxford Book of English Verse*, this takes its name from the watch, or wake, traditionally kept over a corpse, for which the Norse word is lyke (hence lychgate).

Believed to have last been sung over a corpse at Kildale in 1800, the dirge describes the terrible purgatory journey made by the dead person's soul over a frightful moor. To Bill, the dirge's opening lines expressed the spirit of his night-time slog over the trackless wilderness.

> *This yah neet, this yah neet,*
> *Ivvery neet an' all,*
> *Fire an' fleet an' cannle leet,*
> *An' Christ tak up thy soul.*

Twenty-three hours after setting off - eight after their struggle over Loose Howe - Bill's party, minus just one drop-out, reached its coastal destination at Ravenscar. Afterwards, the names of the walkers were engraved on a tankard, and the Lyke Wake Club was born. There is no truth in statements that the Walk follows an old corpse road, of which only two (Staithes-Hinderwell, and Goathland-Pickering) have ever existed in the Moors. And neither follows the route of the Lyke Wake Walk.

Having pioneered his walk Bill, a busy farmer, might have left it at that. But he took pleasure in its growing popularity and played an active part in the Lyke Wake Club, open to all who complete the walk in 24 hours. Possessor of a dry sense of humour, Bill relished devising procedures suitable to the club's ghoulish name. Thus those completing the walk in the prescribed time qualify as Dirgers - their grim achievement recognised by the famous black-edged card of condolence. Further levels of dedication to the walk are rewarded with 'degrees' that rise from Master (or Mistress) of Misery (three crossings, including one in the reverse direction) through Doctor of Dolefulness (seven crossings) to Past Master (fifteen crossings plus exceptional service to the walk). A close friend of mine, the late Alan Waller, a journalist who publicised the walk in its early years, and contributed to humdrum tasks like removing litter, was among the first ten of this elite. More recently, the title of Senile Centenarian has been created for the select few who have done the walk more than 100 times.

Officers of the club hold titles such as Anxious Almoner and Harassed Archivist. Bill, who died in 1994, was The Most Mournful, the Chief Dirger. His own score or so of crossings included a rare ski trek in the winter of 1962-63. The qualifying time for such crossings is 24 hours of daylight.

But the Lyke Wake Walk was by no means Bill's only link with the North York Moors. His love of the region was rooted in circumstances uncannily similar to those of one his heroes - the moorland archaeologist and naturalist Frank Elgee. Both born and raised in Middlesbrough, both also contracted pneumonia as boys. And both fell under the spell of the Moors when sent to recuperate among them - Elgee at Ingleby Greenhow, Cowley at Osmotherley. Bill once told me: 'My life was despaired of. The doctor said: "Get him on to the moors." My mother took me to Osmotherley where we spent a year in a freezing cottage. I never looked back.'

Educated at Middlesbrough High School and Jesus College, Cambridge, Bill entered the Civil Service, with which he served in India from 1939 to 1947. Recalling his days as a magistrate in Taxila, a hilltown in the Punjab, he wrote in his 1993 book *Snilesworth* :

> When I looked at the farmers and shepherds in the village square under the Margalla Hills, my immediate impression was that most of them might have come straight off the Bilsdale or Snilesworth Moors. Exactly the same faces and expressions.

Taking up farming on his return to England, Bill only briefly ran that smallholding at Over Silton before moving to the larger Goulton Grange Farm, near Swainby, which he farmed, together with the adjoining Potto Hill, for almost forty years. He found time to write dialect poetry and several books, including a history of Yorkshire farming. A skilled climber as well as keen walker, at 41, in 1957, he led a Yorkshire Mountaineering Club expedition to the Himalayas. Later, he helped set up the Cleveland Search and Rescue team.

But it is for the LWW that Bill will always be remembered. In the walk's first three years only 191 crossings were recorded. But by the late 1970s about 12,000 people a year were attempting the walk, many in large parties. Purporting to depict a typical weekend on the LWW, a cartoon with one of Alan Waller's articles, in the the Middlesbrough-based *Evening Gazette*, showed mothers pushing prams, youngsters on pogo-sticks, and Humphrey Bogart hauling the African Queen through a moorland bog. The reality wasn't much different. One man humped a 28lb sack of potatoes (King Edward's) along the walk. A Greenpeace party carried a mock-up whale. Dressed as monks, a Scout group bore a coffin, the Lyke Wake emblem. A Mr William Pollitt, of Northallerton, was only half joking when he proposed a sponsored march of brass bands.

Chaos, almost tragic, came 1971. With the Moors lashed by driving rain and wreathed in almost-freezing fog - all in glorious June - village halls had to be turned into emergency rescue stations when the members of a 512-strong party doing the LWW to raise money for UNICEF, the United Nations' children's fund, became hopelessly dispersed. Only one person completed the walk.

The following summer 100 walkers from a sponsored group of 239 were cut off by the swollen Jugger Howe beck, near Fylingdales. Rescue teams had to light flares to guide helicopters to the stranded walkers, many suffering severely from hypothermia.

As uneasy as everyone else by the walk's adoption by big sponsored groups Bill Cowley observed: 'The LWW was never meant to be that kind of marathon. No-one can persuade me there is any pleasure in walking in parties of more than 20.' Extensive fires along the route in the dry summer of 1976 led to the temporary closure of the walk, most of which does not lie on rights of way. As the national park authority and moorland owners considered closing the walk permanently, Bill conceded: 'Reducing the numbers is the only way to keep the walk alive.'

Sustained publicity urging sponsored parties to avoid the LWW has helped to reduce the annual number of crossings to about 3,000. Bill and the LWW club also devised an alternative walk, the 38-mile Shepherd's Round, which is now highlighted in Bill's book on the Lyke Wake Walk. But Bill always bridled at suggestions that his walk had become too popular and spoiled the Moors. In 1989 he commented:

> People are more important than peat. What use is a national park if people can't use it? I am proud to know that well over 100,000 people have had the strength, stamina and courage to complete the 40-mile Lyke Wake Walk.

Few crossings better illustrate what Bill meant than one in 1980 by fifteen-year-old Linda Rutherford, of Gateshead. The first seriously disabled person to complete the walk, she clung bravely to her wheelchair for nineteen hours as friends manoeuvred it with ropes poles and planks across moor, bog and beck. A wonderful achievement.

The last link with the high-profile period of the LWW is the annual Lyke Wake Race, run in July. Set in 1989 by Cumbria's Mark Rigsby, the fastest time is 4hrs 41 minutes. The youngest person to complete the walk, Christopher Turton, of Bridlington, was a month short of his seventh birthday when he completed the walk with his mother in 1972. The oldest Dirger, retired Wakefield vicar the Rev. Clarisford Morgan, was 81 when he completed the walk in 1962.

Four men have qualified as Senile Centenarians, and at the Ravenscar end of the walk a seat commemorates Ben Hingston, whose 212 crossings make him the only person to have achieved the double century.

In 1978 an MP, Alex Lyon of York, became briefly lost on the LWW. Two years later nine miners from Grimethorpe set off with their map upside down. They walked for six hours in the wrong direction before realising their mistake. They then hired a taxi to search for their support party, which was totally mystified by their complete disappearance in fine weather.

For the very reason that it hugs the high moors the LWW lacks variety. And no-one loved the contrasts of the North York Moors more than Bill Cowley. As related in his book *Cleveland Calendar*, he gloried in the thrill of standing

> on Botton Head with cloud and darkness shrouding the whole moor, a deluge of cold rain, thunder crashing above your head, and lightning zipping across the heather...To come down to the lush fields again in the pale evening sunshine, to exchange the scent of peat and wet heather for wild rose and honeysuckle, is to savour life at its best.

Bill was also particularly fond of ancient standing stones. In response to complaints about noise and disturbance in Osmotherley by people embarking on the Lyke Wake Walk, it was Bill's idea to encourage a switch to nearby Sheepwash by erecting a roadside stone engraved with the walk's name. A similar stone was also put up at Ravenscar.

An imaginative way of commemorating Bill would have been to to engrave his name, with dates of birth and death, on the back of these stones. But equally fitting is an engraved stone in Clain Wood, near Swainby. Bearing the simple inscription 'Bill Cowley 1915-1994' it overlooks Bill's former farmland and his native Cleveland. And of course it's by the Lyke Wake Walk.

A. J. Brown

Alfred John Brown was the supreme moorland tramper. The words 'walker' and 'rambler' don't come close to what he was all about. He practised - and preached - what he called the art of tramping. In its highest form this became 'moor wallowing' - wading thigh-deep through heather across a trackless moor.

One moor wallow by Brown, between Bilsdale and Bransdale in 1930, was a virtual dress rehearsal for that imperishable moment, 25 years later, when Bill Cowley named a rough moorland walk after the Lyke Wake Dirge. In his book *Tramping in Yorkshire*, published in 1932, Brown gives this description of his Bilsdale-Bransdale crossing:

> Bilsdale East Moor in the rainy season is a beast, covered as it is with a dense growth of very deep heather, all too frequently interspersed with bogs and 'blind' water-logged holes...And yet, gruelling as my own crossing was, I confess I enjoyed every yard of it, though I should not care to be benighted on those moors. Even in daylight they are apt to be a little sinister. Was it, I wonder, these very moors which inspired the greatest dialect poem in the language - the immortal Lyke Wake Dirge? I was muttering some of those wonderful stanzas as I stumbled over the dense ling.

Usually known as 'A.J.', Brown wrote a string of best-selling books on Yorkshire between the 1930s and 1950s. He dubbed moorland trampers like himself 'moormen.' Those who fit the term today - female as well as - should honour Brown. For *Tramping in Yorkshire* and its predecessor, *Moorland Tramping*, remain unsurpassed in conveying the exhilaration of exploring Yorkshire's high places on foot. In *Moorland Tramping*, devoted largely to the Dales, A.J. explained his 'tramping' concept:

> Tramping is to walking what poetry is to prose. It is walking, if you like, in an intenser air....In an age that craves and discovers more and more fantastic sports, it is astonishing that so few people know the thrill of crossing a moor from end to end in a direct line without any

A discreet tribute - Bill Cowley's memorial stone by the LWW at Scugdale.

A.J. Brown, author, hotelier - and supreme 'moor wallower!'

sort of guide. Yet, given the right kind of day, it is to be doubted if there is any sport in the world to vie with it...The joy of free movement...the feeling of fighting one's way forward in the teeth of the elements...To cross a stretch of moor like this in a gale is something like sailing a yacht singled-handed over an angry sea.

Born in Bradford in 1894 Brown rose from being a boy clerk in a railway superintendent's office to heading a wool export business, a role that took him all over the world. But he was gripped by a love for Yorkshire's uplands, nurtured by walks with his father and his own camping trips on Baildon Moor. An accomplished poet as well as prose writer, he once contrasted the two aspects of his life in a poem inspired by a tramp along one of his beloved green roads:

> *There in that city I by day am mewed;*
> *And sweat and swink in clerkly servitude.*
> *Here on this Road, that climbs to cleave a cloud,*
> *I live: I laugh: I sing: I shout aloud.*

As a West Yorkshireman, A.J. won his tramping - and doubtless wallowing - spurs in the Dales. The first issue of *The Dalesman*, April 1939, contained his itinerary for a Three Peaks Walk, not then established as a Dales' classic.

Serving as an Intelligence Officer in Bomber Command during the Second World War, A. J. resolved that afterwards he wouldn't return to the world of wool. Fortunately his wife, Marie-Eugenie, a French-born typist whom he met at work and married in 1927, shared his wish for a fresh start. So in 1945 they bought the Whitfield House Hotel in Goathland.

The hotel had been closed during the war, and it was certainly not by examining its dusty accounts that A. J. decided his future with Marie-Eugenie lay there. What persuaded him was a sunlit window seat.

A.J. was captivated by the seat, in the hall, when he and Marie-Eugenie were shown round the hotel. He wrote later: 'It was the most inviting window seat I had ever seen. I could not resist the impulse to sit there while the others took chairs.'

On completing their inspection, A.J. and Marie-Eugenie again halted in the hall. He recalled. 'I had the window seat again. The sun was still shining and I felt curiously happy and excited. Short of discovering some unforeseen snags I had already decided to buy High Fell.'

High Fell is the name A.J. gave to Whitfield House in a book, *I Bought a Hotel*, from which the above quotations are taken. Together with its sequel, *Farewell High Fell*, it recounts A.J.'s experience as a country hotelier. With their still-unchanged moorland setting, these two books, rich in character and anecdote and exploiting the escapist dream of running a country hotel, could be the basis of a popular TV series in the elusive mould of James Herriot's All Creatures Great and Small. So it's ironic that while Goathland has in recent years become famous as the location of ITV's Heartbeat, based on the adventures of a village constable who never served at Goathland, the village's authentic crock of potential TV gold remains undiscovered.

'The front seemed all windows...' A. J. Brown's entranced first impression of Goathland's Whitfield House Hotel, holds good today.

Whifield House as illustrated in A.J's brochure – *A Hymn to Yorkshire Hospitality*.

Still a hotel, by the hill down to Darnholme, Whitfield House still looks very much as A. J. described it in *I Bought A Hotel*:

> The front seemed all windows...bulging towards us in four or five bays. There seemed to be a lot of little gates and several doors all painted white...There was a lovely cottage garden, full of daffodils and primroses, with a lawn beyond and an orchard. The quiet lane slipped past the house and disappeared down a steep hill to the river.

Virtually an essay on Yorkshire hospitality, A.J.'s brochure is a masterpiece. It declares:

> The accommodation is limited to about 20 guests, so there is no question of a crowd...Just 20 people - the right sort of people. The kind who seek solitude and quiet after the turmoil of cities; who love to explore the old moorland tracks and neighbouring villages by day; or fish in the local becks; or ride over the moors; and come back in the evening with an edge on their appetites to enable them to appreciate a good dinner. And then to sit round the fireside on chilly evenings and talk or read or play bridge to their heart's content. What more could the heart desire? But for those who disdain the comforts of the fireside and a good selection of books, even at night, the quiet road outside the gate leads straight to the moors where the air is like wine.

Of course the brochure refers to A. J.'s tramping passion: 'All local footpaths seem to lead to the lovely village of Beck Hole, but there are plenty of real walks for hardy trampers,' he wrote.

A. J. and Marie-Eugenie left Whitfield House in 1952. The strain of doing all the cooking - brilliantly, in English style with French touches - had taken its toll on Marie-Eugenie. She and A. J. also regretted the loss of 'family' time with their children, three daughters and two sons, though all helped at the hotel. And A. J. found it difficult to fit in his writing, let alone moorland tramping.

But during his seven years at Whitfield House, A.J. brought out a collection of his Poems and Songs and wrote *Fair North Riding*, still the best general guide to that historic county. In 1958 A. J. adapted its chapters on the North York Moors into the first official guidebook for the national park, designated six years earlier.

Meanwhile, A. J's two Tramping books appeared in the single volume *Striding Through Yorkshire* . He had also written *Broad Acres*, a celebration of all things Yorkshire, from green roads and moorland inns to cricket and ham-and-egg teas. He also published novels, a book about his RAF service, and - his most original work - a tramping opus entitled *Four Boon Fellows*, a Yorkshire walking tour with three friends. Throughout their lives they addressed each other by the names of Yorkshire rivers - Ouse, Aire, Swale and Wharfe.

After leaving Whitfield House, A. J. and Marie-Eugenie spent periods in London, York and Bradford. But the North York Moors drew them back, to a

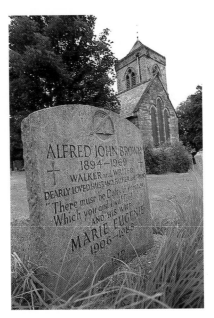

With quill-pen motif and lines of verse A.J. Brown's headstone forms a fitting memorial in Sleights' churchyard.

George Osbaldeston - 'Squire of All England.'

cottage at Sleights called St Joseph's. Shortly before moving there in 1966 A. J., in failing health, spent a long day tramping the Bronte moors, the hills of his youth. In a moving letter to 'My Dear Ouse' [George Heseltine], and signing himself 'Wharfe', A. J. recounted his experience:

> I intended to walk another few miles and then return to my car and be home for tea, as promised . But once I sniffed the air of those moors and felt the eerie atmosphere I got the bit between my teeth and went on and on...It meant another four or five miles back to Haworth but I had every intention of entering the broken threshold of Wuthering Heights again - and did. I touched the walls again and stamped in the kitchen and felt glorious again for a brief moment. I have such memories of that spot! And I felt full of high excitement and gratitude that I had been permitted to walk all that way again; and that my body was still strong and my heart full of fire.

But within three years A. J. was dead. Remaining at Sleights until her own death in 1988, Marie-Eugenie put up a lovely headstone in the churchyard. Engraved with the motif of a quill pen and describing A. J. as 'walker and writer, dearly loved husband, father and friend,' it quotes the opening lines of one of his poems: *There must be dales in Paradise, which you and I will find.*

And, one trusts, a bit of rough heather for A. J. to wallow in.

Squire Osbaldeston

Scratched on the parapet of Ebberston Hall, between Scarborough and Pickering, are the outlines of several hands and feet. They are a bizarre legacy of an Ebberston squire - George Osbaldeston. George liked to take lady friends on to the balustraded roof, where he invited them to have a hand or foot recorded for posterity - or perhaps his own strange satisfaction. Some of the outlines are so close to the edge of the parapet that George might be suspected of having threatened to push his girlfriends off if they didn't co-operate with his hand-and-foot fetishism.

No doubt George would prefer to be remembered by the grand, if unofficial, title by which he was known in his lifetime: Squire of All England. The foremost sportsman of his day, he was an outstanding boxer, oarsman, tennis player and cricketer - fast bowler and belligerent bat. Equally expert with duelling pistols he is said to have been able to put ten bullets through the ace of diamonds on a playing card at 30 paces. Out in the field, he once bagged 97 grouse with 97 shots, and 100 pheasants with 100 shots.

George's stamina was as awesome as his skill. He once played billiards non-stop for 50 hours. In his forties, he won rowing matches on the Thames, and he was 68 when, riding his own horse in a race at Goodwood, he was beaten by only a short neck. At a party one evening, George, stung by a fellow guest's remark that the bouquet carried by his lady companion was inferior to that held

Fetishist? The squire traced these outlines of the hands and feet of lady friends on the roof.

Not quite Castle Howard. But tiny Ebberston Hall was good enough for the 'All England' squire.

by another woman, leapt on to his horse and galloped 50 miles to fetch his partner the best bouquet in the room. It is said that George completed this mission in time to sit down for supper!

A compulsive gambler - his downfall as we shall see - George once wagered he could ride 200 miles around Newmarket Heath in ten hours. Dressed stylishly in a black velvet cap, purple silk jacket and doeskins, he completed the feat in well under nine hours, including a break to dine on partridge washed down with brandy. Afterwards celebrated in pictures and verse, this ride climaxed with George waving his whip to the wealthy racegoers in the stand, before galloping off as though he intended to do it all again.

'Chaffing challenges and the love of fame have always egged me on', George once wrote. Born in Wimpole St in 1787, he was only technically a Londoner. His pregnant mother went deliberately to the capital for what she considered the superior medical care available there compared to Hutton Buscel, the village on the southern slope of the North York Moors near Scarborough, where the family had its estate.

George's sporting prowess emerged at Eton and Oxford. So too did his wild extravagance. At eighteen, for instance, he bought his own pack of foxhounds. This led to spells as Master of fashionable hunts, including the Quorn and Pytchley.

Inheriting the family estate as a child George was still a young man when the family mansion at Hutton Buscel was burned down in about 1810. While some say the fire broke out during a riotous party, others claim George torched the building for insurance money, needed to pay gaming debts. The stone gateposts of the hall survive, and the site of the hall is now occupied by a Victorian school, designed in 1854 by the noted Victorian architect William Butterfield.

In 1814 George bought Ebberston Hall. Facing south, in a shallow valley running up to the moors, it is assumed by many, who see it from the nearby Scarborough-Pickering road, to be the gatehouse or lodge of a larger hall somewhere out of sight. But the modest, pavilion-like baroque building, with just one window on each side of its Tuscan-columned doorway, is the hall. Its architect, Colen Campbell, called it 'a rustic edifice', and George spoke of it lightly as 'a mere chateau in the Italian style.' It is today often described as 'England's smallest stately home.'

It was larger when George bought it. He demolished two wings, using their stone to build stables. From these emerged the 1836 Derby winner - *Ebberston*. She was almost certainly trained on gallops laid out by George in nearby Givendale, parts of which can still be traced.

Even discounting those peculiar visits to the roof, George enjoyed more success with ladies at Ebberston Hall than the man who commissioned the house - William Thompson. MP for Scarborough, and Warden of the Royal Mint, Thompson commissioned the house, in 1718, for his mistress. The site was chosen to allow the creation of elaborate water gardens at the back. Ebberston village, which intruded into the view, was moved half a mile eastwards. But Thompson's mistress, perhaps learning from friends that the hall wasn't quite as imposing as Castle Howard, on the other side of the Vale of Pickering, never even visited the mini mansion.

George is said to have bought it mainly for the water gardens, whose pools he stocked with trout. He might have intended rebuilding the hall on a scale appropriate to the 'Squire of All England.' But his gaming debts, which totalled about £200,000 over his lifetime, thwarted his plans.

To please his mother, who wanted him to at least seem industrious, George also spent a large sum buying a safe Parliamentary seat. But he rarely attended debates, preferring to hunt six days a week. The obligation to meet electors during elections was particularly distasteful, and he once told a friend: 'A dirty fellow approached me, holding out his filthy paw. He said "Tip us your manus, brother sportsman! We are both hunt varmints. You kills foxes, I kills rats." '

As his debts mounted, George tried to reduce them by opening lime kilns, prospecting (in vain) for coal, establishing rabbit warrens (at Scamridge), and even selling trees for railway sleepers. Nevertheless, he had to mortgage his estate, and the ultimate humiliation came when he was reduced to bartering furniture from Ebberston Hall to pay for drinks at the Grapes Inn. Much of this furniture remained at the Grapes until it was auctioned in 1928. The largest item, a seven-piece mahogany table, failed to reach its reserve price and was afterwards bought by the auctioneer for £100. Where is it now, one wonders?

In 1848 George had to sell Ebberston Hall itself. By then he daren't even show his face in the village, where he faced the so-called 'duns' - being sued, or 'dun' for money.

For most of the next 100 years the hall was a tenanted farmhouse. But in 1941 it was restored as a small country house by Major William de Wend-Fenton, who moved there from West Yorkshire. The third generation of his family now occupies the hall, which is occasionally open to the public.

What of Squire George? Shortly after selling the hall he was saved from complete ruin by a strong-minded widow, Mrs Williams. Caring for him like a mother, she allowed him to gamble £1 per night - quite a come-down for a someone who had routinely staked £100 for each trick at whist, and £1,000 for the rubber.

George died in 1866. A larger-than-life example of the squires who ruled rural England for three centuries until the First World War, he relished cock-fighting and badger-baiting in addition to the other pleasures mentioned here. Engraved on the ancient sundial above the church door at Hutton Buscel, George's early home village, are the words: Time Wasted Is Existence, Used Is Life. Into which category did squire George's activities fit?

Sydney Smith

When Frank Sutcliff retired from photography in 1922 Sydney Smith was beginning to hone his photographic skills. On Sutcliffe's death in 1944 he was a master of his craft. Active chiefly just south of Whitby and its hinterland, the district so beautifully captured in the late Victorian photographs of Sutcliffe,

Smith thus continued the 'tradition' of documentary photography pioneered in the North York Moors by Sutcliffe.

Like Sutcliffe, Smith produced an evocative record of local people and places. It is remarkable that neighbouring districts of the Moors nurtured two such outstanding photographers in direct succession. And it is somewhat sad that while Sutcliffe is rightly renowned, Smith, though steadily winning wider recognition, has yet to receive the acclaim he deserves.

The place to discover him is the Beck Isle Museum, Pickering, his native town. Displaying his rare skill and deep feeling for his subject, the many Smith pictures on view there capture probably better than any others the rural England that began to vanish after the Second World War. It is the England of corn stooks and carters, of horse-drawn binders clanking round sunlit fields, and cows being driven languidly to pasture along dappled lanes. Complementing these nostalgic images are others of timeless beauty - the smooth trunks of beech trees, a worn set of stone steps, the delicate tracery of a springtime birch.

Humanity is there too. Counterparts to Sutcliffe's fondly-observed Whitby fisherfolk and Eskdale cottagers are Smith's portraits of, for example, a gipsy woman selling pegs, a farmer's wife hand-rearing lambs, a child absorbed in her book on a sunny doorstep, a milkman making his rounds in the long shadows of early morning.

The parallels with Sutcliffe don't stop at the subject matter. Neither could earn a living from the photographs they took for their own pleasure. Both depended on studio work - and postcards.

Spanning the years 1914 to 1947, Smith's postcards are a phenomenon in their own right. They include not only hundreds of local views but sets of up to 36 cards devoted to events such as a flood, a royal visit, or a circus. When a freak hailstorm hit Pickering in June, 1935, Smith rushed out a set of ten cards. Fires, funerals, and even novelties like the companionship of a dog and a tame fox, were all grist to Smith's postcard mill. One of his last cards showed a local midwife's car abandoned on the snowbound Whitby moor road during the severe winter of 1947.

Born in 1884, the youngest of twelve children of a Pickering builder and his wife, Sydney began work at fourteen as a delivery boy with the local Co-op. Already fascinated by photography, a then new-fangled hobby, he is believed to have taken his first pictures with a pinhole camera that he made according to instructions given by the manager of the Co-op.

Shortly before the First World War Smith took over an existing commercial-photography business in Pickering. He married a local girl, Maud, to whom he taught photography. When Smith was away in the First World War, Maud ran the business.

On his return, Smith opened a garage, in Park St. But in the 1920s he and Maud reverted to commercial photography. Initially based on a studio and darkroom (now flats) near the Station Hotel, their business was later run from a shop, since rebuilt, 13, Market Place.

Extrovert and outgoing, Maud was markedly different in character from the somewhat shy and self-effacing Sydney. Known to friends as Percy, a nickname

Master cameraman at work. Sydney Smith with his giant field camera on Bluebank, Sleights, 1934.

The romantic vision of Sydney Smith. Robert Hogarth's mundane delivery of milk on Pickering's Brand Hill is transformed by slight soft-focus into an early-morning idyll.

she acquired in her tomboy girlhood, she did most of the studio work. This spared Sydney his most disliked task - photographing Pickering's babies. Maud was also a familiar figure at Pickering weddings, usually turning up in her three-wheeler Morgan sports car. Some Pickering folk still remember having to push-start the car on its return journey.

Through his own early ownership of a car, Smith was one of the first photographers to travel widely in the North York Moors. Rare historic pictures in his collection include the summit of Ingleby Incline with its towering drumhouse, roofless Hamer House - the former Rosedale inn that has since completely disappeared - and the ferry that operated on the Esk at Sleights after the road bridge was destroyed by the flood of 1930. And there is arguably no finer photograph of one of the AA's famous motorbike patrolmen than Smith's stirring portrait of local patrolman Jack Hodgson amid snowdrifts at Saltersgate, in that same savage winter than ensnared the midwife.

Many of Smith's pictures were taken with a giant field camera straight from the Sutcliffe era - a Tailgate, circa 1895. Looking not unlike an accordion it is on show with other Smith cameras at Beck Isle, which also displays his former shop sign and other items.

The essence of his photography is its romance. If a trifle overfond of Biblical effects, with sunset-gilded sheep and shepherds, he was nevertheless a masterly manipulator of light and shade. Where it enhances the subject, as with a picture of Ugthorpe windmill in full sail, the definition of his pictures is exceptionally sharp. Others pictures, including Smith's favourite, entitled Tranquility, showing a pipe-smoking countryman leaning on a bridge, are suffused with gentle light. One picture, sunlight filtering through a woodland glade, is so irridescent that when it was displayed in a cabinet at Smith's home visitors thought it was backlit. But its faery glow is the product of only natural light - and the consummate art of Sydney Smith.

Like Sutcliffe, he went to great pains to get exactly the effect he wanted. Photographing High Horcum farmhouse one day he felt there was something missing. He knocked at the door and asked the farmer's wife, Florrie Mackley, if she would mind stoking up the fire - which she did. On view at Beck Isle, Smith's picture shows an appealing curl of woodsmoke - and Florrie standing at the farmhouse door.

But for many years Smith could spend only Sundays on photography for his own pleasure. After the Second World War, however, Maud manned the shop while Sydney spent ever more time recording rural Ryedale. His pictures won numerous camera-magazine awards though nothing, alas, as prestigious as Sutcliffe's Honorary Fellowship of the Royal Photographic Society, the profession's highest honour. But few would doubt Smith deserved it.

After his death in 1958 his photographs lay forgotten in a back room at his former studio. When a furniture company renting the premises needed the unused room, the pictures, in plywood boxes made for them by Smith, who was an accomplised cabinet maker, came to light. They were about to be dumped when local historian John Rushton heard of them. He contacted Smith's widow, and with her agreement the pictures were placed in the care of the Beck Isle Museum.

Stonemason-poet. This modern sculpted likeness of John Castillo adorns his Lealholm birthplace.

Lealholm Chapel: Castillo, one of its builders, also preached here.

This rescue saved Smith's pictures from a second threat, besides the council tip. Woodworm had bored through not only the plywood boxes but some of the mounted photographs. The characteristic tiny holes can be seen on one or two prints in the museum.

Altogether Beck Isle holds about 1,600 Smith prints and negatives, representing 900 separate images. Though extremely proud of her husband's work, which she believed was influenced by Rembrandt, Mrs Smith didn't want the photographs to be promoted commercially during her lifetime. But after her death, at 96 in 1994, the museum put prints of about ten Smith pictures on sale. They proved so popular that more than 100 prints are now available. One buyer bought about 30 for holiday cottages in Rosedale - a role that would probably have gone to Sutcliffe a few years ago.

To its huge credit, the Beck Isle Museum has not simply cashed in on its archive of Smith pictures. Gordon Clitheroe, the collection's custodian, has painstakingly researched the photographs: dates, locations, people. Thanks to this labour of love buyers of, for instance, the photograph that Smith entitled simply Horses Harrowing have the pleasure of not only owning a beautiful picture but knowing that it shows nineteen-year-old Eric Bowes tilling a field near Aislaby, Pickering, in 1938, with Pansy, Daisy and Violet, heavy horses owned by Charles Braithwaite, of Corner Farm, Wrelton.

John Castillo - Bard of the Dales

Very few of the gardeners eagerly choosing plants at Lealholm's Poet's Cottage Shrub Nursery know the origin of the name. If they glanced high up the house-wall near the gate - which few also do - they would gain a partial clue.

Overlooking the unheeding passers-by is a carved sandstone head. Commissioned and installed about 15 years ago by the nursery's creator and present owner Hilda Rees, it is a likeness of the eponymous poet, who lived there two centuries ago. During an absence from the village, he fondly recalled:

> O yes, the cottage once again I see,
> Which oft has proved a safe retreat to me,
> From wintry tempest or my neighbour's frown,
> And piercing frost or scorching sun at noon.

Though the cottage is now much enlarged, Lealholm's handsome bridge, centrepiece of the appealing village, remains unchanged. Spanning the Esk, it still evokes a simple yet especially lovely line by Castillo: 'Where still the swallow comes and dips her wings.'

A stonemason by trade, Castillo often conceived verses while he worked. Calling out 'I've just thought of a few lines,' he would sit on a stone, scribble the lines down, and recite them to his companions. He then stuffed the scrap of paper into his hat, which was full of these jottings. He also expressed himself in stone. For he enjoyed carving faces - a practice that makes his own sculpted head most appropriate. Probably depicting mainly workmates and other locals, Castillo's carved faces adorn several local farms. An exception is an excellent likeness of the young Queen Victoria. It is one of four faces, the others now unknown, carved by Castillo on the corners of the roof of Lealholm Methodist chapel, which he helped to build in 1839, two years after Victoria came to the throne.

Methodism was another strong strand in the story of Castillo. But his path to becoming a fervent lay preacher, travelling around the Moors and their hinterland to win converts, was far from one of meek piety.

Stocky, dark-haired, and with a bearded square jaw, he wasn't quite a native Yorkshireman. His father was an itinerant Irish labourer who met Castillo's mother, Mary Boanas, of Glaisdale, while helping with the Eskdale harvest. Marrying in 1789 at Danby parish church, which then embraced Glaisdale, the couple went to Ireland, where Castillo was born in the village of Rathfarnham, near Dublin, in about 1792.

In 1795 the couple returned to Eskdale, where Castillo's father obtained work in Lealholm's paper mill (demolished 1935). Castillo's three sisters were born in the family's nearby cottage, the far end of today's Poet's Cottage.

But in 1801 or 1802 Castillo's father abandoned the family and sailed to America. Castillo later wrote:

> *In distant lands my father's lot was cast,*
> *And we were left to feel the bitter blast.*

Though occasionally earning a little money by nursing sick or elderly dalesfolk, Castillo's mother depended mainly on meagre parish relief. Aged only ten, Castillo became a servant to a wealthy local man - identity now unknown - with whom he soon moved to Lincolnshire.

The lad's gift for words emerged in verses he made up about what he called 'various occurrences in the neighbourhood' - topical local events. Fitting these to popular tunes, and singing them in taverns in his high soprano voice, sometimes with a chorus or on the flute, he became a local celebrity - The Little Yorkshireman.

Castillo later observed: 'Being much addicted to a lightsome spirit, I became very fond of songs, and got much applause in public company for making folks merry, as the world calls it.' Not choosy about his material, he particularly remembered one song: 'A man's wife having run away with another man, I put the particulars into a fashionable song, and the following Saturday evening sung it at the tavern, as the company said like a nightingale, amid their uproarious laughter.'

As Castillo put it, he 'got almost perfected in the school of vanity.' But one night, staggering out of a tavern half drunk, he stumbled into the churchyard and fell over a grave. Interpreting this as proof that the 'evils of corruptions of the human heart' had begun to 'operate on my life and conduct,' he fled home and resolved to sing no more. 'I began to think seriously about my soul,' he wrote later. 'Singing songs did then appear to me to be among the works of darkness, an insinuating sin which led to drunkenness and all other evils; and which I endeavoured to shun in future.'

Full of penitence he returning to Lealholm as a farmworker and took up Methodism with the customary fervour of a convert. Successful missions to spread John Wesley's gospel inspired him to verse:

> *Old Guisborough the message is receiving*
> *And Skelton is catching the flame...*
> *Upleatham has catch'd the emotion,*
> *And Marske is beginning to sing...*
> *They've wakken'd at Easby, the Lord is amang 'em*
> *Tho' tunned oot o' t' temple 'at used to belang 'em.*

For less fruitful outings, prose sufficed. He reported that at Stockton he and a companion 'carried rather too coarse metal for that refined place.' Ryedale was scarcely more responsive: 'At Wass and Helmsley nothing particular. Found them hard as nails at Nunnington and Hovingham. At Stonegrave some were affected but none would yield. At Rosedale not awake in the cause of God.' Oh dear.

Meanwhile Castillo had become a stonemason, his true vocation. Apart from the chapel examples, the best of his carved faces, including a man with a open mouth, are at Lealholm's Wild Slack Farm. Though another face, on roadside buildings at Stonebeck Gate Farm, Little Fryup, is now featureless, four fine rams-horn carvings still grace the roof of the farm dovecot. A particularly splendid set of buildings, the quadrangular farmyard has a keystone on which Castillo carved the names of the four masons, including himself, and the date 1834.

Now worn away is the inscription on the lintel at Hollins Farm, Farndale, which declared:

> *John Foord*
> *1824*
> *Life is but a Moment.*

But the lintel at Postgate Farm, Lealholm, still says: 'BT and J 1839 Or CY'. Early Methodist services were held at Postgate, and though 1738 is now generally regarded as the year Wesley founded Methodism, CY here refers to Centenary Year. Also boasting yet another Castillo face - on a stable - Postgate has become an appropriate home for a rarer Castillo relic. Given some maggot ridden cheese while working at Glaisdale's Midge Hall, he scratched on its kitchen window the thought:

> *Some ants about a clod imply their cares,*
> *And think the business of the world is theirs.*
> *So waxen combs seem palaces to bees,*
> *And mites conceive the world to be a cheese.*

Through a family connection the pane is now preserved at Postgate.

Legacies of Castillo - two sculpted faces at Wild Slack Farm.

More publicly, a direction sign by Castillo, in the form of two hands, with mileages to Whitby and Castleton, is built into a barn at Stonegate, near Lealholm. He also chiselled his name, spelt with a single L, on the flat top of the Dancing Stone, a rendezvous for local lads and lasses, near Botton Hall in Danby dale. Carvings of ships on the stone might also be Castillo's.

At least twice lack of local work drove Castillo far out of the district - to Leeds, Manchester, Darlington, Hull, Preston, London, Carlisle and other places. He lamented:

> *From a land full of friends where he covets to stay*
> *Poor tost-about Castillo's forc'd far away.*

Anguished at being unable to support his near-destitute mother he added:

> *Though I've no child to drown in tears,*
> *Nor tender wife to load with woe,*
> *Yet I've a mother sunk in years,*
> *And she more weight of want must know.*

At its best, Castillo's verse echoes that of his once-neglected but now justly-acclaimed contemporary John Clare (1793-1864), a superb poet of Nature - and of loss. Of his boyhood wanderings in Fryupdale, Castillo wrote:

> *Oft have I rang'd thy verdant woods,*
> *Where roses bursting from their buds*
> *Have struck my wondering eye!*
> *And oft have I thy woodbines cropt,*
> *While from my hands the sweet flowers dropt:-*
> *I've thought - I too must die!*

The death of a local child - perhaps the son of one of Castillo's sisters? - produced these deeply-felt lines:

> *My little boy! My lovely boy!*
> *Why in such haste away?*
> *Will no embrace or tempting toy*
> *Induce thy longer stay.*

And when a donkey was drowned through careless handling by its brutal master he wrote:

> *Poor little donkey, thy travels are o'er,*
> *Thy day's work is done, and thy feet are not sore;*
> *By thy master's rash hand thou hast now gotten clear*
> *Of whippings and kickings and burdens severe.*

Still of use. A John Castillo direction sign at Stonegate, near Lealholm.

Here lies...a forgotten poet. John Castillo's obscure Pickering headstone.

Nicknamed 'Castee', Castillo resumed versifying local events, but kindly now. The death of a long-serving popular Lealholm publican, Mrs Moon, inspired a poem that played cleverly and affectionately on her name:

> *The full moon then did through her vallies shine,*
> *So bright, some thought she never would decline...*
> *But now in mists and gloom she disappears,*
> *Eclips'd - her light no longer Lealholm cheers.*

Printed as handbills and sold at fairs, Castillo's poems, especially Auld (or Awd) Isaac, a dialect poem about a Glaisdale veteran named Isaac Hobb, were widely read in and around the Moors. But Castillo - in another near-parallel with Clare, who was certified insane and placed in an asylum - suffered bouts of depression, which led him to contemplate suicide. He wrote: 'I was sore tempted to finish my existence. The woods and solitary parts of the earth were the only places I could find consolation.'

But he died naturally, at Pickering on April 16, 1845. On the Dancing Stone someone carved 'NEU HEES DEAD.' Two years earlier, a small selection of his poems, had been published at Whitby. Fuller selections, including one entitled *Bard of the Dales*, followed up to 1902, after which Castillo sank into obscurity.

But in 1985, John Hill, of Pickering, where Castillo was buried in the Wesleyan graveyard, knew enough of him to save his headstone when he removed all others after buying the burial ground, in Hungate, to form part of his garden. Still cherished by Mr Hill, the stone hails Castillo as the 'author of Auld Isaac, The Steeple Chase and other Poems in the Yorkshire Dialect,' and 'an original and successful local preacher among the Wesleyan Methodists for many years.' Also proclaiming that 'he lived for others,' it quotes him in dialect on death, or rather 'deeath'. But his most fitting epitaph is this:

> *But all the treasures I desire*
> *In cities or alone,*
> *Is peace of conscience, health of mind,*
> *And hewing at a stone.*

Runswick Bay.

Hutton-le-hole - 'a dream-come-true sort of place'?

Goathland - a villager relaxes with his dog at the bunker of the 'church hole' of the former golf course.

Lealholm - 'metropolis' of mid-Eskdale

Bare, ruined choirs...Rievaulx Abbey pictured not from the celebrated terrace but the more intimate viewpoint of Ashberry Wood, with the terrace's Ionic temple in the background

Mount Grace Priory in the snow.

Helmsley Castle adorned with fairy foxgloves - a rare botanical delight.

The Moors' most famous postbox - where Major John Fairfax-Blakeborough posted his famous newspaper column.

Staithes...an artist chooses the usually-disregarded view up the beck.

Port Mulgrave...The once-bustling harbour succumbs to the sea.

Runswick Bay...Mediterranean-like on its south-facing cliff.

A pretty corner of Runswick.

Linskill Square - Whitby's best-preserved yard.

Blackburn's Yard, Whitby...once housed the local lock-up.

Saltersgate Inn - inland haunt of smugglers (long before the Fylingdales 'sandcastle' sprouted on the horizon!).

Disappearing history. The barely-discernible remains of Limekiln House are unnoticed by a late-evening walker on the Drove Road. House.

Loveliness - and livelihoods - saved. Haymaking in 1999 at Hall Farm, in the centre of what would have been the Farndale reservoir.

Grim greeting. Nicholas Cheeseman's doom-laden message for his bride on Cropton's Rose Cottage.

Burning off, Rosedale: vital 'management' of the moors.

What it's all about. Vistas of heather, like this breathtaking spectacle at Old Ralph Cross, off Blakey Ridge, underpin the Moors' national park status.

CHAPTER 5

STRANGE

Sarkless Kitty

It would make a gripping opening to a TV drama. Bare-headed and solemn, a large gathering of dalesfolk stands silently by a lonely ford. In the middle, Bible in hand, a priest conducts the funeral service. There is no coffin, and no body that might otherwise be in one. After uttering the familiar words 'ashes to ashes, dust to dust,' the priest pauses meaningfully before adding: 'water to water.' With a profound 'Amen', the assembly murmurs its assent.

This happened in Farndale on the evening of Whit Sunday, 1809. The water-burial without a body was to lay to rest the tormented soul of Kitty Garthwaite - Sarkless Kitty as she had become known. Only when Kitty was granted eternal rest would her spirit cease to plague this ford - and claim the lives of men. Eighteen had died so far...

A ghost-story to rank with the scariest, the tale of Sarkless Kitty opens with the courtship of this Gillamoor girl by Willie Dixon, of neighbouring Hutton-le-Hole. A likeable lad, a good dancer and singer, Willie attracted a succession of girlfriends. But he spent more time with Kitty than most. As Hutton folk wryly observed he was often 'off ti Gillimoor when there warn't no need.'

Keen to marry Willie, Kitty one September afternoon received help from fate. Gathering brambles in Douthwaite Dale, the southerly extension of Farndale that separates Gillamoor from Hutton-le-Hole, she got a painful spell under her thumb nail. As she tried to remove it, crying in pain, up came Willie, on his way home from Kirbymoorside market. He pulled out the spell, comforted Kitty, and the chance meeting moved on tenderly from there. As a Victorian account delicately put it: 'It was quite dark when the lovers reached Gillamoor, but they were both perfectly happy.'

The less-happy outcome - Kitty's pregnancy - put Willie under an obligation to marry the girl. At first he seemed as pleased as she did. He often rode to see Kitty, crossing the unbridged river Dove at the ford at Lowna. Kitty often met him there, where she became a familiar figure, sitting on the trunk of a sideways-grown alder tree.

But Willie kept putting off the wedding day. And six or seven months after that 'happy' moment in Douthwaite Dale, he failed to keep a rendezvous at their trysting tree. Returning to Gillamoor, Kitty heard rumours that Willie had been seen that day with the daughter of a wealthy farmer in Castleton, over the moors. Next time she saw Willie he was evasive about where he had been.

On 29 May 1787 - Whit Sunday - the pair met by the ford for the fateful last time. A quarrel climaxed with Willie galloping off, leaving the distraught Kitty by her tree. The next morning her body, clothed only in her white sark, a kind of shirt or smock, was found in the pool below the ford. Her other garments were strewn across four fields.

Aware of the trouble between Kitty and Willie, villagers concluded that the jilted girl had set off back for Gillamoor but had decided to drown herself. Distraught, she had cast off her clothes as she ran to the ford, where she plunged in naked except for her sark.

Kitty's body was laid out in a barn at Lowna Mill, near the ford. The miller's wife, Mrs Agar, removed and washed the sark and hung it by the body, which was carefully covered with clean sacks.

Kitty's burial posed a problem. With suicide still regarded as an offence against God, the bodies of those who killed themselves were excluded from holy ground. Moorland custom decreed Kitty would be buried at a crossroads, with a stake through her heart. But even that cost money, and Kitty's mother insisted: 'By rights Kitty was Mrs Dixon, and Willie must see to t' burryin.'

But where was Willie? Absent since the row, he didn't reappear until Wednesday - three days after Kitty's death. He said that after the row he had gone on the moor to think things over. Deciding to make it up with Kitty he had galloped to York to obtain a wedding licence. He had forgotten the office was closed on Whit Monday. And although he obtained the licence the next day, his return was delayed by heavy floods. Since Willie had the licence in his pocket, and floods had indeed disrupted the district, this explanation was accepted.

Accompanied by Mrs Agar, Willie went to see Kitty's body. But the body and sark had vanished. Only the sacks, neatly folded in a corner, remained.

Willie spent the rest of the day searching for the body. On his horse, he called on Kitty's family and friends and the vicar of Lastingham, whose parish included Farndale. At dusk he was seen riding along the old bridleway between Low Mill and Lowna. But next morning his horse was found grazing near Lowna Mill. His body lay in the same pool in which Kitty had been drowned. 'Sarkless Kitty', as she was henceforth called, had claimed her first man.

A few weeks later two Hutton-le-Hole children arrived home breathless, claiming to have seen Kitty at the ford - 'stark nakt'. They said she was sitting on her usual tree, from which she smiled at them and waved her sark. Accused of being 'dirty little leears', the children were smartly packed off to bed.

But in October, the horse of a well-known occasional traveller across the moors trotted riderless up to the Royal Oak, Gillamoor. The man's body was soon found - in Kitty's pool.

Over the next few years sixteen more men, all but two of them strangers, were drowned in the pool. Locals were convinced that Kitty's ghost startled the men's horses, which reared up and threw the riders. Several local men claimed to have seen Kitty's ghost as they were 'aiming fer to cross' the ford. Always clutching her white sark, the 'nakt' Kitty was sometimes sitting on her tree, sometimes running on the bank, and sometimes in the ford itself. Understanding what this spectre foretold, the local men turned back.

Of the two who died, one was drunk. But it was the death of the other, Kitty's eighteenth victim, a popular and hard-working young farmer, that persuaded people something must be done. Hence that extraordinary funeral-cum-exorcism. Dressed in full robes the vicar conducted it with the assistance of two surpliced choristers, one holding a lighted candle, the other ringing a bell. Kitty's ghost has never reappeared.

But what had happened to her body? In 1947 Wilf Crosland, a Hutton-le-Hole historian, unveiled a startling explanation. Recounting the saga in his book *Yorkshire Treasure*, he said that among books he had purchased 'quite recently' at a local sale was an old Bible. Against verse 60 of 28 Matthew was a cross, accompanied at the foot of the page by a note in faded ink which said: 'X inside back.' Between the paper lining and the board Crosland found a folded sheet of paper covered in small, neat handwriting.

Consulting a family tree in the Bible, Crosland worked out that initials on the paper, H.A., were those of a Henry Armadale. Born in 1775, he was a son of Joseph and Eliza Armadale, the Bible's original owners. The family tree also revealed that Henry's elder sister, Mary, died on 24 May 1787, six days after Kitty. Aged 18 she was buried in the Quaker burial ground at Lowna.

According to Henry Armadale's detailed note, Mary's burial took place on the Friday before the Monday on which Kitty's body was found. The note said that the day after the funeral, the Armadale family, devout Quakers, sat down after supper for their usual bedtime Bible reading. Selected at random, the passage happened to be Matthew's account of how Joseph removed Jesus's body from the cross, and 'wrapped it in a clean linen cloth and laid it in his own new tomb.'

In bed that night, Joseph Armadale asked his wife: 'Art thou sleeping, Eliza?' She replied: 'Nay. That poor child under the sacks is on my mind.' Joseph said: 'Dost thou think Joseph left the bodies of those two thieves hanging? I think he must have covered them somewhere.' Turning over the phrase 'his own new tomb,' he asked: 'Dost thou think it is a leading?' - i.e: Is it telling us something? Convinced it was he sprang up and declared: 'There can be no delay. It must be done at once.' Agreeing, his now sobbing wife said: 'I must go with thee.'

Loading their mare with a pick, spade, ropes and a clean linen sheet, the couple made their way to the barn at Lowna. There, Eliza re-clothed Kitty's corpse in her sark and wrapped it in the linen sheet. She and Joseph then took it the short distance to the isolated burial ground where Joseph placed Kitty in their daughter's own freshly-dug grave. Years later, he related all this to Henry, who wrote it down.

So said Crosland. But a list of all 114 Quakers buried at Lowna between 1675 and 1854 includes no Armadale, a very un-Farndale-like name. Nor was the marked Bible among the artefacts gifted by Crosland to found what has become the Ryedale Folk Museum. A Cropton resident who recently unearthed these facts, and remembers Crosland as a 'imaginative storyteller', believes he may

115

Lowna Mill, Farndale. Sarkless Kitty's body vanished from here. The mill was once a tannery - hence the air vents.

Lowna burial ground - Kitty's last resting place?

have invented the dramatic denouement, perhaps for fun and/or to present Quakerism, his creed, in an appealing light. But would a serious historian wish to muddy history? Or a devout Quaker to present fiction as fact?

An earlier version of the main story than Crosland's - in Gordon Home's *Pickering: The Evolution of an English Town (1905)* - has Kitty as a 'lewd hussey', mysteriously drowned sometime after being deserted by her husband of four months. That deaths occurred in the ford, and an exorcism took place there, is virtually certain, for the first record of the service, obtained and described about 100 years ago by Richard Blakeborough, an assiduous collector of moorland folklore, was in a manuscript of stories of the moors, written in 1823, less than 20 years after the exorcism, by a man named George Calvert.

Identified by a plaque on its boundary wall, the old burial ground, now host to large trees, is just a five-minute stroll from a small car park at Lowna. No longer discernible, the ford itself was formerly a notorious hazard, with very uneven footing. Like Willie Dixon, who had been warned he would try to cross once too often in dangerous conditions, all its victims probably died when the river was in spate. The building of Lowna Bridge in 1826 finally eliminated the danger.

It's odd that Willie apparently wasn't suspected of murder. But odder is that commerce has never swooped on this fascinating story. Thankfully, no Sarkless Kitty Tearoom or gift shop, with a range of souvenirs, greets visitors in Kitty's old haunts.

An Arsonist Priest?

When Canon John Latimer Kyle became vicar of Carlton-in-Cleveland in 1894 parish morale was at rock bottom. Burned down in mysterious circumstances in 1881, just two years after it had been completed, the parish church stood as a blackened ruin. Told in my book *Inside the North York Moors*, the story of how Kyle inspired the parish to build a beautiful new church, and secured his fame by running a farm, riding with the Bilsdale hunt, and even taking over the village pub, has become quite well known.

But still cloaked in obscurity are the startling events that led to Kyle's arrival. They were hardly less extraordinary than Kyle's outstanding and highly-distinctive ministry. And Kyle's predecessor as vicar, the Rev George Sanger, bears comparison with Kyle as an exceptional priest and remarkable man.

A one-time Wesleyan Methodist, Sanger served as a curate at Stokesley before becoming vicar of Carlton in 1865. The parish church of that time is described in Ord's History and Antiquities of Cleveland (1848) as 'a singular and extraordinary structure.' In contrast to its sturdy Norman-style tower, its thatched nave and chancel were 'little better than a shepherd's hut.'

In the two years 1877-79 Sanger replaced this primitive building with a splendid new church, built largely by himself. In his book *Yorkshire Days and Yorkshire Ways*, Major J. Fairfax-Blakeborough quotes a long newspaper report, alas unattributed, whose author witnessed the vicar at his amazing task:

117

Amid blocks of stone and moss-grown tombstones, the vicar stands besides his workmen, dressed in cotton jacket and apron, mallet and chisel in hand, carving bosses and shaping window pieces...He directs how courses shall shall be laid, what work is to be got forward, or bends his finely-featured face to more accurately follow his designs. Not only has he drawn the plans, but he is his own contractor, clerk of works, master mason and foreman carver. Even at this early stage I can see that the building is to bear the impress of a many-sided genius...

On summer evenings, when the workmen had departed, the vicar toiled alone at the church till dusk. Returning home, he bound books, another of his skills, to raise money for the building. He also sent out 2,000 letters seeking subscriptions.

Opened on March 13, 1879, with a tiled roof and handsome spire, the church was praised in one report as 'bearing the mark of exquisite taste and rare skill.' The vicar's work included the oak lectern and pulpit, and the stone tracery of the much-admired east window.

But on October 19, 1881, a fire which broke out at about 3 a.m. completely destroyed the church. Suspiciion fell on the vicar, who was arrested and charged with arson. Though the magistrates at Stokesley threw out the case, concluding there wasn't enough evidence to send Sanger for full trial, Carlton opinion had found the priest guilty. Probably as a sop to local feeling, the Archbishop of York suspended him for five years for a supposed ecclesiastical offence.

Protesting his innocence in a letter to parishioners, Sanger remarked: 'In a period of 16 years I can safely challenge anyone to bring forward any act of mine which could by any possibility be construed into unkindness.' Perhaps exhibiting a little lack of Christian humility he added that his work at Carlton had been 'without parallel in the Church of England for the last three centuries.'

The main evidence of arson against him was that of a 13-year-old boy who had seen the vicar leave the church the previous evening with a basket containing a bottle of paraffin oil - hardly incriminating in those oil-lamp days. Other witnesses claimed Sanger had spoken 'jocularly' at the scene of the fire, advising them to go home or risk catching a cold. One added that the priest seemed 'rather unwilling' the next day to accept a small cross recovered from the ruins.

In his defence Sanger spoke of the 'annoyances and vexations' to which parishioners had subjected him. He suggested that the fire had been seized upon by his enemies as an opportunity to vent their spite. Only weeks before the blaze, his greenhouse and some garden trees had been vandalised. He had also received a poison pen letter urging him to leave the parish, or face departing through the agency of a bullet.

Described in that newspaper report of him working on the church as a man of 'singularly gentle countenance,' erect in bearing and with a high forehead and deep-set eyes, Sanger wasn't without friends. Between his arrest and his court appearance he became engaged to a local girl, Miss Kingston. Cheers greeted his announcement of this during the packed court hearing, and the 'hurrahs' were even louder when he thanked his supporters 'very heartily' for their 'kind sympathy.'

But while Sanger chose to stay put following his acquittal, his flock ostracised him. He spent days wandering the moors above Carlton alone. Even when his suspension ended he remained largely an outcast. Most parish burials took place elsewhere.

Occasionally the vicar held a service in the dismal ruins of his church. The reporter who pictured him building the church was also present at one of these:

> Rain began to fall as the vicar commenced his sermon on the well-known words of Shakespeare, 'There's a Divinity that shapes our ends....' The congregation stood under their umbrellas, but the bare-headed Vicar stood unprotected. His utterances were those of a pious, thoughtful and widely read man... He concluded: 'Often man is condemned, probably not so much from malice as ignorance, but to all such sufferers it is a happiness to know that what is mysterious to the maligant and ignorant is revealed to God, who will be the final Judge of all.'

A clue to what lay behind this tragic tale came when Canon Kyle was organising the building of a second new church. In his parish magazine he observed: 'Great dissatisfaction was often expressed that when the church was rebuilt in 1880 the parishioners were not consulted. I therefore determined that this time they would be consulted.' So Sanger suffered, and Carlton lost a church and a dedicated priest, because the cleric was perceived as high handed.

Apart from a bazaar that raised £172, locals contributed only £28 (£2 less than the sum raised by Sanger's bookbinding) towards the £886 cost of the church. As the project neared completion, Sanger published this plaintive notice in newspapers: 'The Revd Geo Sanger, vicar of Carlton in Cleveland earnestly begs churchmen to help him. He has built a new church, having done a great portion with his own hands. He needs £200 more to pay outstanding accounts. Will churchmen help him...?' Following his acquittal he entreated parishioners to build a new church with these blunt words: 'Money is not wanting in the parish, where one parishioner can boast of being able to command £70,000, and the united income of the wealthy landowners is not much less than £1m a year.' Diplomacy was obviously not among Rev Sanger's skills - and the parish remained church-less for 15 years.

A week before his death in 1894 Sanger addressed a valedictory note to his parishioners, which the blacksmith agreed to pin up at his shop. It said: 'Let us all look upon the past to gather wisdom for future steps, regarding our neighbour's feeling as our own. "Put yourself in his place" is not a bad motto when tempted to say an unkind word to someone. You may lose, perhaps, a little momentary gratification of revenge, but the sunshine afterwards in your own heart will be - well, try it, it can't be described.'

Moved by this simple message, many villagers trekked to the vicarage to make their peace with Sanger on his deathbed. But though this brought the priest great comfort, his grave, near the stump of the Saxon cross in Carlton churchyard, has never been marked. When Canon Kyle accepted the Carlton

Carlton-in-Cleveland - pretty setting for the sad story of the Rev George Sanger.

Gravestones galore near Carlton's Saxon cross, but none for vicar George Sanger.

post, the Archbishop of York, perhaps forgetting his own harsh treatment of Sanger, advised him: 'You will have to exercise the highest form of charity - that is, charity to the uncharitable.' A century later, what more fitting act of charity could there be than to award Sanger the dignity of a headstone?

A Maharajah at Mulgrave

Exploring the Whitby district for his *History of the North Riding*, published in 1859, Thomas Whellan came across perhaps the most incongruous sight ever seen on the North York Moors. He duly noted:

> We were enormously aroused by a motley crew marching in line across the moors. In the centre was a fine stalwart man of some five and twenty summers, arrayed in gorgeous oriental dress - the Maharajah Duleep Singh. On either side of him were two swarthy sons of India, his Royal Falconers, with belled hawks on their shoulders, while six English gamekeepers in scarlet uniforms, and a crowd of domestics filled up the picturesque tableau. It was His Royal Highness taking his sport a-hawking across these wilds. A picture, in truth, worthy of the limning [artistry] of a Landseer.

The encounter was on the moors at Ugthorpe. How did a Maharajah come to be 'a-hawking' there, in full princely costume? The explanation is an extraordinary tale, whose best introduction is a feature of the Whitby district used by thousands of people every day. For the coast road between Sandsend and Whitby was built by the Maharajah. Legend has it that he ordered its construction to spare his elephants the discomfort of sand between their toes as they carried the Maharajah to and from Whitby along the beach.

Alas, the Maharajah didn't keep elephants at Mulgrave. But the story behind that surreal tableau on the moors loses little colour by their absence.

The tale began in 1849 when the British annexed the Punjab, the Maharajah's principality. Just eleven at the time, the Maharajah surrendered his throne to Queen Victoria. With it came riches that included the fabulous Koh-i-Noor diamond - the 'mountain of light.' In return, the Queen granted the Maharajah an annual pension of £40,000.

But where would he live? Baptised a Christian in 1853 he came to Britain soon afterwards. And in 1859, aged 21, he rented Mulgrave Castle, at Lythe, near Whitby. Home of the Earls of Mulgrave, the castle was temporarily vacant while the Earl, who had recently taken the new title Marquis of Normanby, was serving as British ambassador in Florence.

The young Maharajah brought more than Eastern promise to the then remote North Yorkshire coast. His mother came too, with her pet monkey. There was also a large retinue of servants and the Maharajah's several wives. When Lady Normanby expressed surprise at the harem the Maharajah told her he could find nothing in the Bible restricting a man to one wife.

The Maharajah as caricatured by Spy.

Monument to a Maharajah. Built to control the Maharajah Duleep Singh's toll road to Whitby, whose gates appear in this 1920s photo. This house still stands, overlooking Whitby golf course.

Britain's first Sikh, the Maharajah routinely wore jewelled, richly-embroidered clothes, including the turban. With his many Indian servants also dressed in national costume, the effect proved a bit overpowering for Lady Normanby. After visiting the Maharajah, she sighed: 'It rather seems to me when I see queer Indian figures flitting about that the heathen are come into my inheritance.'

But the Maharajah was popular with local people, who liked his easy manner and generosity. When his mother's monkey smashed a gardener's watch, the Maharajah apologised profusely and gave the gardener a much superior replacement. Only once, when he found an estate foreman mucking out stables, was the Maharajah seen to be angry. By doing a task beneath his status, the foreman had breached the strict caste system imposed by the Maharajah in running the estate.

Nevertheless, the Maharajah adopted something of the role of an English squire. He took up shooting, stocking the farmland with pheasants and partridges for the purpose. The hawking witnessed by Whellan was his greatest pleasure, and any estate worker who told him of a hawk's nest from which trainable chicks could be taken was rewarded with more than a week's pay. The Maharajah also went hunting at sea - with cormorants. In a method still practised in China, the birds were released on light chains. A ring fitted round their necks prevented them swallowing their catch. In compensation they were instantly fed with other fish.

Though elephants were never kept at Mulgrave the Maharajah did own a string of horses, on which he and his retinue, all dressed in flowing robes, often rode furiously along the sands - another stirring sight. But the Maharajah disliked horse racing. Refusing to give a subscription to Lythe races, he observed: 'If a man feels tired he can stop or lie down, but a horse is spurred and whipped long after it has had enough.'

The Maharajah was a great favourite of Queen Victoria, who dined with him once at Mulgrave Castle. In return, she allowed his eldest son to be christened in the chapel at Windsor Castle. In her journal after her Mulgrave visit the Queen noted that the Maharajah was 'extremely handsome and has a pretty, graceful and dignified manner. He was beautifully dressed and covered in diamonds...I always feel so much for these poor dispossessed Indian princes...' But not enough, naturally, to restore their inheritance.

What of the Maharajah's road? It removed a considerable inconvenience. The lack of a coast road between Sandsend and Whitby compelled people to use either the beach or a road that climbed - and still does - from Sandsend to Dunsley and then twists back down to Upgang on the outskirts of Whitby.

Though no-one knows precisely why the Maharajah built a direct road, one theory is that it was to ease the delivery of coal to Mulgrave Castle, up Lythe Bank. This was previously carted up the hill from flat-bottomed boats that beached themselves at Sandsend - an impossible task in a rough sea. Perhaps the castle's fuel had run out during cold weather, leaving the Maharajah shivering.

Today's road doesn't exactly match the Maharajah's. At its Whitby end his road was closer to the beach. Swinging inland between Upgang ravine and the

the club house of today's golf course, it also looped into the shallow valley of Raithwaite, thus avoiding the need for an embankment or bridge.

But the modern road and the Maharajah's coincide for a short distance on either side of a two-storey sandstone cottage that overlooks the golf course. This was the toll house of the Maharajah's road. Tolls were charged until 1925, when the county council built the present road. Including an embankment to cut out the Raithwaite loop this was opened by the Minister of Transport, no less. After a landslip closed the road for six weeks in 1968, part of it was rebuilt on section of the former coast railway, which closed in 1958.

By then the Maharajah was a vague memory. He left Mulgrave Castle in 1863 for Elveden Hall, Norfolk, where he spent the remaining 30 years of his life. But though he transformed the interior of Elveden into an Indian palace, Norfolk never produced any image of him to compare with that amazing vision of him and his followers in full Indian finery, 'a-hawking' in the wilds of the North York Moors.

John Wesley at Whitestone Cliff

During a preaching tour of North Yorkshire in the summer of 1755 John Wesley learned of a recent large landslip and rockfall near Sutton Bank. In his journal he wrote:

On Tuesday March 25th, 1755, being the week before Easter, many persons observed a great noise near a ridge of mountains in Yorkshire called Black Hamilton [now Black Hambleton]. It was observed chiefly on the south-west side of the mountains, about a mile from where the Hamilton races are run, near a ridge of rock called Whiston Cliffs, or Whiston White Mare [now Whitestone Cliff, pronounced Whissoncliff], two miles from Sutton, about five from Thirsk. The same noise was heard on Wednesday by all who went that way.

On Thursday, about seven in the morning, Edward Abbot, weaver, and Adam Bosomworth, bleacher, both of Sutton, riding under Whiston Cliffs, heard a roaring (as they termed it) like many cannons, or loud rolling thunder. It seemed to come from the cliffs, looking up to which they saw a large body of stone four or five yards broad, split and fly from the very top... Between ten and eleven, a part of the same rock, about fifteen yards thick, thirty high and between sixty and seventy broad, was torn off and thrown into the valley.

About seven in the evening, one who was riding by observed the ground to shake exceedingly, and soon after several large stones or rocks, some tons of weight each, rose out of the ground. Others were thrown on one side, others turned upside down, and many rolled over and over.

On Friday and Saturday the ground continued to shake, and the rocks to roll over one another. The earth also clave asunder in very many places, and continued to do so until Sunday morning.

Whitestone Cliff across a placid Lake Gomire. Why was John Wesley obsessed with its huge rockfall?

Since then, countless guidebooks have quoted from this account. The reader naturally assumes that Wesley recorded the huge convulsion as an incidental, if spectacular, event during his journey. But the founder of Methodism wasn't a diarist in that sense. Fully-absorbed in his religious mission, he had little interest in chronicling the world at large for its own sake.

So why did he pay so much excited attention to the Whitestone Cliff rockfall? The mystery deepens when you learn he went specially to see it, and recorded it in more than his journal. Longer and more detailed than the paragraphs quoted above, his full account first appeared in a London newspaper, *The Public Advertiser*. Wesley followed this up with a pamphlet containing what he called 'some thoughts' on the landslip.

Catching the public interest generated by a recent large earthquake in Lisbon, Wesley's pamphlet asks why the lesser earth movement at Whitestone Cliff deserved similar wide attention. Revealing a disdain, even contempt, for the general public - his intended flock - Wesley wrote:

> What shall we say to the affair of Whitson Cliffs of which, were it not for the unparalleled stupidity of the English, all England would have rang long ago, from one sea to another. And yet, seven miles from the place, they knew little more of it in May last, than if it had happened in China or Japan.

The place where they knew 'little of it' was Osmotherley. And it was from there, where he was preaching, that Wesley set out to visit the rockfall. His journal records:

> Being at Osmotherley, seven miles from the Cliffs, on Monday June the 1st, and finding Edward Abbot there, I desired him the next morning to show me the way thither. We came thither soon after nine. I walk'd crept and climbed over the great part of the ruins. It was an awful sight...One part of the solid stone is cleft in a perpendicular line and as smooth as if cut with instruments...Nor is it barely thrown down, but split into many hundreds of pieces, some of which lie at a distance of four or five hundred yards.

Wesley also tells of 'an oval piece of ground removed whole with all its load of rocks, some as large as the hull of a small ship.' Also 'transplanted entire', as he put it, was an even larger piece of ground, forty or fifty yards (36.5 - 45.7m) across, with a tree still growing out of a rock. Altogether, the slumped boulder-strewn ground covered thirty or forty acres (twelve to sixteen hectares) and Wesley was particularly struck by an outer fringe of turf, ripped from the hilltop and now protruding as a 'vast number' of upright strips, 'exactly resembling the graves in a church yard.' Wesley added that the 'cliff from which the rest is torn lies so high, and is now of so bright a colour that it is distinctly visible to all the countryside round, even at the distance of several miles.'

This brings us close to what Wesley regarded as the profound significance of the dramatic landfall. Asking 'was it effected by a merely natural cause?', he identifies the three possible culprits - fire, water and air. But he rules them all out, saying there was no 'mark of fire', the weather had been dry for months, and it was inconceivable that sufficient 'imprisoned air' could have built up within the cliffs to explode with such devastating force.

So what did it? Wesley declared: 'I believe it was God, by himself or his Angel, who arose to shake terribly the Earth.'

But why should God strike at Whitestone Cliff? A clue comes when Wesley pinpoints the landslip as occurring near 'the course where the Hamilton races are run.' Still used as training gallops today, the level summit of the escarpment, with its close-cropped turf, was once a racecourse, as fashionable in its day as York is now.

Sternly opposed to gambling, Wesley concluded that God 'purposely chose such a place, where there is so great a concourse of nobility and gentry every year,' to demonstrate his own displeasure at this debased activity. He added that God

> wrought in such a manner that many might see it and fear, yea, that all who travel along one of the most frequented roads in England [the Great North Road, ten miles away] might see it, whether they would or no. It must likewise for many years be a visible monument to his power, all that ground being now so incumbered with stones and rocks that it cannot be either ploughed or grazed. Nor can it well serve to any other use than to tell all beholders: who can stand before this great God?

No doubt the symbolism of the turf 'gravestones' weighed strongly with Wesley. And he would certainly consider it no coincidence that the rockfall and its after-rumblings lasted almost a week, up to Easter Sunday, the day of the Resurrection.

A theory for the physical cause of the landslip is that it was the delayed result of a great storm that struck the Thirsk-Helmsley district on 18 October 1754. From accounts of the extensive damage in the two market towns, both of which lost their bridges, it seems likely that the storm's epicentre was over Sutton Bank. Filtering slowly through the limestone strata, the rainwater could have accumulated in one or two cavities, ultimately causing a landslip at the base of the crumbly cliff, whose unstable face then sheered off.

It's possible, however, that a small earthquake undermined the cliff. A Victorian catalogue of British earthquakes records a 'subterranean noise at York, unaccompanied by any shock' on 25 March 1775. Rumblings were heard over the next two days. Though sometimes attributed to the Whitestone Cliff fall this is unlikely over the distance of 20 miles and a period of three days. And even if the noise did stem from Whitestone Cliff, that doesn't prove the cause was an earthquake. But the Victorian catalogue also records a 'violent tremulous motion' at York on 27 March. Though the Whitestone Cliff fall itself could never have literally shaken the ground in York, it could have been caused by the same earth tremor felt at the city.

127

Though the turf gravestones have long gone, the many huge boulders that still litter the foot of Whitestone Cliff testify to the scale of the rockfall. And, of course, the shattered limestone cliff is still visible far and wide, especially when sunshine picks out its gleaming limestone. Wesley would doubtless regard its enduring prominence as confirmation of its divine origin - God's warning against degenerate pleasures.

CHAPTER 6

BY THE SEA

Staithes

Few visual contrasts are more sudden and dramatic than the one that greets visitors to Staithes. At the end of a half-mile-l\ong lane lined with an unpromising raggle-taggle of bungalows, semis, Edwardian terraces and old mining cottages, the road plunges abruptly. With seagulls wheeling and screaming overhead, Staithes appears in its cleft in the cliffs. Formerly painted in large rough letters on its gable, but now more discreetly announced on a neat sign, the name of the nearest cottage, First and Last, at the foot of the 1-3 hill, symbolises Staithes as a place apart.

The sudden view of the limpet-like colony was no less striking when its prelude was open countryside rather than today's mish-mash. In the 1860s, Samuel Gordon was certainly impressed. In his *The Watering Places of Cleveland,* published in 1869, he observed:

> The situation and aspect of this village are about as picturesque and romantic as can well be conceived. As it lies several hundred feet below the tops of the cliffs, it cannot be seen until the spectator stands on the verge of the overhanging rocks, when all at once the quaint village rises before him as if by magic.

For good measure, Gordon also describes the equally 'magical', though less often seen, view enjoyed by anyone passing at sea:

> All at once they perceive a deep chasm-like opening in the cliffs, revealing a cluster of houses rising one above another from the beach, and huddled in the strangest confusion. In a few minutes one of the bold, frowning cliffs intervenes and shuts the village out of sight, as suddenly as if the chasm had swallowed it up.

Perhaps few would say today that the two headlands enclosing Staithes - Cowbar and Penny Nab - 'frown.' But they lend a rugged strength to the village, gripping it like the claws of one the millions of lobsters landed here down the centuries.

Picturesque yet spurning the chocolate-box prettiness of its sister villages of Runswick Bay and Robin Hood's Bay, Staithes is a place of powerful atmosphere. Often dour but never grim, it retains the feel of a living, working community. About half its 250 or so cottages are still occupied by locals. And though most residents are either retired or work away, chiefly at either the nearby Boulby potash mine or on Teesside, the village still supports a number of full-time fishermen. Only Staithes, among all North Yorkshire's so-called fishing villages, has never ceased to draw some of its living from the sea.

When first recorded, as Seaton Staithes in 1451, it was probably just a landing place for the since-vanished village of Seaton, a mile or so inland near Hinderwell. But it seems to have gained its own identity by 1539, when 'muster rolls' of men recruited into Henry VIII's navy list 'fishermen' from 'Staithes.'

Until the advent of steam trawlers, which were too big to berth at Staithes, the village was a leading East Coast fishing port. At its peak, around 1885, it supported 120 boats, manned by about 300 fishermen.

A similar number worked in related activities, such as boat building, sail making, and fish curing or selling. The women also played a part, or rather several, repairing lines, mending nets and collecting bait, especially limpets, known as *flithers* . Old photographs show the women carrying bait baskets or coiled fishing lines on their heads. But many other items, such as cans of water, collected from the beck, and dough, taken to the common bakehouse, were carried the same way. In 1872, a *Northern Echo* reporter noted:

> Even the very houses have been borne piecemeal on these invaluable heads. Horses and carts cannot get into the back streets or up the steep sides where the houses are, and so, when these need rebuilding the heads of the women bear the stone, mortar and wood, for the fishermen rarely undertake these kinds of labour.

Small wonder the double-crowned 'Staithes' bonnet', worn by village women to protect their head and hair, became a famous Staithes' feature. With local variations in style, such bonnets were once common in most fishing villages. But the Staithes' bonnet lingered long after its counterparts vanished. Its last two regular wearers, fishermen's widows Eva Hanson and Olive Cole, died within weeks of each other in 1995. Only on Lifeboat Day - a Saturday in mid August - is the bonnet now seen on Staithes' streets. But it is worn in the Post Office and general store, whose female staff have adopted it to meet hygiene regulations covering the sale of cooked meats. The bonnet thus retains its role as working headgear. In a neighbouring shop, bonnets made by local woman Ann Lawson are sold as souvenirs.

In pre-railway days, relays of horses took Staithes' fish to York, 75 miles away. After the coast line opened in 1884 a special fish train left the village station three times a week. The catch included huge numbers of crabs and lobsters, for which Staithes remained a main supplier until well after the Second World War. Though this shellfish trade has dwindled, lobsters landed between Whitby and Teesmouth are still stored in tanks at a modern fish factory at Staithes' bank top.

Since the First World War the number of full time boats at Staithes has rarely exceeded ten. In 1998 there were just four, worked by seven men. Sadly, only one of the boats was a coble, the North-East's traditional inshore fishing craft, which evolved from the Viking longboat. With its high prow and semi-flat bottom the coble is ideal for operating straight off beaches. There are still half a dozen among the twenty or so part-time boats that also fish out of Staithes. Like their full-time counterparts, their crews pot for crabs and lobsters from March to October, after which they switch to line fishing, mainly for codling.

But Staithes has seldom been entirely dependent on fishing. From 1672 to 1871 many of its men were employed at the nearby Boulby alum works, turning alum shale into crystals, used chiefly to fix colours in tanning, dyeing and paint-manufacture. The Staithes' women were involved in that too. They gathered and burned seaweed, which was stirred into the alum liquor. Also added was human urine, collected in casks on Staithes' streets. Imagine the odours from this mingling with the all-pervading smell of fish, and you begin to understand why Staithes' was nicknamed 'stinkin' Steeas.'

As the alum trade declined, ironstone mining took over. In the early 1850s, four men from the Whitby district began working deposits in the cliffs at Penny Nab. One of them, Staithes' fishmonger William Thompson, is credited with discovering the ore in Rosedale, thus sparking that valley's spectacular mining boom. Still visible at low tide at Staithes are the remains of a dock and tramway cut into the rocky scaur at Penny Nab by either Thompson and his partners or the Tyneside industrialist Charles Palmer, who took over the venture in 1854.

To justify such effort, the ironstone must have been regarded like gold. Sixty miners were ultimately employed. They lived in three terraces - two up on Cowbar, the headland across the beck, and the third at bank top. In 1915 a miners' hospital was built. Easily identified by its original glazed cupola, this is now a bungalow, by the main coast road at Staithes' lane end.

But its succession of activities has never made Staithes look outward. The village was - and some say still is - astonishingly insular. Almost within living memory, any outsider who courted a Staithes' girl was virtually driven away. Superstition, too, was once rampant. Fishermen considered it bad luck to speak of a pig, the epitome of a land animal. If a pig had to be mentioned, it was referred to as 'the gentleman of the sty' or a 'grecian' - from *gris*, the Scandinavian word for pig.

Whistling at sea was an invitation to disaster. Nor would a fisherman accept a new boat, or place new gear on a boat, on a Friday - he 't'devil's day.' Staithes' women never wound wool by artificial light, which symbolised winding seamen overboard.

Though most of those beliefs have died out some fishermen still tie a 'lucky stone', a pebble with a hole in it, to their boats. When Prince Charles visited the village in 1978, a young boy, Howard Jackson, stepped forward unannounced and handed the Prince a lucky stone. After being told its significance, the Prince put it in his pocket, saying: 'Then it will be lucky for me.'

The Prince's visit was to inaugurate a Capt Cook Trail through North Yorkshire. Raised in the farming country of Great Ayton, Cook came to Staithes at the age of seventeen to learn the drapery and grocery trade from shopkeeper William Sanderson. The probably-crucial influence of Staithes on him is graphically expressed by J. C. Beaglehole in his classic biography, *The Life of Capt James Cook*:

> There it was, the little fishing port, the most considerable port, indeed, on that part of the coast, at the foot of a gash in the cliffs, alive, active. Strong Yorkshire figures took out their boats or brought them in, heaved up their baskets of fish, bent working over their pointed flat-bottomed cobles...ropes were coiled, nets dried in the wind; the smell of the beach, of seaweed and tar, was diffferent from that of the farmyard, it blew into the shop; the children playing on the beach, in and out of the boats, the youths of seventeen, seemed a different race from those land-bound beings a few miles westward; how could another youth of seventeen, glimpsing all this at door or window, or gazing out to the procession of sails north and south on the horizon, half the traffic of the North Sea, and then turning back to the groceries and ribbons, not be stirred to restlessness?

The seafront shop in which Cook worked for eighteen months, before being apprenticed to Whitby shipowner John Walker, was washed away in 1830. Bearing a 'Cook Trail' plaque unveiled by Prince Charles, the harbourside house named Capt Cook's Cottage, became Sanderson's shop after the original shop was destroyed. A direct link with the shop is a bill made out there for ship's candles in 1787. It is exhibited in a full-size replica of the shop in Staithes' Heritage Centre, a museum in a former Methodist chapel at the foot of the bank.

Together with sixteen cottages swept away in the same storm, the shop stood in what is now the open harbour - in front of the Cod and Lobster Inn. The inn itself has been severely battered by the sea five times. But for the defence of the three harbour breakwaters built in 1928, the inn and nearby cottages would almost certainly have been completely destroyed by the great East Coast storm of 31 January 1953. Pictures in the inn show how its front was ripped away. The sea remains such a threat that in 1994-95 the breakwaters themselves were protected with a barrier of 'rock armour' - huge boulders, brought by barge from Holland. In 2000 a £1.94m scheme was announced to raise the height of the existing breakwaters, build a new spur breakwater on the eastern (Whitby) side, create a 'wave barrier' at the Cod and Lobster slipway, and instal more rock armour.

Around the turn of the nineteenth century the wildness of Staithes attracted a colony of artists. Less well known than the famous group at Newlyn in Cornwall, the 'Staithes Group' nevertheless produced the largest quantity of high-quality paintings inspired by a single English place over such a short period - 1894-1909.

Among the youngest of the 30 or so artists was Laura Knight (1877-1970), ultimately a Dame and now regarded as one of Britain's finest twentieth-century artists. Of her time at Staithes she wrote:

> It was there I found myself and what I might do. The life and place were what I yearned for - the freedom, the austerity, the savagery, the wildness. I loved it passionately, overwhelmingly. I loved the cold, and the northerly storms when no covering would protect you. I loved the strange race of people who lived there, whose stern almost forbidding exterior formed such a contrast to the warmth and richness of their nature.

A number of Staithes' Group paintings can be seen in Whitby Museum. Dame Laura's studio was by the harbour on Cowbar. Reached by a footbridge over Roxby beck, the photogenic mooring place of the Staithes' boats, Cowbar is technically a separate community from Staithes. It is even in a different local-authority area. An eye-catcher in many Staithes' group paintings, the linking footbridge used to be a picturesque trestle-legged wooden affair. Recreating this appealing feature would have made an imaginative millennium project.

Built into a wall bordering a pathway upstream from the bridge, on the 'Staithes' side, are weathered sandstone carvings of unofficial Staithes' emblems: a coble, a cod, a lobster, and a seagull. On the Cowbar side, a slanting road to the mining cottages also leads to the much-photographed bird's eye view of the village - almost obligatory on Yorkshire calendars.

Back in the High Street, a barometer and clock commemorates fisherman George Hanson, husband of bonnet-wearer Eva, who died trying to rescue a drowning schoolmaster in the harbour in 1957. The plaque doesn't mention that George, aged 52, had already saved a boy in the same incident. Incredibly, he slipped away and was never traced.

In steep Church Street, off the quayside, Staithes' Anglicans worship not in a church but a chapel on the upper floor of a former school. The street gets its name because it was the route to Staithes' mother church at Hinderwell, where the Staithes' dead are still buried. The chapel is a satellite.

Since 1979 only local traffic has been allowed into the village. Leaving their cars at bank top visitors invariably walk straight down the steep bank and into the cobbled High Street. This is the best route. But there is no need to return the same way. Beloved of children, a more adventurous alternative begins with a squeeze through the eighteen-inch (0.45m) gap of Dog Loup, a passage between buildings in Church St, a few yards from the 'Capt Cook' house. From there a flagged and stepped footway climbs among the cottages. At the top, a knoll by a white cottage commands a panorama nearly as good as the better-known one from Cowbar.

Port Mulgrave

Walkers gazing down from the cliffs between Staithes and Runswick Bay see a tantalising scene. A shattered stone pier pokes into the sea. Waves break over, or lap against, a second pier, now reduced to a spit of rubble. One or two small fishing boats might bob in a silty pool. Others are hauled up above the shore, amid a ramshackle collection of fishermen's huts.

It's difficult to imagine steamships once plying from here, with ironstone for hungry North-East blastfurnaces. But Port Mulgrave, as this sad, disintegrating harbour is called, played a big part in the Victorian ironstone boom in the North York Moors.

By uncanny coincidence the historic name of the section of coast occupied by the harbour is Rosedale, whose inland namesake experienced the biggest 'ironstone rush' in the Moors. To avoid confusion, Charles Palmer, the man who created the harbour, named his brainchild Port Mulgrave. This honoured the main local landowner, Lord Normanby, of Mulgrave Castle, who formally opened the harbour in 1857.

The extraction of iron ore in the area, from the cliffs, had been begun a few years earlier by the same four men who pioneered the iron trade at Staithes. Still traceable in the rocky seabed a short distance south of the harbour are the postholes of a jetty built by the partners in 1854. And at the base of the cliffs, near the foot of the present main pier, are some heavy baulks that supported an inclined tramway, up which the ore was carried to the clifftop.

In 1857 the partners built a second jetty at the southern end of this small bay - Rosedale Wkye. But Palmer, a Tyneside industrialist who had taken a lease on land in the area in 1854, soon began to dominate the scene.

Born in South Shields in 1822 Palmer is best known for founding Jarrow, where he erected blasfurnaces and, with brother George, opened what became a world-famous shipyard. Launched there in 1852 was the world's first screw-propelled tramp steamer. Soon, a fleet of these vessels, faster than paddle steamers, was plying between the North-East and London. But for their speed, the North-East would probably have lost its coal trade with the capital to the nearer Midlands.

At what became Port Mulgrave, Palmer initially built a wooden pier, on much the same line as the present main pier. But in 1856, when he had acquired the mining rights over some 700 acres (283ha), he set about developing a proper harbour. Enclosed by two stone piers, which provided a safe anchorage of about three acres, this was completed within a year at a cost of £45,000. Taking the full force of the waves, the northern breakwater, today's rubbble strip, was itself defended by a ramp, or apron, of stone blocks.

At first the port handled ironstone mined immediately nearby. But in 1865 Palmer bought the 1,250-acre (505ha) Grinkle estate, which stretched inland from his harbour to the Guisborough-Whitby moor road. A tunnel that had already been dug a short way into the cliffs for the local mines was extended a mile inland. Ore from a new 'Grinkle' mine, opened in 1875, was transported through this tunnel to Port Mulgrave.

Adieu the bonnet. Eva Hanson (left), pictured here in 1978 with Alice Jackson, became the last everyday wearer of the fishwife headgear once synonymous with Staithes.

Staithes old trestle bridge - a strong feature in this typically-vigorous painting by Dame Laura Knight.

Secret Staithes. Few visitors spot these carved symbols of the village, overlooking the beck.

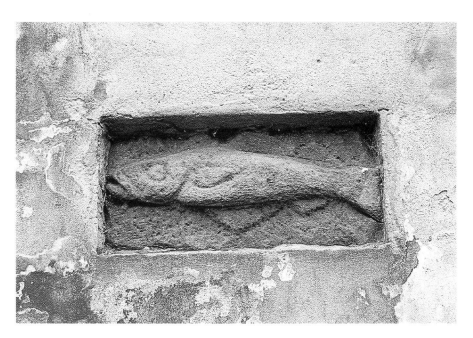

The tunnel emerged partway up the cliff. From there the ironstone wagons ran along a tall wooden gantry built on top of today's surviving pier. Discharged into bunkers below the gantry, the ore was then fed into vessels via chutes, at the rate of 200 tons in fiteen minutes. With the Grinkle mine providing the bulk of the ore, the tonnage shipped peaked in 1880 at 170,576 tons - an average of almost 3,300 tons per week.

About 200 vessels a year were handled by the port. The first were sailing ships, but these were soon replaced by steamers, paddle and screw. Featuring specially-strengthened holds, to withstand the force of the ore shot from those gantry bunkers, at least two screw steamers, Grinkle and Runswick, were built specially for Port Mulgrave. The others towed barges and lighters filled with the ore.

Though some ore went to blastfurnaces at nearby Skinningrove and on Teesside, most of it was shipped to Palmer's Jarrow steelworks. Returning vessels often delivered coal for the harbour and mines. But though the harbour could accommodate three 400-ton ships, its narrow entrance proved a serious drawback. Skippers were reluctant to enter in any sea heavier than a mild swell. And even then, the paddle fenders of the steamers had to be removed.

The harbour's heyday ended with the First World War, when the Grinkle mine was linked to the Whitby-Middlesbrough coastal railway, considered safer than the sea. But shipments continued at a reduced rate until 1921 when the mine closed. Three years later, the harbour's final consignment of ore was despatched - but not to sea. Left in the storage bays when the mine closed, it was sent through the tunnel to the Grinkle mine and then on by the Whitby-Middlesbrough railway. And though the mine reopened in 1927 the harbour remained idle except for one day in 1929 when an oil-powered barge loaded with ironstone nosed in. Said to be testing for the possible re-use of the harbour by the Grinkle mine, this was probably a ploy by the mine company to persuade the railway to reduce charges.

The Grinkle mine closed for good in 1930. During the removal of the harbour equipment five years later the impressive gantry was destroyed by fire. At the start of the Second World War in 1939, the outer breakwater was blown up by the army as a precaution against enemy landings. Port Mulgrave has been in its death throes ever since.

Apart from the bricked-up tunnel, its most enduring feature is the clifftop cottages that housed the 300-400 workers from the mines and harbour. The terrace closest to the cliff edge was lodgings for single men, who were kept as far as possible from the married couples. These occupied the three terraces set back from the cliff.

As a further discouragement to the mixing of these two groups, the homes of mine officials were built between them. Overlooking the whole complex from a small rise was the manager's bungalow, and beyond that, discreetly out of sight, was the sycamore-shaded 'lodge' used by Palmer when visiting his harbour. All these still survive.

In 1881 Palmer built the baronial mansion of Grinkle Park, now a hotel. Knighted in 1886, he served as Jarrow's MP for more than 30 years, up to his death in 1907. But his summers were spent at Grinkle Park, and he chose to be buried at the local parish church - Easington.

If he returned today he might be pleased to find that part of his former ironstone mine lies within the Boulby potash complex, perpetuating its link with industry. But he would surely grieve at the decay of his harbour - now Port Melancholy as much as Port Mulgrave.

Runswick Bay

On a sunny summer's day, there are few better occupations along the North Yorkshire coast than to spend an hour or so wandering among Runswick Bay's maze of twisting lanes and stairways. Here a hollyhock leans across a flagged path. There, a wisteria garlands a charming cottage. Cordon pears ripen on a sun-baked wall, while a shady spot is brightened by a purple clematis watered by a gushing spring. And seldom out of sight, over cottage gardens or across a jumble of pantiled roofs, is the glorious azure-blue bay.

The scene can, and very often does, look Mediterranean. Basking on a south-facing headland, which protects it from northerly winds, Runswick enjoys an exceptionally sunny position. Seen from the shore, with its creamy cottages set against a backdrop of hanging woods, it has a southern softness. How appropriate that virtually on the sea wall stands a thatched cottage - the prettiest of finishing touches to Runswick's fair face.

But all that charm masks a grim struggle to survive - against relentless landslip. One night in about 1682 every house bar one fell into the sea. Fortunately, a party of villagers was returning late from a funeral 'wake'. Sensing the ground move - and reckoning it was not the effect of the 'wake' - they roused their sleeping friends and neighbours in the nick of time.

Though the village was rebuilt, the landslip menace has never diminished. In January 1873 the *Whitby Gazette* reported: 'Almost every house is moving and numbers have been made completely uninhabitable.' In 1961, the only road into the village, with a hairpin bend directly behind the cottages, slid so dangerously it had to be abandoned. Prudently, its replacement was built to the side of the village.

But in 1966 the remains of the old road slipped again, sending two boulders crashing into the chapel. On 27 February 1977, the occupants of Ileene Cottage, alarmed by what they described as 'a noise like a stampede of elephants,' escaped just before a telegraph pole and a tree, carried on a slithering mass of earth, embedded themselves in the empty Rose Cottage next door. Jim Romanes, village shopkeeper and chairman of the Runswick Bay Association, declared: 'In the long term the whole village will go.' In 1995 Square Rig Cottage had to be demolished when subsidence made it unsafe. And in 1998, cracking in the 'new' seawall, built in 1971 to protect the new road, was adjudged so serious that within a year work began on a £2.4 million scheme, mainly funded by the Government, to repair the wall, defend it with 'rock armour' - ten-ton boulders shipped from Scandinavia - and stabilise the cliffs with interconnecting concrete piles. An engineer warned: 'If allowed to continue the deterioration could ultimately result in the failure of the sea defences.'

In Runswick, the term 'sea wall' is almost a misnomer. For the main threat comes from the land. Seeping into the heavy boulder-clay cliffs, rainwater builds up until pressure causes a section of the cliff to sheer off. An engineering report to the County Council in 1969 concluded:

> For all practical purposes there is nothing that can be done to stabilise the land...Those who live in the village, those with long experience of the soil, and those who have bought properties there in recent years are well aware of the inability of man to control this environment.

In a recognition of beauty rare in an engineering document, the report's authors apologised for 'having to write in this depressing way about so attractive a locality.'

As if to draw attention away from this landward threat, Runswick's most prominent building is its Lifeboat House. A reminder of the perils at sea it thrusts forward over the beach.

Runswick and Staithes co-star in the story of lifeboats along this stretch of coast. But Runswick enters first and has the larger role. Opened in 1866, its lifeboat station served both villages until a boat was placed at Staithes nine years later. Launching difficulties in the often rougher sea at Staithes led to the closure of its station in 1922.

Though the completion of the Staithes' breakwaters six years later allowed its station to reopen that year, it closed again in 1938, not re-opening again until 1978 - as an inshore station. Meanwhile, however, Staithes men served with the Runswick-based boat, officially assigned to both villages.

In 1934 Runswick fisherman Robert Patton, cox of the station's first motor lifeboat, *The Always Ready*, died from injuries received in an outstanding example of lifeboat heroism. Attending a steamship sinking in a heavy sea on 17 February, The Always Ready inched herself into position to rescue a man clinging to the stricken vessel's side. Leaning out of the lifeboat, Patton grasped the man and shouted to him to let go. But the terrified man hung on.

As a huge wave pitched the lifeboat towards the steamer Patton could have released the man and leaned back out of danger. But knowing the man would be swept to his death, he grasped him even tighter. The man survived, but Patton, crushed between the boats, died of multiple injuries nine days later. Aged 46, he was posthumously awarded the RNLI's Gold Medal - the lifeboat service's VC. Thousands gathered to see Patton's widow receive the medal from the Princess Royal, who also renamed the lifeboat *Robert Patton - The Always Ready*. It seems a shame that subsequent Runswick lifeboats haven't kept this inspiring name.

In a nationwide 're-structuring', the RNLI closed the Runswick station in 1978 when it also reopened the Staithes' station with its inshore craft. But Runswick residents and the bay's many pleasure sailors felt Runswick still needed a lifeboat. A meeting in the former Fishermen's Institute, a community

How it was. Port Mulgrave harbour with its elaborate ironstone gantry.

Unseen Runswick: a crumbling ironstone kiln at the aptly-named Wreckhills.

hall, resolved to buy and operate an independent 'Rescue Boat'. Launched in 1982, the inflatable they acquired has since been succeeded by three larger and faster inshore craft. With 20 fully-trained crew-members, the boat provides year-round cover and is fully recognised by the Coastguard Service. It has so far carried out more than 70 rescue missions, details of which are proudly logged on boards in the Royal Hotel. The boat is berthed in the tractor shed of the former Lifeboat Station, which is now a private boathouse.

At least twice, in 1901 and 1940, the Runswick lifeboat was launched by the village women. This was no mean achievment, as the heavy boat had to be hauled across the foreshore, a task that usually required about 30 men.

With the older men of the village forming a makeshift crew, the first of these launches was to escort home the local fishing fleet, caught in a storm. Prompted by a wartime shortage of manpower, the 1940 launch - at 2a.m. incidentally - resulted in the saving of the six crew of a floundering motor vessel. The delivery in June 1940 of an RNLI launching tractor saved the women from making further wartime launches.

A poem praising Runswick's women is displayed in the tiny white-painted Methodist chapel. Written by former Minister, the Rev Joseph Toyn, it salutes not only the 1901 launch but the women's equally hard labour in building the chapel. As the poem explains:

> *Husbands and brothers with eager glee*
> *Quarried the stone that was given free,*
> *And the women bore it - a heavy load -*
> *For two long miles on a rugged road.*
> *And their grand memorial stands today*
> *- the little chapel in Runswick Bay.*

Also in the chapel, a simple little building, is a picture of Robert Patton, to whom the organ is dedicated. A nearby cottage wall is built of stone cut from the boulders that crashed into the chapel in 1966.

At the far (Kettleness) end of Runswick's beach, a cave is the reputed home of a *hob*, the North Riding word for hobgoblin or imp. Runswick's hob was credited with power to cure whooping cough, and Runswick mothers used to carry their sick infants the half mile or so to his cave and call out: 'Ma bairn's gotten t'kink cough. Tak't off, tak't off.' The success rate isn't known.

Runswick children learned an unusual prayer. Indicating the prevalence of 'wrecking', the plundering of ships that came to grief in the bay, it went: 'God bless Ma and Pa, and send us a good wreck by morning.' Along the entire North Yorkshire coast any unforeseen bounty of the sea is still swiftly and gratefully seized upon. In 1993 a container of clothes, mostly T-shirts, was washed up below Boulby cliff, near Staithes. Before Customs officers arrived, its contents vanished. A local fisherman observed: 'I've never seen so many well dressed people in Staithes for years.'

A sister fishing village to Staithes, Runswick had 38 boats in 1848, when herring houses occupied what is now the bank-foot car park. Its population was almost 500. But by 1998 this had dwindled to just 22, with only 12 of the village's 92 homes permanently occupied. Even part-time fishing has now more or less ceased, though Runswick Sailing Club has 70 members - more than three times the resident population. The many self-consciously nautical house names - Capstan, The Tackle, Achorage Cottage etc - mirror Runswick's chief contemporary roles as holiday haven and weekend retreat.

Few incomers know it once had an ironworks. Opened in 1858 on the aptly-named Wreckhills - a slumped section of cliff just north of the village - the Victoria Iron and Cement Works seemed pre-destined to fail. Under tow at sea from Whitby, two of its three boilers sank, a debacle that spawned an expensive court case. Only two months after production started, most of the works, which included two blast furnaces, a boiler house and several kilns, collapsed in a landslip - that old adversary again.

The works' owners, mainly businessmen from Leeds, spent four years rebuilding the works. But though iron was produced for seven years, the initial investment of £30,000 was never recovered. Abandoned in 1869, when their salvageable material was sold for a mere £1,005, they have since crumbled away. Visible from the nearby beach, but dangerous to visit, their only surviving structures are a bank of kilns. But on the clifftop are two ponds, now silted up, that fed the boilers.

The ponds are where the Cleveland Way takes a sudden right-angled turn to Runswick's bank top. Why this long distance trail fails to use a right of way that goes straight on at the ponds, to a magnificent viewpoint over the bay, is a mystery. Blocked at the time of writing this right of way, the natural climax of the cliffwalk from Staithes, should be re-opened.

From bank top, the Cleveland Way is signposted down the 'new' road. But this too is unsatisfactory. The most enjoyable way to enter Runswick on foot is down the twisting old road. Now a track that a starts near the Cliffemount Hotel, it connects with paved lanes and steps, whetting the appetite for the enchantment to which they lead.

Robin Hood's Bay

A romantic name and a romantic situation invest Robin Hood's Bay with rare appeal. Its million or so visitors each year make it easily the most popular village in the North York Moors.

Obliged to leave their cars at the bank top, many of the annual million do little more than stroll down the Clovelly-like steep main street, marvel at how it terminates in a slipway, which brings the sea into the village at high tide, and then wander back.

But the essence of 'Bay', as the village is locally called, is the Lilliputian world behind the main street. On each side is an delightful network of tiny lanes, yards and steps. A diminutive pair of doors in Sunnyside, a narrow lane on the west side - the right hand side going down - could be an entrance to Wonderland, where Alice had her rendezvous with the White Rabbit.

Across the main street, Sunnyside has an eastern counterpart in Sunny Place, a small square. As these two 'Sunnys' suggest, Bay is a surprisingly balmy place. A large plane tree, a species that generally struggles against the salt-laden North-East winds, flourishes in that main street. A fig tree graces a cottage off Fisherhead. And in the hot summer of 1995 I came across tomatoes ripening outdoors at Ocean View Cottage, within 30 yards (27.4m) of the North Sea.

Winds tend to blow straight over the notch in the cliffs, carved by King's Beck, occupied by the village. The notch itself is sheltered because it is part of a strip of the North Yorkshire coast, about three miles long and half a mile broad, that dips down from the higher ground inland. Forming a huge natural ampitheatre with the moors at its back, it enfolds a gentle patchwork of woods and pastures more reminiscent of Devon than the bleaker North-East. Its boundary headlands - North Cheek and the more towering South Cheek - create the bay itself.

The connection with Robin Hood? Hazy, to say the least. The outlaw himself might well be entirely mythical, of course. But among the 40 or so ballads about him is one in which he gives up robbing Nottinghamshire's rich for the supposedly more lucrative fishing off Scarborough. Try telling that to a Scarborough fisherman! But this could be the origin of the legend that Robin kept a boat at Bay as a last, desperate means of escape from the Sheriff of Nottingham. He is said to have selected the spot by shooting an arrow from Stoupe Browe, two miles away near Ravenscar.

This prodigious shot is nearly matched by others in a different legend. This tells of Robin and his Merry Men arriving in the district at the invitation of the Abbot of Whitby, who recruited them to fight off Danish invaders. The abbot is said to have arranged an archery contest between Robin Hood and Little John, to see who could shoot an arrow furthest from the abbey tower. Still marking where the arrows supposedly fell, a few yards from each other about one-and-half miles from the abbey, are two stones engraved 'Robin Hood Field' and 'Little John Field'. They stand a short way down the footpath opposite Manor House farm, on the minor road between Hawsker and Whitby.

Near Stoupe Browe stands a group of Bronze Age burial mounds named Robin Hood's Butts. Though these might have been used for archery practice, the bowmen were more probably the local medieval militia than Robin and his outlaws.

A possible clue to the village's name is that the earliest record of it - 'Robbyn Huddes Bay' in Whitby Abbey registers of 1534 - dates from the period when legends about the outlaw were very popular. The registers also reveal that in the 1530s Bay's 'herrynge house' was run by a John Smith, who came from Wakefield, where Robin Hood reputedly died. Perhaps that link caused Smith to be nicknamed Robin Hood, and as he was a key local figure, the village acquired that name as well. But no-one knows.

With Danish raiders plaguing the coast until well into the Middle Ages, Bay's earliest fishermen, like those at Staithes, lived inland - in their case at Raw. Once settled at Bay, however, they built up its fishing trade to surpass Whitby's. In 1538, John Leland, Henry VIII's antiquary, recorded Bay as 'a fischar tounlet of 20 bootes.' And though he also described Whitby at that time as 'a great fischar toune', a Dutch North Sea chart of 1586 omits Whitby yet gives a compass bearing from Rotterdam to Robinhoodes Bay .

Concentrating on its whaling and alum trade, Whitby had only nine fishermen in 1816. Bay had 130 - more than anywhere else on the Yorkshire coast.

For generations Bay was also Yorkshire's hottest hotbed of smuggling. In the eighteenth century smuggling became so rife along the entire North Yorkshire coast that in 1775 sixteen Dragoons were billeted in various villages. Bay had the largest contingent - six. In 1817, with the illegal trade as bad as ever, the Customs' and Excise deployed two patrol boats. Each manned by six well-armed men, these were based at Bay and Staithes.

The smugglers were ruthless and violent. In 1779 Customs men swooped on a Bay inn and seized 200 smuggled casks of brandy, 150 sacks of tea, and a large quantity of firearms. But a band of twenty smugglers fought back and regained most of the contraband. A newspaper reported how they paraded their spoils through the streets, threatening 'death and destruction to all their opposers.'

The most determined Bay smugglers had armed ships, including a schooner with fourteen large cannon. In an incident just off Robin Hood's Bay in 1778 it shot away the sails and damaged the hull of a pursuing Revenue cutter, one of whose Excisemen was also injured.

Bay's smuggled goods usually began their inland journey up the large tunnel that still leads King's Beck on to the beach. At low tide the first few yards of the tunnel can be entered safely. Further in, side tunnels, now bricked up, led to various houses. From these contraband was swiftly passed to other houses through secret doors in back-to-back cupboards. It is said that a cask of brandy or bolt of silk could be shifted from the shore to the bank top without emerging into the open air.

When the Revenue swooped, the smugglers often fled along The Bolts, a short lane leading to woods - as it still does. This was also an escape route from the Press Gang, whose arrival was signalled by a drum.

As smuggling declined in the mid nineteenth, it was perhaps the vast tax-free wealth it had created that enabled Bay to switch to a maritime activity not usually associated with a small village: shipowning. In 1867, an astonishing 174 ocean-going vessels were owned by residents of Robin Hood's Bay. Most were registered at Whitby, from where they plied the shipping lanes of the world. There is a record of one Bay-owned ship, a barque sailing to Hull with cotton from the West Indies, being attacked and robbed by pirates off Gibraltar. Most of the large Victorian houses at Bay's bank top were built by Bay shipowners. But as steam replaced sail, ship-owning gravitated to ports able to handle the larger vessels.

Though there is no record of a quay at Robin Hood's Bay, post holes identified on the foreshore in 1995 suggest the former presence of at least a mooring pier. But Bay's present-day 'Dock' is merely a small square by the slipway. And though a dozen or so boats are often hauled up there, very little fishing has been done from Bay since 1939, when Oliver Storm, last in the unbroken line of full-time Bay fishermen, retired.

Living in the four-storey white-painted house by The Dock, Storm was also cox of the last Bay lifeboat - a rowing vessel withdrawn in 1931. The lifeboat house is now a shelter and toilets, at The Dock. The anchor attached to its wall served as a 'holdfast' for the lifeboat. Close by is the old coastguard station. Originally a seventeenth 17th century inn, which became a watch post two centuries later, it served as a marine research laboratory from 1911 to 1982. In 1965 it suffered an unsympathetic rebuild. But since 1998 it has been restored to its original appearance by the National Trust. Reopened in 2000 is houses displays on the building's history and the conservation of the Yorkshire coast. Also given a new lease of life was Bay's (probably) centenarian cod. Photographs prove that since at least 1904 the metal fish has been fixed vertically to the coastguard station wall, open mouth uppermost to receive coins: a unique RNLI collecting box.

The coastguard station was probably where, on 19 January 1881, the alarm was raised when the brig Visitor foundered off Bay, in seas too rough for the local lifeboat to turn out. As described in my *Inside the North York Moors*, the Whitby lifeboat was hauled six miles over snowdrifts to save the six crew. A plaque erected on the centenary of the astonishing rescue stands at bank top.

Shortly before the advent of steam, so many sailing ships were wrecked in the bay that a mortuary was built in the village. With its euphemistic name, Coroner's Room, engraved over the door, this handsome Tudor-style building, in Fisherhead, now houses a good local museum. Particularly apt is its display of fishermen's ganseys, whose distinctive patterns, each peculiar to a particular place, helped identify drowned seamen.

As its name, New Road, implies, Bay's main street is not the original main road. That was King's Road, of which only a rump, off The Dock, survives. Believed to get its name because much of its property belonged to Henry VIII, the road, or rather most of it, fell into the sea in 1780. In the two centuries since then, 193 Bay homes have suffered the same fate. As the number of surviving homes is about 200, virtually half the village has vanished.

Once extending to about today's low water mark, the boulder cliffs are retreating at the rate of ten feet (three metres) a year. In 1843 a predecessor of the Bay Hotel, which bears the full brunt of the waves, was washed away. Fifty years later the bowsprit of a wrecked ship protruded through an upper window.

The survival of the entire village was in doubt until a 40ft (12.1m) tall sea wall, the highest in Britain, was built in 1973-74. The consulting engineeers calculated that without the wall fifteen properties faced imminent destruction, and the sea would penetrate to the heart of the village within 30 years. The wall's completion inspired some stirring lines by the Yorkshire poet, the late Ronald Scriven:

> *Now men have built a great sea wall,*
> *Immensely strong, immensely tall,*
> *Protecting with its massive stone*
> *Boats and buildings, flesh and stone.*

Unfortunately a walkway on the wall doesn't live up to its inviting name-the Quarterdeck. It would be much improved by facing the harsh concrete parapet in stone, and raising the public seats to give a decent view over the top.

Each May a band of literary pilgrims arrives in Bay. Members of the Walmsley Society they hold events to honour once-popular novelist Leo Walmsley (1892-1966). He grew up in Bay, where his former home, in King St, is marked by a plaque. Several of his books are set in Bay, which he re-named Bramblewick – hence the Bramblewick Tearoom. Unveiled at the Dock as part of the British film industry's centenary in 1996, another plaque recalls that J. Arthur Rank's first feature film, Turn of the Tide, filmed in Bay and Whitby in 1935, was an adaptation of Walmsley's best seller Three Fevers .

The appeal of Walmsley's books was well expressed by a correspondent to the *Whitby Gazette* in 1941, who said they evoked 'the tang of the clean salt air, the cry of the gulls, brown sails in the wind, and above all the queer characters who reside by the North Sea coast.' But the correspondent wrote not to praise Walmsley but upbraid him - for ploughing on Sunday! A man of many parts, Walmsley dabbled in farming - and also fishing. He once caused amusement by trying to adapt a parrot's cage into a collapsible lobster pot, using parts from a pram and a bedstead. Leo's father, Ulric, was a noted painter, and a book of his watercolours, including scenes of Robin Hood's Bay, has recently been published.

Bay's roots at Raw, a mile from the coast, explain why its first parish church, built in 1108, stood in open countryside - at Raw lane end, by the road to Hawsker. Its successor, built in 1821, still occupies the same spot. Very simple and dignified, with a small bellcote instead of a tower, it reflects the strong influence of Methodism.

John Wesley preached at Bay eleven times, and his ideas probably determined the unusual position of the church pulpit - half way along the nave. The aim was to concentrate the congregations's attention on the Word rather than the trappings and rituals inherent in a view of the altar. Some Bay worshippers sat with their backs to this traditional heart of the church.

The church contains a rare set of 'maiden's garlands.' Carried by village girls at the funeral of any unmarried young virgin, these coloured ribbons were afterwards left hanging until replaced by a fresh set at the next 'maiden' funeral. The origin and meaning of the custom are a mystery, but since the dozen or so places where it is recorded are all on the coast it seems to have had something to do with the sea. Bay's garlands date from the last occasion the custom carried out, in 1869.

Among the gravestones are more than 260 of Bay seamen. The view from their last resting place, across a chequerwork of fields and woods to the bay, backed by the towering 700ft (213.3m) South Cheek, is rivalled only by the one down Nidderdale from Middlesmoor church as the finest from any church in Yorkshire. Smack in the centre rises the tower of Bay's present church, at bank top, which replaced the one at Raw in 1870. Designed by Edward Street, architect of the London Law Courts, and somewhat dark inside, it contains the font of the original church. Unearthed from a field in 1895, this had probably served as a trough. Scenes of local life - fishing and farming - feature on an oak

Robin Hood's Bay sea wall - 'immensely strong, immensely tall.'

St Stephen's old church - last resting place of more than 200 seafarers.

porch screen made by Littlebeck woodcarver Tom Whittaker (1910-1991), whose gnome trademark also appears on several other items. There is also a vigorous stained glass scene of fishermen hauling in their nets.

By the doorway, a framed certificate, dated May 22, 1930, bears the rare signature of Edward, Prince of Wales, later the abdicating Edward VIII. As President of the Royal National Lifeboat Institution, he conveyed the institution's thanks for 100 years of 'devotion and courage' by Bay lifeboatmen, who had 'never failed to maintain the high traditions of the lifeboat service.' Within a year their station was closed.

The Resort That Never Was

In October 1893 a magazine entitled *The Tourist* - a journal surely well ahead of its time? - reported:

> One of the most interesting and perhaps astonishing features of our English coast lies in the fact that fresh places of interest and beauty are constantly cropping up. It might be thought that the most had already been made of the Yorkshire coast, yet its attractiveness between Scarborough and Whitby may be said to be just beginning to be fairly realised.

The writer went on to extol the antiquity of Robin Hood's Bay, recently made accessible by the Whitby-Scarborough Railway. But his words became even more apt a couple of years later. For what then 'cropped up' was not the discovery of a quaint old village but a plan to create a spanking new resort. The attractiveness of the 'Yorkshire coast between Scarborough and Whitby' seemed set to be realised in most spectacular fashion.

The location of the intended town was Ravenscar, the towering headland overlooking the wide sweep of Robin Hood's Bay. Bronze Age folk dwelt there, burying their dead in the mounds, or howes, still to be seen at Stoupe Brow.

Early in the fourth century came the Romans. The foundation stone of their headland fort, with a Latin inscription telling how 'Justinian, governor of the province, and Vindicianus, prefect of soliders, built this fort,' is on show in Whitby Museum.

Though the name Ravenscar might be derived from a Celtic word pronounced raif, which means a huge rock or cliff, legend has it that the name stems from the arrival of the Vikings, who planted their raven banner on this dominating 708ft (188m) headland, which was also for long known simply as Peak.

But all this pales besides the unfulfilled plan to create a second Scarborough at this improbable spot. The prelude to the astonishing scheme was the building of a mansion on the clifftop in 1774 by a Capt Child, of London. It was during the construction of this house, which Child named Raven Hall, now the well-known hotel, that the Roman foundation stone was unearthed.

The hall soon passed to Francis Willis, a physician to George III (1760-1820), who married the captain's daughter, Ann. The royal connection has fostered a claim that the mentally-unstable George was nursed at Raven Hall during bouts of madness. Though there is no evidence for this, the hall, remote from London and its gossip, was certainly well placed to be a royal sanatorium.

It was Richard Child Willis, son of Francis and Ann, who added the clifftop battlements to Raven Hall. Legend has it that he planted the hall's grounds with metal trees, whose tin leaves tinkled in the breeze. A possible origin of this fanciful tale is that he planted an American shrub called Ironwood, a variety of hop, and local wits did the rest.

A reckless gambler, Child Willis is reputed to have lost Raven Hall when he staked it as a bet on a race between two woodlice crossing a saucer. The winner, autioneer and land agent William Hammond, of Chancery Lane and Bell Yard, London, used the hall as a holiday retreat. His nine children spent their summers there, apparently liking it well enough to eventually send their own children there. Thirty-six of them in all, they stayed with their grandfather at the hall in relays. Meanwhile Hammond turned much surrounding moor into farmland. Housing his farmworkers in new 'model' cottages, he also built a church, manse and schoolroom, all still in tact, and a now-ruined windmill.

Hammond campaigned strongly for the construction of the Whitby-Scarborough railway - with the proviso that it crossed most of his land in a tunnel! Where it surfaced, he urged contruction of a station, probably chiefly for his own convenience.

Hammond died the year the line, complete with its 'Peak' station and tunnel, opened in 1885. Other speculators saw potential in Hammond's 1,800-acre (729ha) clifftop estate. Buying it on the death of Hammond's widow in 1895, a group of businessmen, mainly from West Yorkshire, formed the Peak Estate Company with the aim of creating the resort of Ravenscar. The driving force was John Septimus Bland, whose family had made money developing Scarborough's South Bay, part of which is still known as Bland's Cliff.

Displayed in the National Trust's information centre at Ravenscar is a plan of the town envisaged by Bland and his partners. Centred on the railway station and covering 750 acres (303.5ha), it was intended to occupy virtually all the land between the clifftop and the Whitby-Scarborough road. Its 1,200 building plots were laid out along broad boulevards with names like Marine Esplanade and Cliff Road. Ravenscar's history was mirrored in Dane Road, Saxon Road and Roman Road - though the latter was curved! The shop-lined Station Road linked Station Square to Raven Hall Road, the town's main highway. The existing Bent Rigg Lane was widened and straightened to become Church Road, with Hammond's church at its junction with Raven Hall Road.

A labour force of 300 to 400 men was recruited to turn this dream into reality. So confident were its promoters that they opened a brickyard alongside the railway, to make bricks for the resort. Several roads, including Station Road and Church Road, were built, and drains and sewers were installed. Plots were offered for sale at a series of auctions. The prospectus for one of these, held at Ravenscar in 1898, announces: 'There are some splendid shop plots and sites for marine villas of every size.' Costing about £80 a typical plot could be bought outright or in instalments over nine years at five per cent interest. The prospectus advertised a special train from Scarborough to the sale, with the fare refunded to anyone who bought a plot.

But neither this sale nor any other drew many takers. Only a dozen or so villas were built. Most were near the station, where a row of shops and a hotel were built. Now private homes and a tearoom they form one side of a Station Square that is vacant on all other sides. Two have never had buildings, but the third once had the station, whose grass grown platform survives. Nearby, a short terrace of houses faces the unmade-up Loring Road, where rusting manhole covers and drainage grilles peep through grass. Various other roads and avenues are now just tracks between fields.

The ill-judged enterprise was abandoned in the 1920s, when the Peak Estate Company went into voluntary liquidation. Its failure was probably inevitable. Subject to sea frets, the exposed clifftop is so windy that even while Bland and Co. were promoting its merits, a gale blew away the wooden station buildings. The proposed resort also lacked a promenade or beach - just a rocky shore, reached down a steep, twisting path. Not even the magnificent view across the bay could compensate for those deficiencies.

But in good weather today Ravenscar draws many visitors. The Raven Hall Hotel, with splendid gardens, swimming pool and a nine-hole golf course, thrives. The hall's conversion into a hotel was the first act of Bland and his associates on acquiring the estate. That part, at least, of their rash dream defies the overwhelming odds.

CHAPTER 7

ON THE ROCKS

Ruts 'n' Rails

Vanishing twice a day, perhaps the least-known feature of the Yorkshire coast is a series of cart-tracks and former tramways along the rocky scaurs. Covered by each incoming tide, more than a score of these remarkable arteries exist along the 40 miles of coast between Saltburn and Scarborough.

Neptune's highways? Not exactly. But they're none the less fascinating for that. Very much a human enterprise, they rival the Rosedale Railway, that standard gauge line thrust across the moors to reach coveted deposits of iron ore, in illustrating the lengths to which men would go to exploit the rich mineral wealth of the North York Moors.

Alum was probably the first prize for which it was considered worthwhile to hack cart roads and tramways on the rocky seabed. Turning alum shale into crystals, used in tanning, dyeing and parchment-making, a string of alum works operated along the alum-rich coast between the sixteenth and nineteenth centuries. They were served by flat-bottomed boats, which fetched coal and shipped the finished crystals to London and other ports. The boats either beached themselves near the works or berthed in shallow docks blasted from the seabed.

The ease the passage of carts, and speed up the turnround of the ships, ruts were cut in the rocks for the cart wheels. Sections of six such rutways can still be traced below Hummersea Point, Skinningrove. They almost certainly ran from alum works at Loftus, some traces of which also remain, to Skinningrove beach about half a mile away.

Some of these Skinningrove rutways merge, like railway junctions. One that doesn't heads for a crude dock on Hummersea Scar. And another, now less complete, seems to have served a similar dock below The Warren.

Discernible between the two Cowbar headlands north of Staithes, a faint and fragmentary rutway might have been cut for the Boulby alum works, which operated from 1672 to 1871. Kettleness also has an alum rutway, on foreshore rocks called Fillet Tail. And from Saltwick Nab, south of Whitby, site of another alum works, a much-eroded rutway runs for half a mile to Whitby harbour. Difficult to pick out except when highlighted by the low midsummer sun at dawn or dusk, this rutway was probably linked to a stone ramp at Saltwick, still a prominent feature on the foreshore, which led to a pier.

Near Ravenscar, the Peak alum works, whose remains have been conserved and put on display by the National Trust, were linked to the shore by an inclined tramway. Ships berthed in a dock cut in Billet Scar, which was the termination of a number of rutways. Among them is one double the usual width and with a centre rut - apparently some form of dual-carriageway. But how did the carts pass each other?

When trade in ironstone, initially based on samples collected from the beach, began, a number of alum rutways, including the one at Kettleness, were pressed into service. But many new rutways were soon cut. The longest so far identified adopts a serpentine course of one-and-a-quarter miles around Saltburn's Huntcliff. Venturing further from dry land than any other rutway it reaches about 120 yards (110m) below the high water mark.

Fragments of another rutway probably cut for ironstone exist west of Hole Wyke, near Boulby. More easily visited is a 50-yard (46m) section of rutway under Penny Nab, Staithes. A little further south, at Old Nab, the outlines of more than 60 sleepers, running out to sea, are still visible. Their narrow-gauge tramway was one of four that operated at various times on the three-miles of foreshore between Staithes and Port Mulgrave.

Only in recent years has this extensive complex of seabed cartways and tramways been thoroughly charted and chronicled. According to the late John Owen, the Cleveland industrial archaeologist who found and researched most of them, their earliest-known predecessors are rutways on Malta, believed to date from the New Stone Age.

The Romans and Greeks also created rutways in Mediterranean countries. In Britain, rutways constructed of stone blocks exist at a nineteenth-century granite quarry at Haytor, Devon, and an eighteenth century limestone quarry at Conisborough, South Yorkshire. But North Yorkshire's coastal rutways are the only known British examples chiselled from the natural rock.

That they were cut for carts is certain, because the distance between the ruts is invariably the four feet four inches (1.3m) of a standard heavy-duty cart. The three-inch (76.2mm) width of the ruts also matches a heavy cart's wheelrims.

The most southerly rutways, a group of about four near Scarborough's South Bay bathing pool, are believed to have been cut for the transport of slabs, hewn from the seabed, used to build the town's east pier in the nineteenth century. The last-known use of any rutway was shortly before 1914, when an old rutway about half a mile north of Robin Hood's Bay, probably originally for ironstone, was adopted by carts recovering steel from a wrecked ship.

But perhaps the most intriguing of these North Yorkshire rutways is the only example NOT on the seashore. Cut into an exposed bed of sandstone on a steep hillside at Howdale, a small valley near Ravenscar, this rutway has locally always been associated with a quarry. But since it doesn't run into the quarry, but skirts its rim and continues beyond, this is unlikely. According to John Owen it could predate the foreshore rutways and be their model. Aiming for Ravenscar it could have been part of a Roman road to the fort there. On its steep exposed

Ghost of industry. The grooves of a foreshore wagonway head for the now 'rock-armour' defended Staithes' harbour.

An astonishing road. This little-known grooved cartway at Stoupe Browe perhaps served the Roman signal station at nearby Ravenscar.

section, about 200 yards (180m) yard, its surface has been chipped to provide grip for horses.

A more impressive feature than the Roman road on Wheeldale Moor, yet still virtually unknown, this well-preserved stretch of rutway is probably one of the most ancient and historic highways in the national park.

The mv Creteblock

For an hour or two either side of high tide, a puzzling sight from the cliffs just south of Whitby is a black object that protrudes from the sea like a shark's fin. Submerged at high tide and often unnoticed on the wide scaur when the tide is out, this is the starboard bow of the motor vessel *Creteblock* . Easily visited by a half-mile walk along the scaur, the shattered vessel is not only Yorkshire's most accessible shipwreck, but one of the most unusual.

The *Creteblock's* rare claim to fame is that she was built of concrete - hence her name. The concrete was reinforced with steel wires, which are now exposed on that snapped-off bow. Lying about a quarter of a mile from the cliffs and pointing out to sea, it is at a right angle to the former stern section, which rests on its keel about twenty yards (18.2m) away. Other pieces of the ship litter the surrounding scaur, from which they, like the main sections, are almost indistinguishable through a crust of barnacles and lichens.

How did the ship come to be built of concrete? An obscure fact of naval history is that the British Admiralty commissioned ships of concrete in the First World War to make good a shortage of steel. With the latter reserved for battleships, the substitute material was used for support ships, usually built in small yards.

Among these was Whitby's Whitehall shipyard. Closed in 1902, after the last Whitby-built merchant ship, the 3,860-ton *Broomfield*, slid down her slipway, the yard, on the east side of the upper harbour, was reopened in 1917 to build concrete 'lighters' for the war.

Two vessels, each 109 feet (33.2m) long, were built. They were intended for use as seaplane tenders or moveable platforms for manned balloons, which kept a lookout for submarines. But by the time the first vessel was launched, in May, 1919, the war had been over six months. And though both vessels were completed, no more ships, concrete or otherwise, were ordered from the Whitehall yard.

For a while, the Whitby ships ferried supplies to RAF seaplanes, chiefly in the Solent. But their top speed of four knots proved unsatisfactory, and they were soon scrapped.

Understandably, local memories of the construction of these these two concrete ships at Whitby have bred a belief that the *Creteblock* is one of them. But she was built at Shoreham, Essex. It is pure chance that Whitby, one of few places to build concrete ships, has a rare concrete shipwreck.

Built for similar war tasks to the Whitby ships, the Creteblock also missed the deadline. Launched in 1919 she entered service the following year as a seagoing Royal Navy tug. Propelled by a single screw she was 125ft (38.1m) long, with a beam of 27.5ft (8.3m).

Like her Whitby counterparts she enjoyed only a short military career. Bought by Smith's Dock, she worked at this busy Teesside shipyard until about 1935, when the company moved her to Whitby. There she was stripped of her fittings, the removal of which might have been the reason she was brought to the port. Though adopted as a store by a fishermen, her decaying hull, in the upper harbour, became an eyesore.

When the harbour authority ordered Smith's Dock to remove the ship, the company patched her up and arranged for her to be scuttled in deep water. But as she was being towed from the harbour, in a choppy sea at 4.30 a.m. one day in 1947, she began taking in water very fast. So she was beached on the nearby scaur, where she rests today, forlorn amid a big bed of mussels.

Inshore fishermen curse her for sometimes snagging their gear, a large collection of which has accumulated in that hollow bow. But half a century's erosion by weather and the North Sea hasn't yet planed away the vessel's stamped-out name. The severed hull remains remarkably in tact. Not only a rarity, this concrete shipwreck looks capable of enduring as long as any of iron and steel.

An improbable shipwreck. The remains of the concrete-hulled Creteblock litter the scaur at Whitby.

CHAPTER 8

IN WHITBY

The Swing Bridge

Few communities are more closely bound together - and yet divided - by a bridge than Whitby. The east and west communities of the town intermingle largely by courtesy of the venerable swing bridge. The ringing of a brass handbell is the signal for the bridge, and Whitby, to split asunder. Scurrying across at the last minute, the bent, urgent figures on the bridge are an image straight from L. S. Lowry.

Having opened, the bridge sometimes obstinately refuses to close. While waiting townsfolk fume, workmen struggle to hand-crank the bridge back into place. If this fails, those wishing to cross must detour a mile or so over the High Level Bridge, where the Esk enters the harbour. Before this opened in 1980 the nearest alternative was at Ruswarp, four miles inland.

Can Whitby's temperamental linchpin be considered beautiful? Fully in view, the bulky girders that carry the swivelling roadway might suggest not. But the bridge's gentle arch and trellised iron parapet give it an unexpected grace. A turreted bridgehouse, with shingle-tiled roof, adds a cosy, homely touch. The centrepiece of many Whitby views, the bridge holds the historic harbourside scene together like the well-worn clasp of an antique necklace. 'Comely' is the word it most brings to mind.

Visitors certainly love it. Cameras in hand they rush to photograph the bridge in motion. This is a rarer spectacle than most realise. For the bridge is Britain's only double-opening swing bridge - i.e.one whose two cantilevered sections, or *leaves*, both open. Unfortunately this distinction doubles the chance of things going wrong - as they not infrequently do.

But inconvenience has been the stock-in-trade of virtually every 'Whitby Bridge', of which the swing bridge is but the latest in a long line.

Exactly when the first bridge was built isn't known. For centuries, the Esk was crossed by a ford, still visible at Bog Hall, between the present swing bridge and the High Level Bridge. Though a footbridge was probably erected soon after the advent of the Norman Abbey in 1075, the earliest record of a bridge comes in a will of 1327, which mentions 'shops at the bridge foot.'

In 1351 Edward III granted the abbey a seven-year right to collect tolls for the bridge's repair. These might have been paid as 'donations', in a bridge chapel where travellers prayed for a safe journey. Demolished early this century the chapel stood on the west side near the present Midland Bank. It appears in some Frank Sutcliffe photographs as a wine store.

The abbey's bridge was probably a drawbridge. That was certainly the form of its first two successors. Built about 1609, the earliest of these figured in a legal dispute heard at the North Riding Quarter Sessions in 1661. Townsfolk complained that the bridge was 'in danger to be pulled down' because ships were being moored to it. The court authorised 'the present bridge master...assisted by the constable' to 'cut the cables wherewith such ships are fastened.' But on another occasion, the court allowed a shipbuilder to saw sections off the bridge so his newly-launched vessel could pass through!

If this bridge was too small, its replacement, whose gap for shipping was a mere 32ft (9.8m), can't have been much better. Built in 1766, this drawbridge appears in many old prints. They reveal that it occupied much the same place as the present bridge. Attached to chains hanging from a huge gallows-like frame, its carriageway was raised in two halves by an elaborate system of weights and pulleys. The clumsy superstructure often fouled the rigging of sailing ships.

So Whitby rejoiced when a modern 'swivel' bridge was constructed in 1835. Designed by Whitby's harbour engineer Francis Pickernell, with well-proportioned stone arches supporting a central span of cast iron, it epitomised Georgian elegance. Its iron railings were a precaution against a repeat of a recent tragedy. In 1830, John Brown, the driver of a hearse crossing the bridge in a gale, was blown into the harbour and carried out to sea. His body was never recovered.

Though thirteen feet (3.9m) wider than its predecessor, the new bridge was soon too narrow for iron steamships. This handicap contributed to the closure of Whitby's last important shipbuilding yard, Turnbull's Whitehall Yard, which shut down in 1902.

More generally, Whitby folk had begun to chafe at the disruption to their ever-busier town caused by the bridge's now frequent opening. In August 1871 a tradesman grumbled: 'We are approaching the herring season, when there will be the usual amount of complaining about the bridge; and no effort has been made to lessen the inconvenience.'

That 'effort' came in 1909 when, with a parade of dignitaries, the present bridge was opened, an event commemorated by a plaque on the parapet. With its 70ft (21.3m) span and weight limit of 15 tons - set to accommodate a traction engine - it served Whitby well for its first half century or so. And its future seemed assured when it was extensively renovated, including the fitting of a new twenty-three horse-power electric motor to each leaf, in 1955.

But when construction of the High Level Bridge, a project first mooted in 1827, was agreed in 1972, the county council announced its intention to replace the swing bridge with a footbridge. With maintenance reduced the bridge became less reliable and began to look shabby and neglected. Highlighting its 'deplorable condition' in a letter to the *Whitby Gazette* in 1978, Church St resident C. R. Dunton noted:

Whitby Bridge - holds the harbourside scene together 'like the well-worn clasp of an antique necklace.'

The bridgeman rings his bell - signal to scurry.

The structure lacks paint and is streaked with rust. There is a total absence of grease on the moving parts, one of the doors of the control box and one of the warning lights appear to be tied on with string. One can only conclude there is a deliberate policy to ensure an early collapse or serious breakdown.

Shortly afterwards, a community campaign persuaded the county council to retain the bridge, which soon benefited by a £400,000 renovation scheme. 'Not an inch has been left untouched,' declared the consulting engineer on completion of the two-year programme in 1986. His team had found that the girders had rusted to half their original thickness of half an inch (12mm). No wonder each opening and closing of the bridge had produced what local councillor Dorothy Clegg, a tireless champion of the bridge, called 'a fearful juddering.'

Due mainly to the creation of a marina in the upper harbour in 1979, the bridge had been working harder than ever. Between 1974 and 1988 the annual number of 'openings' rose from 1,647 to 2,789. To reduce disruption, opening on demand was scrapped. Vessels wishing to pass through must now do so at the designated opening times of on the hour and half hour for two hours either side of high water - plus an extra evening opening on summer Saturdays and Sundays. Of course the bridge doesn't open at those times if if no vessel wishes to go through.

But the bridge, wayward as ever, has shown little gratitude for this easing of its workload. In May 1989 it was out of action for two days. 'It's been like a town of the dead for the East Siders,' complained one trader. Backing him, local MP Sir Michael Shaw referred to a long catalogue of breakdowns: 'Bread and butter are being taken out of the mouths of east side shopkeepers,' he said.

On September 20, 1993, the bridge's east leaf swung beyond its stopping point and crashed through the lounge window of the Dolphin Hotel. Luckily, it was early morning and no-one was injured, though a cleaner had a narrow escape. Could the accident have been caused by the bridge's loss of an old companion? For just weeks earlier, Whitby's veteran dredger, *Esk*, which had been sold to the Port of Lancaster after 57 years faithful service to Whitby, had passed through the bridge for the last of countless thousands of times. As precious an antique as the swing bridge, the dredger, was, and still is, Britain's oldest working seagoing vessel. Whenever she passed through the swing bridge Whitby provided Britain's best display of living industrial archaeology - free.

Today the bridge alone splendidly fulfils that role. Iron gates clang before and after it opens. Great steel cogs turn slowly to move the leaves. And one of the two bridgemen rings that bell.

To top-off its 1980s' renovation, the bridge was fitted with replica Victorian gas lanterns and painted in an attractive livery of red and dark grey offset by gold bands. Its proud rebirth, with a predicted 40 year life from 1989, converted at least one former adversary into a friend. Announcing in 1991 that it no longer believed 'the bridge should have been scrapped,' the *Whitby Gazette* declared: 'Let's make the most of what we have. The bridge is a major tourist attraction, which we should cherish despite its inconvenience.'

Quite right. More should be made of the bridge. A simple measure to enhance its tourist value would be to announce the next opening time, with details of the vessel due to pass through, at the bridgehouse, perhaps on the blackboard already used to state the tides. The bridge would at last be recognised as the fascinating, if also at times infuriating feature of Whitby that it is. How about it, Whitby Harbour Office?

The Piers

Probably no day passes without someone walking along Whitby's broad West Pier. In summer, it usually teems with visitors. Strolling, sitting, angling, taking photographs or being photographed, they turn the West Pier into probably Britain's most popular 'pleasure' pier.

But neither the West Pier not any of Whitby's three other piers was built for pleasure. Though all act as promenades, they never feature in books and articles about Britain's piers, which are perceived exclusively as the cast-iron structures of Victorian England. And most of the millions who enjoy them each year know very little about them.

And yet Whitby's piers give the town much character. Without them Whitby wouldn't even be a town. For while the history of human activity around the mouth of the Esk goes back to the New Stone Age, significant growth of a community here was impossible without major protection from the sea. Even in the heyday of the great Norman abbey, Whitby, at that time with only primitive piers, remained little more than a village. Its emergence as a port, ranked seventh in the United Kingdom in 1828, was the outcome of ambitious pier-building that followed the abbey's suppression.

The exact beginnings of the piers are vague. In 1307 Edward I granted the abbey money to maintain a 'new quay.' The abbot was authorised to collect tolls from vessels using the quay, which was probably just a simple landing place. But in 1534 John Leland, compiler of something like a Domesday book for Henry VIII, described Whitby as 'an haven help with a pier, and a great fischar town.' He reported: 'A new quay and port is in the making, of stone fallen down in the rocks.'

The stone was probably assembled into a pier of boulders, encased in an oak frame. For in 1545, six years after the abbey was dissolved, advisers to Henry VIII urged him to

> reserve all the woods within the parish of Whitby...for the maintenance of the King's tenements and cottages in Whitby and Robin Hood's Bay, and of the pier against the sea at Whitby, where the King's Majesty has already employed great sums of money.

This sixteenth-century pier is believed to have been the earliest predecessor of today's Tate Hill Pier, which thrusts into the harbour near the foot of the 199 steps. Now in the lee of the larger East Pier, it originally bore the full brunt of the

Whitby piers - practical AND pleasure-giving.

Whitby's Tate Hill pier - the town's oldest.

North Sea. Its first name was the Burgess Pier, from the burgesses, or leading citizens, who built it. They continued to manage the harbour until special trustees were appointed in 1702.

By then Whitby had also gained a forerunner of today's West Pier. On a different line, it jutted from Scotch Head, now occupied by the bandstand, towards Tate Hill Pier. Exactly when it was built isn't known, but it must have been before 1632, when both piers were reported to be in serious disrepair.

Their renovation, and with it the future growth and prosperity of Whitby, were due to the Lord of the Manor, Sir Hugh Cholmley. A member of a family whose ancestral home was at Roxby, near Thornton-le-Dale, Sir Hugh (1600-1657) adopted the family's second home, Abbey House, Whitby, as his principal residence in 1626. Often hailed as the Father of Whitby, he built a new drawbridge over the Esk, opened alum works at nearby Saltwick, laid out gardens to produce food, and reclaimed the harbourside land on which Grape Lane, the street with the 'Capt Cook' house, was developed.

In striving to restore and improve Whitby's piers Sir Hugh faced immense public apathy. His memoirs state: 'In Easter term, 1632, I went to London for obtaining something for re-edifying the piers, having, not without difficulty and trouble, persuaded the townsmen to petition the Council Table [the King's Cabinet] for that purpose.'

But though the Council authorised Whitby to raise 'a general contribution throughout England', the townsfolk could not be bothered to organise it. Sir Hugh complained: 'I could not get a townsman to employ themselves [sic] in it, every one so intent on his particular profits as it made them neglect the public.'

But with the help of what he called 'two honest neighbours' Sir Hugh raised £500, which he used to rebuild the West Pier, probably on its present line. He afterwards remarked that this work 'in the judgement of all men hath preserved a great part of the town from being ruined by the sea, and kept the harbour open.' The reduced incursion by the sea also transformed three miles of Esk tidal swamp, up to Sleights, into usable land.

But Whitby remained ungrateful, prompting Sir Hugh to observe: 'Yet will not the townsmen bestow care and pains to lay up one stone, or fill up a breach when the sea has made one.' The cost to the town was indicated in 1763 by visitor Richard Blome, who wrote that the fishing fleet, then comprising 100 vessels, 'would be more considerable were its [the town's] pier finished.'

The growth in coastal shipping, especially the coal trade, eventually shook Whitby out of its lethargy. As the only safe harbour in the 100 miles or so between the Tyne and the Humber, Whitby was often used by ships seeking refuge. In 1772 it obtained a Parliamentary Act which required every passing collier to pay a duty for the upkeep of the piers. Other duties on goods landed at Whitby also went into pier maintenance. Renewed in a series of Acts up to 1812, these powers soon earned Whitby an average of £2,000 a year, which rose to £4,000 in the first half of the nineteenth century. Prudent use of this cash created the piers much as they exist today.

In 1766 the Tate Hill Pier was rebuilt and extended. Now celebrated as the place where Count Dracula, in the form of a large black dog, leaps ashore after being shipwrecked in Whitby harbour, it was the mooring place of Whitby's rowing lifeboats between 1822 and 1863. A tablet recording this is set where the lifeboat was suspended from stone davits. Unforgivably, these were destroyed by Scarborough district council in 1981 as part of a scheme to restore the pier to its eighteenth-century appearance. Since the davits dated from the 19th century, they had to go!

Whitby's present lifeboat is moored at the nearby Fish Pier. The harbour's shortest, this was built sometime before the earliest record of 1790, which notes its reconstruction. Protected by the older Tate Hill, or Burgess, pier, it was almost certainly built as a fish quay, the purpose it served until the fish trade switched to the west side in the nineteenth century.

Meanwhile, the Burgess Pier itself gained protection in the form of the new East Pier. First built in the late 17th century it was widened and extended between 1844-50. The stone deck still shows the bull-nosed head of the original pier.

Visitors wonder why this pier is detached from the cliff. A gap was left as a cartway to Cholmley's Saltwick alum works. But sand washing through caused serious silting. In 1879 harbourmaster Robert Gibson remedied this by building a low ramp, later replaced by a concrete wall. Soaring above was, and still is, a steeply angled footbridge linking the pier to the cliff. Known as the Spa Ladder, from a chalybeate spring that once gushed nearby, the bridge is due to be replaced in 2001 by a more convenient causeway, on top of rock armour dumped around the old wall. Thus made accessible for the first time since 1992, when the Spa Ladder was declared unsafe, the pier itself will improved with rails, seating and lighting - a precious Whitby feature properly available to the public for the first time.

Back in the 18th and 19th centuries, the most ambitious pier works were on the west side. Though few realise it, a West pier walk really begins at the swing bridge, a good quarter of a mile away. For the west side harbour frontage was entirely rebuilt as a result of the 1702 Act.

At that time, much of the present west side was under water at high tide. Near the bridge, houses on stilts projected into the harbour. To reach the pier it was first necessary to climb the short Golden Lion Bank into Flowergate, the street behind today's Woolworth's, and then go along Cliff Street and down Pier Lane, now an attractive flagged footway. The last lap was a raised narrow lane, still there behind the harbourside cafes, shops and amusement arcades. The steps into this at each end were an escape from the high tide.

Between about 1734 and 1750 Cholmley's West Pier was lengthened by 100 yards (91.4m) to the present termination of its stone section. Towards the town it was extended in the form of a new quay - today's Pier Road. Built in the late eighteenth century this eliminated the need to use the harbourside lane. A further extension created the Marine Parade. And the logical final step was the removal of the stilt houses to complete a clear, level way between the bridge and the pier, which opened up the west side for commerce.

The West Pier itself underwent yet more change. Its rebuild of 1734-50 left it on two levels - the inner half lower than the outer. Though the inner half formed a sheltered walkway, it was raised between 1782 and 1814 to strengthen the whole pier. The join is still evident. The pierhead was also widened by the addition of a sixth gun embrasure to the original five. Each housed an 18lb cannon, to defend the port in the Napoleonic wars.

A further eight cannon stood in a new crescent-shaped battery at the pier foot. Now named Battery Parade, this still has its original guardhouse and two turreted powder stores. Though the cannon were removed after the Battle of Waterloo in 1815, the military purpose is symbolised by a First World War naval gun recovered from a local wreck. Preserved on the pier itself are capstans used for winching-in sailing ships.

The massive sandstone blocks of the two main piers came from the quarry at Aislaby, in the Esk Valley, that also supplied the stone for London Bridge and the neighbouring Waterloo bridge. Weighing six tons, the blocks were hauled to Whitby on wagons drawn by oxen - usually four to a wagon, in a procession of four or five. An encounter with them in a narrow local lane could be a fearful affair, as once recounted by a Whitby resident, Robert Holt:

> The big horns and straining eyes of the huge brutes were bad enough, but instead of keeping upright, they sloped their legs outwards, so your only choice was to turn back, find a refuge in some gateway, or scramble into a hedge and hold on till the creatures had lumbered past.

For maximum resistance the great blocks were both mortised and riveted together.

But the piers did not eliminate a tendency by vessels approaching the harbour, whose entrance channel is at an angle of about 45 degrees, to overshoot and end up on Saltwick rocks. In the early nineteenth century so many ships foundered that a rope ladder was kept in St. Mary's church. Chimneysweep William Turner became adept at swarming down the ladder to help stranded seamen to safety.

To ease navigation, lighthouses were erected - the West Pier in 1831, the East in 1854. Previously, the only night-time guidance was a lantern on the West Pier or a bonfire on the east cliff. And they were lit only when it was considered unsafe to enter!

Designed by harbour engineer Francis Pickernell, the 75-ft (22.8m) West lighthouse, with its fluted Doric column, is particularly handsome. But despite the new lights, ships still came to grief.

Between 1909 and 1914 this hazard, together with a troublesome build up of sand at the harbour mouth, was tackled by the addition to the main piers of the distinctive double-deck extensions. With their planked upper decks, and footbridge links to their parent piers, they provide the pier stroller with as potent a nautical experience as any 'pleasure' pier. They were constructed with the aid of a moveable oil-rig-like contraption, locally dubbed 'the world's tallest walking man.' A picture of this marvel keeling over in a storm in 1912 made a popular postcard.

Among the millions who have enjoyed Whitby's piers is William Wordsworth, who confided to a friend:

I have been to Whitby several times. Once, I remember seeing a most extraordinary effect from the pier, produced by the bold and ragged shore on a misty day. The appearance was as of a set of huge faces in profile, with noses of prodigious prominence.

This view - the coastal headlands northwards - is unchanged today.

Writing in 1817 of the West Pier itself, Whitby historian George Young noted: 'It now forms an admirable piece of workmanship, which may vie with any pier in the kingdom for strength or beauty.' He hailed the pier and its associated new quay as 'a most excellent promenade.'

Nearly two centuries later they remain so. And it's a safe bet that all Whitby's piers will still be giving pleasure long after the last 'pleasure' pier has finally rusted away.

The Yards

Whitby's east side has its Arguments Yard. Not to be outdone the west side has a Loggerheads Yard, which sounds equally quarrelsome. Mistakenly regarded as less picturesque than the east, the west once also had an Arguments Yard. Like its east side counterpart, it gained its name not from any notoriety for squabbles but a large Whitby family called Argument.

The west side 'Arguments' was at The Crag. Until swept away by 'slum clearance' in the 1950s, this warren of cottages, tiered into the cliff behind today's harbourside amusement arcades, was a magnet for tourists and artists: 'a rummy spot,' one old book called it. Its loss was matched on the east side by the destruction of a network of yards and lanes on Boulby Bank, between the upper harbour and the abbey. Though the fact is forgotten now, the layout of the flats that replaced them was designed to echo their original character.

But no concession was made to nearby Tin Ghaut. One of Whitby's most charming corners, where pantiled cottages overhung a cobbled cartway running down to the harbour, this old lane, another great favourite of artists, was bulldozed to make way for the Grape Lane car park. Whitby still mourns this loss.

But the town still has 82 named 'Yards'. Together with another 30 or so places of similar character, but perhaps named 'Steps', 'Lane', 'Square' or ''Place', they form a hidden Whitby - secret cameos full of the atmosphere of the old town. Largely ignored and neglected until recently, many have now been sympathetically restored through a partnership between English Heritage and Scarborough district council. With their new sandstone paving, period lighting, attractive ironwork, and often well cared for cottages, they are now a feature of Whitby worth getting to know.

Created largely in the eighteenth and early nineteenth centuries the yards were the haphazard outcome of a rapid rise in population as Whitby's whaling, alum and shipbuilding industries boomed simultaneously. With little level building land available, houses were squeezed into the gardens, or garths, behind the properties on the main streets. A square provided the maximum number.

The problem of the steep harbourside was overcome by erecting the houses in tiers, called stacks. Access to the upper stacks was by steps and wooden galleries, which also brought in precious light and fresh air. As in modern flats, the weekly wash was draped over the galleries. At least one of these survives - in the private Nicholson's Yard, off Sandgate.

An attractive larger yard, with a right of way through it, is Linskill Square. Reached by passages off Station Square and Baxtergate - the main shopping street - this yard still has its original cobbles and central drainage gutter. In most yards this gutter was constantly blocked with residents' rubbish, producing a serious health hazard.

Linskill Square is sometimes said to be named after Mary Linskill, a Whitby-born Victorian novelist (1840-91). Once compared to George Eliot, her work was admired by Prime Minister Ewart Gladstone, who once entertained her at Number 10. But the Linskill of Linskill Square was Reuben, an eighteenth-century ancestor of Mary, who owned alum works at Sandsend.

Mary was born and bred in another Whitby yard - Blackburn's, off Church Street. Her father, a local constable, was in charge of a jail at the foot of the yard. Though their home has been demolished, a plaque once incorporated in it marks the spot. It is by a flight of steps that climbs from the yard to Abbey Terrace East, which in turn joins Church Lane, an ancient cobbled cartway by the 199 Steps. Known to few, this makes an enjoyable alternative to the 199 Steps as a link between the town and St Mary's Church.

Commonly called the Donkey Road, from its long use by beach donkeys quartered in a field at the top, Church Lane is believed to have been the original way from the town to the church. If so, it predates the 199 Steps, first recorded as a wooden stairway in 1370.

Mary Linskill is buried near the south wall of St Mary's church, from where the views, out to sea or across to the moors, illustrate the titles of the books she set in the town: *The Haven Under The Hill*, and *Between The Heather And The Northern Sea*.

Back in Baxtergate - or rather just off it - the sadly-nondescript Angel Yard is where, around 1809, Isaac Greenbury opened Whitby's first jet shop. Further along the street, a weathered ship's figurehead advertises the Old Smuggler tearoom, whose beamed and inglenooked premises are claimed to date from 1401. The entrance is down Loggerheads Yard, a passage between Baxtergate and New Quay Road, facing the upper harbour.

A loggerhead was a piece of timber on a whaling ship over which lines were hauled. How Loggerheads Yard acquired that name isn't clear. But the harbour once covered the area of New Quay Road and extended almost up to Baxtergate. With Whitby's shipyards nearby, the Old Smuggler, originally known as the Old Ship Launch Inn, was a favourite place where shipbuilders celebrated a launch.

It was also a notorious haunt of smugglers, and some historians say the figurehead is from a smuggling vessel captured by the excise men, who put it up as a warning to others.

In 1816, 126 people lived in the since-demolished America Yard, off Baxtergate. Eighty-six were crowded into the smaller Post Office Yard off St Ann's Staith, also now vanished. Concern about public health in the yards led to an annual inspection of all yards by the Whitby's Medical Officer. This was still taking place in 1909, when the MO reported:

> In Bolton's Yard [off Church St, demolished], there is a stack of property that has tenements over a warehouse, and in these the following state of things exists: There is a small bedroom with a bed and a very small bedplace, for a man and his wife and two children. In the second there is a room with a bed in it and a small bedplace for a man, his wife and three children. In the third there is a room with two bedplaces, for a man, his wife and four children. The whole is in bad repair and there is only one privvy for the lot. In addition this privvy is under the pantry of the second house. In the yard the channel is bad.

In Peck's Yard, off Cliff St, the MO found seventeen people sharing one privvy. In Loggerheads Yard the drainage channel was broken and 'the urinal is a nuisance in warm weather.' Matching its name, Paradise Yard, Haggersgate, turned out to be 'one of the clean ones, well kept and containing some nice little houses.' But in the east side Arguments, the MO found 'only one house inhabited, the rest being left to their fate.' The backdrop to many Frank Sutcliffe photographs, the same yard today is spick and span. As in many Whitby yards most of its cottages have become weekend retreats or holiday homes.

Outlining the obstacles to improvement back in 1909 the MO observed:

> The difficulties are very great, partly because much of the worst property belongs to the small capitalist who, perhaps, has nothing to spend on repairs, and who depends on the rents for a living; partly because the tenants are, in many cases, so filthy in their habits that it is impossible to keep the property decent.

Ruling out the employment of street sweepers to clean the yards, he added: 'The rubbish is generally thrown about by the tenants, who ought for their own comfort and health to see that this state of things is not allowed to go on.'

Among the filthiest yards was Black Horse Yard, off Church Street. Rubbish-dumping there had a distinguished pedigree. Excavations for a jet workshop in the 1860s exposed a former midden of St Hilda's abbey. Items unearthed included a bone spoon, a bronze comb and a seventh century lead seal from Rome, which could have been handled by Hilda herself. These are now in Whitby Museum.

Most Whitby yards, including Arguments, are private. The best with public access are Blackburn's, Linskill's, and McLacklins - the latter between Flowergate and Cliff St, with a view of St Mary's church. Footways worth seeking out include Ellerby Lane. Linking Church Street and Sandgate this originally continued to the harbour, which could be crossed at low tide by stepping stones. A blank wall in Sandgate and blocked-up archway in the harbour wall indicate its route.

Off the upper-harbour, Salt Pan Well Steps, lined by pretty cottages, have a Cornish flavour. Their name comes from short-lived salt works established in the nearby harbour in the seventeenth century by the redoubtable Sir Hugh Cholmley.

On the West Side, Bakehouse Yard is in reality another stairway, which climbs from the harbourside at Haggersgate to Cliff Street. Honoured by a recently-installed plaque at the top, Whitby's best-known lifeboatman, Henry Freeman, lived here. The only survivor of Whitby's 1861 lifeboat disaster, he is immortalised in Frank Sutcliffe's picture of him wearing the cork lifejacket to which he owed his life. His decision, on his first day in service, to wear the new-fangled device, scorned by his 12 crewmates, testified to considerable strength of character. This was borne out in 1881 when, as cox, he masterminded the famous 'Pull' - the heroic hauling of the Whitby lifeboat across six snowbound moorland miles, to rescue the crew of a brig floundering off Robin Hood's Bay.

A stepped footway only, Bakehouse Yard is matched further down by a handcart link, Pier Lane, now attractively paved. But better known than both, because it opens off Khyber Pass, where its frames a much-photographed view of the abbey, is a tunnel that leads to steps descending The Crag.

In 1995 Whitby gained an addition to this extensive heritage of yards and lanes. From Green's Yard, near the junction of Bridge St and Church St, a flight of 65 stone steps was installed. Named Caedmon Steps, after Whitby Abbey's cowman poet, the steps will offer a more direct route to the abbey's new visitor centre than the the 199 Steps, which will thus be saved from some visitor-pressure.

Easily mistaken in photographs for the 199 Steps, the new steps are a fresh vantage point from which to appraise Whitby's endlessly fascinating townscape - yards, lanes, steps and all.

Morte D'Arthur

Parent: What did you like best about your day in Whitby? The sands? The abbey? The 199 Steps? The fishing boats...?

Child: Morte D'Arthur.

This imaginary exchange could be real if Whitby made more of one of its minor treasures. Virtually unknown, it is the legacy of tale that will touch young hearts - and those not so young.

The story's setting is Whitby railway station. One day in the 1960s a stray black and white cat, lame in a back leg, hobbled in. Befriended by station workers it adopted the station its home, where it lived for more than 10 years.

The staff christened the newcomer Arthur. Signalman Charles Hart, now retired, remembers his pitiful arrival. 'He was a scruffy old cat, but we all loved him,' he recalls. Regular station users, too, soon became very fond of the limping station cat. 'People were more often heard asking "Where's Arthur?", or "How's Arthur?" than "When is the next train due?" ' says Mr Hart.

Arthur's disability didn't appear to impair his hunting prowess. He repaid the kindness of rail staff and travellers by keeping Whitby station virtually mouse-free. And when he died, in 1975, the staff, who had enjoyed his company as well as valuing his hard work, buried him by his favourite haunt - the buffers at the end of the unused Platform 3.

A rough piece of sandstone was selected to mark Arthur's grave. As the station workers were about to set it up, a passenger arrived. He didn't know about Arthur, and when told his story, he laughingly suggested that the railmen carve on the stone Morte D'Arthur - title of Tennyson's epic poem on the death of the legendary King Arthur.

One of the railmen carved the phrase, in the style of a medieval scroll. Together with the date of Arthur's death, 8.8.75, this was then painstakingly picked out in gold paint, as if for a monarch. 'We spent hours on it,' remembers Mr Hart. In the 1980s Platform 3 was levelled to make way for the new Co-op Supermarket. During the work, Arthur's headstone vanished. Letters inquiring about its whereabouts appeared in the *Whitby Gazette*.

Initial inquiries established that the platform had been dismantled and removed to Grosmont, to be re-erected for the North Yorkshire Moors Railway. But the volunteers who had shifted the stone blocks didn't remember seeing Arthur's gravestone. There were fears it had been destroyed.

But former Whitby porter George Jennison had carefully rescued the stone before the platform was dismantled. He kept it carefully at his home in Robin Hood's Bay until the supermarket was completed in 1990. The Co-op then re-erected it on the railway side of the boundary wall between the store and the station.

A perfect ending? Not quite. For the stone is awkwardly sited a few yards beyond the end of the platform, making it hard to see. Casual visitors can't reach the platform end anyway as it is now part of the Whistle Stop Tearoom. And even to those who see it, the stone's inscription means nothing unless they already know the story.

In 1996 Whitby Civic Society began erecting plaques on places of interest. Moving Arthur's headstone to a public part of the station, and outlining its story, perhaps deserves a place in this admirable project. Arthur's makeshift but lovingly-fashioned headstone is the kind of curiosity on which tourism thrives. And many Whitby visitors, especially children, would be touched by the tale of Arthur, the stray station cat.

CHAPTER 9

PUBS - PRESENT AND PAST

The Lion, Blakey

Walkers on the Rosedale railway between Ingleby Incline and Blakey Ridge tramp a good five miles through the heart of the moors without seeing any dwelling closer than a distant farm in Farndale. Then the long skyline ahead is broken by a pitched roof, with often-smoking chimney. Soon, a thin path leaves the cinder trackbed and winds up through heather towards this seemingly-lonely habitation: the Lion Inn.

But a surprise awaits on the last few yards. Traffic hurtles along a sometimes-busy highway, within a few yards of the Lion's door. Coaches as well as cars often stand in the pub's large and dusty car park. Able to seat 154 in its three restaurants, the inn draws as much business, perhaps more, from wedding receptions, family anniversaries and office parties as walkers slaking their thirsts after a hard trek across the moors.

Yet within living memory the Lion, which at 1,325ft (404.2m) above sea level is the highest inhabited building in the Moors, was a rudimentary wayside alehouse. A. J. Brown, who turned up there in lashing train after walking from Danby, wrote in his 1931 book *Tramping in Yorkshire* : 'The little Lion Inn is not a luxurious house. It is simply a primitive roadside cottage with an ale licence.' A. J.'s hosts fed him with ham and eggs and gave him a change of clothes while his own dried out.

As the Lion lacked accommodation, A. J. pressed on to the Feversham Arms in Farndale. The next morning, walking to Hutton-le-Hole, he met a group of road workers. He recalled:

> To my astonishment, one of them stepped forward to offer me a pair of gloves - my own. I saw that it was the innkeeper of the Lion at Blakey. He had found my gloves on the table after I had gone, and, on the off-chance of meeting me the next day had taken them with him to his work. It seemed odd that we should meet again a good seven miles from Blakey.

At that time the road past the pub, an ancient link between Cleveland (Castelton) and Ryedale (Hutton-le-Hole) was merely a rough track. But it was surfaced just two years later. And though the inn is still sometimes cut off for a day or two in winter, the improved road spelt the end of its 'remoteness' if not its physical isolation. Extensions to the inn in recent years, when it has become a stopping point on Wainwright's Coast to Coast Walk, have increased the number of its letting bedrooms from four to 10. Though still an independent pub run by its owners, the Lion is big business.

Happily its interior retains the snugness visitors expect in a moortop haven. Warmed by two open fires, one with a spit, is an intimate honeycomb of four formerly separate rooms, which now open into each other at different levels. There are massive old beams and an abundance of settles. Somehow, a grand piano does not seem out of place. Tiny windows - the priority up here is to keep the weather out, not provide vistas - give glimpses of the wild moors.

The pub is among the oldest not merely in Yorkshire but Britain. Tradition has it that a wayside refreshment house stood here in Roman times. A Victorian landlord exploited the claim by setting up a stone engraved with the the Latin words for 'Traveller's Rest'.

Whether or not Roman legions ever halted here, the road by the pub almost certainly predated them. A line of prehistoric cairns parallel to the road, on the Lion side, probably indicates a Bronze Age track. A route was certainly established by 1200, when a Gisborough Priory charter mentions a road at *Blakenhow*. This name later became Black Howe, ultimately shortened to Blakey.

In 1348 Edward III granted the bizarrely-named Order of Crouched Friars, a religious sect based on York, a small enclosure, or *toft*, with ten acres (four hectares) of land at Blakeshowe . The grant was described as being 'for the building of an oratory [chapel for private prayer] with other edifices for habitation.' Though some historians believe the oratory was in Farndale, near the present church, the walled enclosures at The Lion amount to exactly ten acres. And traces of a building once existed near a spring by one of the walls.

With beer a staple part of the diet in those days, it's possible that the Friars opened a small public alehouse as a means of raising money from passers-by. At least two such monastic inns existed at Scarborough, and there was a third at Arden, near Hawnby. Blakey House, as The Lion was called until early this century, might have been yet another.

Modestly, the inn claims no earlier date than 1553. About that time, a bunch of leaves was hung outside to advertise each fresh brewing of ale. Historians suggest this might have been a gimmick to drum up custom for a new inn, or gain more business for an established monastic inn, which had changed hands on the recent Dissolution of the Monasteries.

Whichever, the inn doubled for centuries as a smallholding. Its owners still have rights to cut peat and run sheep on the moor. In the eighteenth century corn and bacon from nearby farms, and woollen goods made by Hutton-le-Hole's cottage weavers, were bartered at the Lion. In the 1780s a landlord tried to grow his own corn and potatoes at this bleak spot. His Victorian successors dug coal, from shallow pits near the pub. Together with coal from other small pits in the north of the moors, it was traded in exchange for lime from Ryedale. The packhorse teams that conducted this trade provided much of the Lion's business.

The Lion Inn - a lonely landmark as viewed from the Rosedale Railway at Farndale head.

The Saltersgate legend, vigorously depicted on the inn sign.

Other custom came through cockfights, staged in Cockpit Howe, a scooped out burial mound immediately north of the inn. The last recorded fight was in 1760.

Just over a century later, in 1861, the opening of the Rosedale ironstone railway sparked a boom at the Lion that anticipated the later one brought by the motor car. A short way south of the inn, where the railway passed under the moorland road at the Farndale turn-off, a sizeable community of miners and rail workers sprang up. The site of their demolished homes - a terrace of cottages, four houses and a three-storied lodging house - is a cleared area by the railway overlooking Rosedale. The miners worked in Blakey mine, south of the Farndale road, which operated between 1876-95. The Lion was extended twice to cope with the extra business. This explains the three-foot (0.9m) thickness of some interior walls.

In the rumbustious ironstone era the Lion often witnessed what Joe Ford, Danby historian and staunch Methodist, called 'riots of merriment'. In his 1953 book *Some Reminiscences and Folk Lore of Danby Parish and District*, he observed: 'In those days, when beer was usually served in half gallon jugs, Blakey saw many strange happenings that it is as well should not appear in print.' Accordingly, he didn't mention a brawl involving the vicar of Westerdale, whom some say provoked the fight.

A less troublesome Lion regular was Fish Willy. In the early decades of the twentieth century he carted fish from Staithes to Ryedale, always changing his horse at the Lion.

But from the 1890s the inn declined with the ironstone mines, which finally closed in 1926. A subsequent landlord worked on a farm at Church Houses, Farndale. Another was A. J. Brown's council roadman. After his visit, A. J. declared: 'If I were brewer-in-charge, I would convert the Lion into a real noble tavern, as an inn standing at such a breezy altitude deserves to be.'

But he would doubtless have drawn the line at an extension proposed in 1985, which would have doubled the size of the inn. Turned down by the national park, it also alarmed the Council for the Protection of Rural England, which feared the enlarged building would resemble a prison.

The more modest scheme carried out has preserved the spirit of this fine old moorland pub. Those who enter on a rough day still find that sense of refuge felt by generations of moorland travellers.

Saltersgate Inn

Blazing or smouldering in its burnished cast-iron range, the fire at the Saltersgate Inn has reputedly been burning since 1800. Why must it never be allowed to go out?

The cynical might reply: 'Because the inn would lose its claim to fame.' True. But who would want to invite bad luck to plague the entire neighbourhood? And for the superstitious that is why the fire must be kept alight.

Legend has it that one night at the lonely inn, a landmark on the moors between Whitby and Pickering, a Customs and Excise officer disturbed a band of smugglers who regularly met there. The smugglers are said to have murdered the intruder and buried his body beneath the inn's hearthstone. To make sure the stone was never disturbed they invented a colourful tale.

In this, the Devil bursts into the inn and threatens all present with damnation. To humour him, drinkers offer him the chair closest to the fire, but as he sits down they push him into the flames. They believe that if the fire ever goes out, the Devil will escape and wreak revenge on the district.

This yarn rests on strong local associations with the Devil. The nearby Hole of Horcum, the impressive ampitheatre created by moorland springs, is said to have been scooped out by the Devil to form his punchbowl. The sharp road bend where the inn stands, at the foot of Saltersgate Bank, is known as the Devil's Elbow.

The pub's swinging inn sign imaginatively captures the legend. With one side showing the smugglers handling their contraband, the other has the Devil's face flickering in the flames of the inn's fire as the smugglers slake their thirst after burying the Excise man with a shovel now propped against the wall. What a shame the effect is marred by depicting the all-important fire in a nondescript fireplace rather than the inn's magnificent historic range.

Ten miles - wild moorland miles - from the sea, the inn might seem an unlikely smugglers' den. But a network of smugglers' routes once threaded the North York Moors. A house at Yoadwath, near Hutton-le-Hole, is believed to have been a hiding place for brandy. Westerdale's Gin Garth, a now-ruined enclosure on Hograh Moor, was certainly used to store smuggled liquor, which was also sometimes consumed there by parties from far and wide.

Gin Garth was a link on a route from the coast to York that probably also included Bilsdale's Sun Inn (better known as Spout House), and Wether House, on Bilsdale's west moors. Now a ruin but once a pub called The Sign of the Withered Tree, Wether House was a noted hiding place of Flemish silk and lace. Prized for wedding dresses for daughters of Yorkshire gentry, much of this was sold from a shop in Stonegate, York.

Though Saltersgate Inn handled smuggled gin and brandy, its main illicit trade was in - salt. This vital commodity was very heavily taxed from 1798 to 1825, during which the remote Saltersgate Inn was an ideal clearing house for smuggled supplies. Fishermen from Whitby and Robin Hood's Bay either carried the salt home or salted their fish at the inn. Hung from nails partly banged into slats on the cellar roof, which were removed only a few years ago, fish might even have been smoked at the inn.

But traffic in salt at Saltersgate long predated smuggling days. The trade probably began with the packhorse consignments of salt carried inland from Rievaulx Abbey's extensive saltings at Teesmouth. The records of Pickering's Royal Forest include references to a Saltergate in 1292 and 1305, when a cache of poached game was found there. Salt pans in Whitby in the seventeenth century only partly satisfied local demand, and the salt smuggled in a century or so later probably came from Cheshire.

The salt trade gave its name to the track passing the inn - the Salt Road. Heading for the coast, it went north-east from Saltersgate, crossing the area now occupied by Fylingdales' Early Warning Station. Diverging into two branches - Whitby and Robin Hood's Bay - soon after crossing the 959ft (291.6m) Lilla Howe, with its seventh-century cross, this was one of the most daunting routes in the North York Moors. In 1779, the Whitby historian Lionel Charlton noted:

> Till 1750 all the roads about Whitby lay in a state rough, rugged, uneven. It was dangerous for a man on horseback to come into the town in winter...more so for any laden carriage... A road was made within two miles of Saltersgate in 1760, before which time no stranger should presume to come to Whitby without a guide.

From such difficulties came the traditional saying: 'The only road to and from Whitby is the sea.'

The new road referred to by Charlton was a turnpike between Saltersgate and Sleights. Now the A169, this departed from the original track about a mile north of Saltersgate, avoiding Lilla Howe. But it didn't instantly dispel the fear of travelling over the inhospitable moors. It was another 28 years - 1788 - before a regular coach service began running between Whitby and York. And its passengers routinely made their wills before setting off! But from 1812, a Royal Mail coach, christened Neptune, made the journey three times a week. The horses were changed at the Saltersgate Inn, where the postboys slept. Tolls were collected at a the now-ruined tollbooth, opposite the inn.

Built as a seventeenth century cottage, the inn evolved through the initiative of a Thomas Massenger, an eighteenth century chaise driver. Employed by John Yeoman, of the Black Swan, Pickering, he was often required to drive the Earl of Mulgrave home from Pickering to Mulgrave Castle, near Whitby. When Massenger pointed out that the journey would be quicker if the horses were changed midway, the Earl gave or loaned him £100 to stable horses at Saltersgate.

Initially called The Wagon and Horses, the inn became popular with lime-carrying packhorse teams. Whitby whaling men recruited from the Pickering area roistered at the inn on their way home. Its strong nautical connection continues to this day. Suspended near the imperishable fire is the tiller of the *Helga Maria,* the venerable fishing smack in which Whitby seafarer Jack Lammiman made arguably the most extraordinary voyage ever undertaken from the port, in 1991. Jack's homage to the Whitby whaling skippers William Scoresby Senior and Junior, his 2,600-mile round trip to the Arctic circle and back was achieved in defiance of a nit-picking Department of Transport order confining Jack's 62-year-old vessel to port because of petty infringements, like a too-small bell and insufficient sand in the fire buckets. Much of the planning for the voyage, in which Jack's volunteer crew consisted of a retired welder, a Scotsman he had met at a bus stop, a local vicar and two elderly widows, was carried out in the Saltersgate, to which Jack presented the tiller. His adventure is celebrated in a film, *Capt Jack*, starring Bob Hoskins.

Somewhat stark in appearance, the Saltersgate commands a magnificent panorama west and south, where a broad swathe of moorland, sliced by the great glacial trench of Newton Dale, sweeps up to the headland of Saltersgate Nab. Looking down on the inn from there locals could see a warning of prowling Excisemen in the form of lantern in a small window near the fire, where one is still kept today.

What of the fire itself? Made by F. Dobson, of Pickering, the splendid range in which it burns is believed to date from around 1800 - contemporary with the 'Devil' legend. Some people remember a period before the Second World War when turf cakes, a kind of unsweetened scone, were baked in the side oven and served at the inn.

Still sometimes popped into the oven today is - wait for it - the precious fire! This is its temporary home while the chimney is being swept. More routinely, the fire is damped down each night with its own ashes. Sadly, the peat and turves, the top fibrous layer of heather moor, that were the original fuel have yielded to coal and (whisper it) slow-burning sawdust 'brickettes'. The old peat store is now the landlord's house.

Concerned that too much profit was vanishing up the chimney, the landlord applied in 1994 for a tourist board subsidy to keep the fire burning. Though this was refused, even on the hottest day the fire still burns.

But has it really never gone out? Presumably the Devil would know if it had - and would be fulfilling his vow to torment the district. And since just about the worst recorded event at Saltersgate in the last two centuries was an occasion in 1856 when the vicar of Lythe, near Whitby, dashed into the inn pursued by a swarm of bees, we must assume the fire has always burned.

Of course that's if we believe the legend.

Limekiln House

Limekiln House is now virtually nothing but a memory. But look closely. Just visible among the grass-grown mounds of limestone rubble where the old inn stood is a tiny segment of arched brickwork. This is the cellar's vaulted roof.

From slightly higher ground nearby, the pattern of various rooms can be made out amid a confusion of humps and hollows. They reveal that the inn had a surprisingly long frontage of about twenty yards (18.2m). It was broken by a gap wide enough for carts, some of which doubtless trundled to the inn down a now barely-discernible track crossing the grassy moor behind the inn.

At the front is the better known Drove Road, that broad green highway along the edge of the Hambleton Hills. Renowned as a drovers' inn, Limekiln House is, or rather was, one of its celebrated landmarks. But its history, like that of the Drove Road itself, goes back much further than the drovers who made it famous.

Possibly Yorkshire's oldest highway, the Drove Road was very probably created by the first inhabitants of the North York Moors. Nomadic pastoral and arable farmers of the New Stone Age (3000-1500BC) they settled thinly along the southern and western limestone fringe of the Moors. A rare example of their long burial mounds, or barrows, is by the Drove Road above Kepwick.

The imperishable fire: why must it always burn?

A simple way-side inn. The postman calls at the Lion in the mid 1930's.

Their Bronze Age successors dug a series of defensive ditches near the road - Casten Dyke, Hesketh Dyke and Cleve Dyke. Followed in the Iron Age by a fort at Boltby all these ancient earthworks suggest considerable prehistoric movement along the road.

In Saxon times a Bronze Age burial mound at Sunnybank, between the Drove Road and Hawnby, was reused for the interment of an obviously-important young woman, perhaps an earl's daughter. Around her waist was a garnet-studded leather girdle, with clasp and rivets of gold, and her hair had been secured with gold and silver pins. Her obviously-wealthy family would almost certainly choose to live somewhere with good communications - which points to the Drove Road again.

In pre-droving days the road was called Hambleton Street. In 995, the bones of St Cuthbert, moved from place to place by his followers for more than a century after Holy Island was sacked by the Danes in 875, are believed to have been carried along the Street from Crayke, near Easingwoold, to their final resting place at Durham.

William the Conqueror probably marched his troops along the road during his Harrying of North in 1069. And it was certainly a well-used highway in the fourteenth century when the Scots made frequent raids along it. The so-called Scotch Corner, near Oldstead, is where the Scots in 1322 routed the troops of Edward II, who was lucky to escape.

But as easier routes became available in the Vale of York, the moorland highway fell into disuse. Its revival as a drove road was due to the eighteenth century turnpikes. To avoid the tolls, Scottish drovers, herding cattle, sheep, and sometimes geese to English markets, adopted the old highway.

For their animals and themselves, drovers needed a resting place, or *stance*, about every ten miles. Farmhouses alongside the road became inns - the service stations of the droving era. Three farms along the Hambleton Drove Road - Dialstone Farm, near Sutton Bank, Chequers, near Osmotherley, and Black Lion Farm, Swainby - underwent this change.

It is generally assumed that Limekiln House, a stance between Dialstone and Chequers, was another existing building turned into an inn through droving. But its history as an inn is probably much older. It might even have been built as an inn.

Only a mile or so away, at Arden near Hawnby, where a side valley of the upper Rye penetrates deeply into Black Hambleton, Benedictine nuns founded a priory in 1119. Virtually forgotten today it survived till the end of the monastic era. On its Dissolution in 1536 it housed eight nuns, including two pensioners, and 12 servants. A chimney breast of the priory is within Arden Hall, the core of which was built with the priory's stone in 1574. Recently restored in nearby woods is a 'Nuns' Well', still brimming with crystal-clear water.

The priory's history isn't entirely of Christian piety. In 1306 a nun gave birth to a baby, probably by a servant who was expelled at about the same time. In 1311 another nun confessed to an affair with a bailiff. Meanwhile, an Archbishop ordered the removal of the nuns' pet dogs, which the nuns had been feeding with scraps intended for the poor.

In the fourteenth century the nuns also opened an inn. But this wasn't a further act of decadence. With beer part of the everyday diet, most monasteries had a brewhouse. And small monastic communities like Arden, which lacked land to make themselves self-sufficient, often opened wayside alehouses as a means of earning money.

As already explained, the Lion Inn at Blakey probably originated as a monastic wayside inn, run by friars who had a cell nearby. The Arden nuns, who were so poor that they managed without candles, and used a vestment to sift flour, might have copied this idea. And where better for their wayside inn than the junction of the busy Hambleton Street with a track up to it from their priory? Long abandoned, that track is the one at the back of Limekiln House. It was a predecessor to the present rough road from Arden over to Kepwick.

Limekiln House certainly existed not long after the nuns departed. For it is mentioned by name in a 1577 deed of the Tancred family, who bought the land in 1574. It was they who built the original Arden Hall. Still there in the eighteenth century, they rebuilt it in its present form. A lovely Queen Anne house, built of particularly attractive creamy sandstone, it became the home off the Earls and Countesses of Mexborough in 1900, when the long tenure of the Tancreds finally came to an end.

As Limekiln House was known by that name when the Tancreds took over, it must already have been noted for limeburning. But though several old limestones quarries exist near the house, the site of the limekiln has never been established.

When droving collapsed with the advent of railways, the inn, more remote than others on the Drove Road, fell on very hard times. By mid-Victorian days trade was so slack that the landlord and his wife both worked as stonewallers. That fragment of cellar roof would stir a memory for them. In their absence, the inn was looked after by their two young sons. They were under strict orders that if one had to fetch beer from the cellar, the other must stay with the customers. Yes, those were the days when everyone was honest and trustworthy.

The last occupants of the inn were the Kendall family, who left in 1890. There were five of them - 39-year-old Luke Kendall, his wife Elizabeth, their two young daughters and Luke's 76-year-old mother, Elizabeth, the last licensee. Luke and his wife later had a son, another Luke. In 1960 I met him at Swainby sheep sale - a spare, Viking-like figure with a drooping moustache. He recalled that the last busy night at Limekiln was in 1877, when a bonfire marked the Golden Jubilee of Queen Victoria.

For safety, the inn was demolished in 1953. A clock bought at the sale of its contents still ticks away in a Bilsdale farmhouse. Stone from the ruin has been used to repair field walls - perhaps the very ones originally built by the inn's former stonewalling-tenants. But so little of Limekiln House is now left that few of the thousands of walkers and cyclists who pass by each year notice it.

Perhaps a token section of wall should be rebuilt, and a plaque attached. For it will be a great pity if so much history vanishes completely beneath the Drove Road turf, splendid though it is.

Chequers

A landmark on the lonely moorland road between Osmotherley and Hawnby, Chequers is by far the best known of the four inns that served the ancient Drove Road across the North York Moors. Unlike the others it still aims to attract passers-by. For while Dialstone Farm, near Sutton Bank, and Swainby's Black Horse Farm are now private homes, and Limekiln House is a ruin, Chequers augments its main role of working hill farm with those of a popular tearoom and farm shop, and a small holiday-cottage complex. It thus caters for visitors as busily as in its droving-inn heyday.

And ale - or the devious promise of it - still figures at the former inn. Fixed to its outside wall, the historic inn sign makes its famous sales pitch: Be Not in Haste. Step in and Taste. Ale Tomorrow For Nothing. It is said that last century, this clever version of 'jam tomorrow' persuaded one traveller to stay overnight. Told the next morning that he was expected to pay for his beer, but the promise of free ale tomorrow still held good, he stormed out, swearing never to set foot in any pub again.

In the Yorkshire Dales, the former Crook Seat Inn, now a barn by Swaledale-Kirby Stephen road, also had a sign that promised 'Good Ale Tomorrow for Nothing'. Did one copy the other? And which was first? We'll never know. But the Chequers' sign, which shows a chessboard, went missing after it was taken down in 1960. In 1983 Mary Priest, head teacher of Osmotherley Primary school, and Denis Arnold, a local historian, tracked it to a Northallerton school. A plaque by the sign records its restoration and return to Chequers by the Osmotherley Society in 1984.

Why Chequers - an uncommon pub name? One theory is that it stems from the Wild Service tree. With maple-like leaves, this is sometimes known as the chequer tree because its bark splits into a pattern of small squares. Its tiny fruits, also known as *chequers*, were used to make an anti-colic drink. The late Alan Mitchell, Britain's foremost tree authority, suggested that inns which brewed this drink, with fruit from a tree in their garden, took the name of the tree, but when this reason was forgotten adopted a chessboard for their sign.

But there is no record of a chequer tree ever being at Chequers Inn, where it would probably have struggled anyway. An alternative explanation is that inns called Chequers were much-used by itinerant tradesmen. The commercial taverns of their day, they customarily provided marked boards and metal counters to help the traders to do their sums. Unconvincing? Well, it is certainly easier to imagine the drovers settling down to tot up their profits over a glass of Chequers' ale, even if not free, than sipping a form of gripe water.

The Drove Road Chequers is probably at least 300 years old. When the present owners, John McDonald and his wife Gladys, arrived in 1959, the wall facing the road was leaning out by almost a foot. The limestone mortar was only skin deep, and the main bonding was by a mixture of soil and sand. The sand was probably dug from a deposit up the hillside.

Located where the Drove Road, having climbed steeply to 728ft (252m) from Swainby in the Vale of Cleveland, levels off before making a head-on

Chequers - still thriving as a farm and tearoom.

The fabled tongue-in-the-cheek sign.

ascent of the 1,257ft (399m) Black Hambleton, Chequers was well placed to cater for the Scottish drovers. But even though its stretch of the road doubles as part of the highway between Osmotherley and Hawnby, the demise of droving in the mid nineteenth century still plunged it into decline. Ironically, though the inn survived to witness the Osmotherly-Hawnby road being metalled in 1940, it closed five years later. Had it lasted just another five years or so, the motor car would surely have saved it.

Illuminating its twilight years are three vivid cameos. Describing a visit early this century in his *Rambles in Cleveland* William Heavisides tells how he was met by 'two neat and trim maids, busily engaged preparing a dinner and hot girdle cakes for a small party.' On a later visit, Heavisides found the 'sturdy landlord' stacking turves, the shaved off top layer of heather moor, for the inn's fire. He wrote: 'Re-entering the inn, I find they have a pet lamb, and presently it appears, amusing us with its antics.'

A. J. Brown stopped overnight at Chequers in about 1930. In *Tramping in Yorkshire* he described how he found the little parlour full of hikers, singing sentimental songs and consuming quantities of tea. 'They created such a commotion I could not obtain any lunch with my ale nor get anywhere near the imperishable fire...The main attraction is the antiquity of the place, the shining pewter, the old peat fire with its hanging kettles - and the moors beyond.'

Together with the range in which it was said to have been burning for two centuries, the 'imperishable fire' - a counterpart to the one yet burning at Saltersgate - has long gone. But the scones and cheesecakes served in the tearoom, an extension built with stone from a derelict farm, are baked on the premises by Mrs McDonald. And most of the products in the shop, the former inn's scullery, are from Chequers' too. Besides free range eggs and heather honey is bottled mineral water, drawn from Chequers' own borehole. A century ago, a local farmer named Metcalfe used the very pure water to run an illicit whisky still up at now vanished Moor House. The local place name Jenny Brewster's Gill perhaps indicates the source of his supply.

Now run mainly by the McDonalds' son Andrew, Chequers farm supports 750 breeding ewes and an 80-strong herd of beef catttle on its 1,400 acres of moor and 116 acres of adjoining grassland, plus 60 rented lowland acres. Enough ramblers and motorists turn up to keep the tearoom and shop open daily from about Easter to November, and at weekends and on Fridays in rest of the year. John McDonald observes: 'When we came we saw one or two walkers a week. Now they pass in droves all day long.' Chequers' 'droving' days are far from over.

CHAPTER 10

ISSUES - OLD AND NEW

The Farndale Reservoir

In August 1967 a Yorkshire ghost arose and sent a shiver throughout the county. The Water Resources Board, the body changed with overall responsibility for Britain's water supplies, announced that a reservoir should be developed in Farndale - 'immediately'. The battle this provoked echoed the bitter clash almost a century earlier over Thirlmere in the Lake District. But this time the reservoir builders were routed. Their defeat proved a turning point in the protection of Britain's countryside. For the scale and intensity of opposition to flooding the moorland valley virtually guaranteed that never again would a national park landscape be sacrificed to slake the nation's thirst.

Still generating interest, the reservoir scheme dated back to 1933, when Hull Corporation bought land for it from the Feversham Estate. Still waiting to be carried out before the advent of the Second World War, and virtually forgotten afterwards, this scheme was the ghost that arose, in slightly different guise, in 1967. Intended to serve Sheffield and Leeds as well as Hull, the reservoir would flood 425 acres (172ha) of the upper dale. More than two miles long and over half a mile wide, it would impound 8,000 million gallons of water, providing a daily yield of 88mg.

From a wooded knoll just north of Church Houses, a 151ft (46m) high stone-faced dam would stretch across the valley to near Monket House on the far hillside. Behind it, the reservoir would drown the dale above Church Houses up to the 550ft (177.6m) contour. While water would lap almost at the front door of Long Causeway farm, four other farmhouses - Wake Lady, Minthorpe, Oak House and Hall Farm - would be completely submerged. Altogether, 28 farm holdings would vanish.

The narrow lane that links the east and west side of the valley between Church Houses and Monket House would be obliterated by the dam's one-in-three embankment. Skirting this would be a new road, bulldozed through the meadows near High Mill. And another new road would replace the one serving the east side of the upper dale, parts of which would be submerged.

To accommodate the construction traffic, the twisting Blakey Bank, the steep descent from Blakey Ridge to Church Houses, was to be widened and straightened. Two car parks overlooking the reservoir, with spaces for 650 cars, were suggested, and a clubhouse for a proposed boating and yachting club was pencilled in near Monket House.

The scheme's impact spread far beyond the reservoir. Four miles downstream, south of Lowna Bridge, a pumping house with access road was to be built. From there, water would be pumped back up to the reservoir - an aspect of the scheme rightly dubbed 'Gilbertian'. More water was to be pumped from two points in Bransdale, each requiring a pump house and access road. Before reaching the reservoir, these supplies would be united in a balancing tank on Harland Moor, which required yet another access road. And finally, to boost the water supply in Whitby and Scarborough in times of drought, a tunnel was to be driven through the moors at the head of the valley, to feed water into the Esk.

The promoters, the Yorkshire Ouse and Hull River Authority (later the Yorkshire Water Authority) admitted that their reservoir would have an exposed shoreline of up to to about 100ft (30.4m). But they were proud of their intended handiwork. Mr D. G. Thornley, the authority's landscape architect, declared: 'This is an opportunity too good to miss.' Visiting Farndale, Coun Thornton Lambert, chairman of Sheffield's water committee, announced: 'The reservoir will not detract from the amenities but add to them.' His words recalled those of Manchester's Ald James Harwood who, during the Thirlmere struggle, insisted: 'Thirlmere will not be damaged; the reservoir will improve the district.'

Some of those who might have been expected to challenge Coun Thornton's sanguine view apparently agreed with him. In the July issue of the York and County magazine, Sir Martyn Beckett, of Nawton, near Helmsley, an eminent architect and president of the Ryedale branch of the Council for the Protection of Rural England, wrote: 'There is no reason why the reservoir, if properly handled, should not enhance this beautiful landscape, the only deficiency of which is the absence of any large expanse of water.' Adopting the view that the reservoir was 'in the national interest' his branch decided it could not 'effectively protest.'

Equally defeatist was the North York Moors National Park authority. Its response soon came down to considering ways of reducing the reservoir's impact, the chief of which was to move it to Rosedale! Meanwhile the Countryside Commission, the nation's official guardian of the countryside, endorsed the reservoir as 'an obvious need.' And so Farndale teetered on the brink of disaster.

Its salvation arrived chiefly through the efforts of two local men - farmer Matthew Clark, of Cropton Mill, and retired solicitor John Capron, of Gillamoor. Motivated to defend Farndale by their deep love of the valley, they nevertheless chose to fight less on an appeal to the emotions than solidly practical grounds.

In a tightly-argued thirteen-point rebuttal of the reservoir, which they circulated widely to the media and conservation bodies, Capron and Clark identified a major flaw in the river authority's case. As they stressed, the claim that the reservoir was vital to meet an urgent need for a new supply seemed inconsistent with statements that the reservoir would not reach full output until 1992 - seventeen years after the first water was expected to flow. Capron and

Clark argued that boreholes and river abstraction outside the Moors could provide as much water as the reservoir in its first decade. This would allow time to consider other possible sources. Though initially ridiculed this strategy was eventually adopted. So far no major new source has been needed. Boreholes and river abstraction still provide most of the water that would otherwise have come from flooding Farndale.

The victory inspired by Clark and Capron was the more remarkable because the reservoir faction enjoyed a virtually free run for more than two years before the pair launched their last-ditch struggle in January 1970. Swift support from their local MP Robin Turton - later knighted and made a life peer - lent weight and credibilty to their crusade.

Headlined Who Will Fight For The Lonely Places? an article in the *Yorkshire Post* by Malcolm Barker also struck a chord among Yorkshire folk. Under the banner The Drowners, *The Northern Echo* had already launched an anti-reservoir campaign, to which I contributed an article that was circulated to all MPs and members of the House of Lords.

Belatedly, the CPRE challenged the reservoir. Meanwhile, volunteers from all parts of Yorkshire and the North-East came forward to help Clark and Capron organise a petition. Within three weeks early in 1970 this attracted 10,930 signatures, including those of 98 per cent of the population of Farndale.

But on 19 March 1970, the House of Commons gave a second reading to the reservoir Bill by 167 votes to 61. Stating that he had studied the issue more closely than than any other matter put before him, Local Government Minister Denis Howell declared there was an 'overwhelming' case for the Bill to proceed. But in May, a Commons' select committee rejected it on technical grounds. This followed a hastily-arranged meeting of the national park authority, which agreed unanimously to oppose the reservoir until alternatives had been examined. No explanation of these strange events has ever emerged.

But with the river authority still determined to build the reservoir, Capron and Clark didn't relax. Their campaign blossomed into the Farndale Defence Committee, an alliance of the CPRE, Youth Hostels' Association and Ramblers' Association. At daffodil-time in Farndale volunteers handed out 16,000 Save Farndale stickers. Requested in bulk by groups like Women's Institutes and rambling clubs, the stickers soon appeared all over Yorkshire. A 'Save Farndale' Christmas card was another initiative. Selling these in Helmsley market during a blizzard, my wife and a friend, Hazel Pallan, perhaps narrowly escaped paying the ultimate price to save Farndale. During their brief absence for a cup of tea, their stall collapsed with a mighty crash.

On 29 June 1971, the river authority announced it was postponing the Farndale scheme indefinitely. Though not formally laid to rest until 1988, when the water authority agreed to sell to the sitting tenants the land set aside for the reservoir, the scheme was effectively dead.

As the reservoir's promoters liked to point out, the popular daffodil walk between Low Mill and Church Houses would have been untouched by the reservoir apart from the dam's slight encroachment at High Mill. Nevertheless, a third of Farndale's 2,000-acre (810ha) Nature Reserve would have been

185

inundated. The daffodils in the remainder of the reserve, below the dam, might have been affected by the possibly-raised water table and controlled flow of the river Dove.

But even if not a single daffodil had been threatened, or if none had bloomed in the valley, the key arguments against the reservoir would have held good. The wild dalehead would have been tamed, and the dale would have been permanently overwhelmed by visitors. If boating had been permitted, the pleasure craft, scudding about near the heart of the national park, would have diminished the sense of remoteness. John Capron observed: 'We don't want Farndale to be a pale reflection of the Lake District, nor saddle ourselves with congestion, noise and litter, and the loss of a true recreation atmosphere and quietude.'

John died in 1990, aged 93. Matthew died the previous year, aged 74. A stone bench in John's memory stands in Gillamoor churchyard. But the pair deserve a memorial in Farndale. Ideal would be an engraved stone, amid the daffodils at High Mill in what would have been the shadow of the giant dam.

Cook's Cottage

In February 1934 the SS *Port Dunedin*, a vessel of the Commonwealth Dominion Line, sailed from Hull Docks. Packed in her hold, in 253 cases and 40 barrels, was a rare treasure of North Yorkshire. But it was better appreciated elsewhere. For the *Port Dunedin's* cargo was the dismantled cottage of Capt Cook's parents. Reassembled after its 12,000-mile journey amid the calm lawns and trees of Melbourne's Fitzroy Gardens, it is now Australia's most popular and prized historic attraction.

Great Ayton, where the cottage originally stood, now bitterly regrets its loss. But it did little to prevent the cottage being exported. While the owners of the cottage were shrewd enough to use its its Cook connection to promote its sale, most local opinion, echoing that of Cook scholars, dismissed the cottage as of no significance in the story of the great nagivator.

It is true that Cook never lived at the cottage. The second of eight children of a farm labourer and his wife, he was born at Marton, near Middlesbrough, in 1728. His birthplace was demolished long ago, though the site is now occupied by a modern Capt Cook Museum.

At the age of eight, Cook moved with his family to a cottage at Airyholme Farm, Great Ayton, where his father, also named James, had gained employment as bailiff, or foreman, to the local squire Thomas Skottowe. Enlarged and much-altered since Cook's day, Airyholme Farm, at the foot of Roseberry Topping, is still a working farm.

In 1744 Cook left Ayton for Staithes - the vital move that ultimately took him round the world. It was not until 1755, when Cook joined the Royal Navy, that his parents moved to the cottage that was later exported. Cook Senior built the cottage himself, on a small triangle of land given to him as a retirement gift by his grateful employer. A mixture of mellow brick and sandstone, with pantiled roof and the traditional 'Yorkshire lights' - horizontal sliding sash windows,

Asset stripped. Cook's Cottage comes down.

Despatch - or deportation? The stones of Cook's Cottage are numbered for their journey to Australia.

designed for low rooms - it stood near the river Leven, not far from the parish church on the opposite bank. Above the cottage door Cook, a skilled stonemason, engraved the date and the initials of himself and his wife, Grace.

It used to be said that Capt Cook probably never visited the cottage. But there's no doubt he did.

On 14 December 1771, Cook, not long back from his first great voyage of discovery, in which he charted Australia's east coast and established New Zealand to be two islands, wrote to the Admirality asking for three weeks leave. His letter explains he had 'business to transact in Yorkshire, as well as to see an aged father.'

With his wife, Elizabeth, and their three sons, Cook arrived for this visit in Great Ayton on Boxing Day. Apart from New Year's Day, when he visited old friends in Whitby, Cook spent the next eight days in Ayton. In a letter dated 'Ayton 3rd Jan 1772' Cook wrote to a Capt Hammond, of Hull, saying he would be unable to meet him, 'Mrs Cook being but a bad traveller.'

This cancelled meeting was almost certainly the 'business' Cook referred to in his letter to the Admiralty, for Hammond was a shipowner who had supplied the Royal Navy with two Whitby colliers for Cook's next voyage. Probably wanting to discuss modifications with Hammond, Cook reports in his letter that 'the Admiralty have altered the names of the ships from *Drake* to *Resolution* and *Raleigh* to *Adventure*, which in my opinion are much more proper.' Of course the name of the vessel on his first voyage, also a Whitby collier, had been changed from *Earl of Pembroke* to *Endeavour*.

On his second voyage, started in August 1772, Cook became the first navigator to enter the Antarctic Circle, after which he extensively charted the South Pacific. His Great Ayton visit was therefore in the interlude between two voyages that dramatically changed the map of the world.

A diary kept at that time by Ralph Jackson, brother-in-law of Commodore William Wilson, of Ayton Hall, reveals that Cook and his family stayed with Wilson at Ayton Hall. Perhaps his parents' cottage, where Cook's father had lived alone since the death of his wife in 1765, was too small, or too primitive for Cook's wife, who was pregnant. But there can be no doubt that Cook would visit his widowed father in the cottage, probably daily, since the cottage was just across the river from Ayton Hall.

The 'family' purpose of Cook's 1771-2 visit is believed to have been to persuade his father, then 77, to go and live with a married daughter, Margaret, at Marske, near Redcar. Cook Senior moved to Marske in May, 1772, after which the cottage was sold.

Very little is known of its subsequent history until it was shipped to Australia. But in the 60 years preceding its export it was owned by a prominent Great Ayton family, the Dixons. Running a farm and a hardware shop they gave little attention to Cook's Cottage. Without sanitation and electricity, it had been empty for several years and had become a virtual hovel when Arnold Dixon and his wife, Annie, put it on the market in June, 1933.

The briefest of adverts in the *North Eastern Daily Gazette* - now the Middlesbrough-based *Evening Gazette* - announced:

Great Ayton. For sale or to let, Capt Cook's house, five rooms, large garden, garage added.

Publicity in the national press drew a mini avalanche of inquiries, which persuaded the Dixons to auction the cottage. A poster for the aution described it as the 'renowned home of Capt Cook's early days.'

On 13 June, a short report of the sale appeared in the *Melbourne Herald*. Nine days later, just forty-eight hours before the aution, Russell Grimwade, a Melbourne industrialist, offered to present the cottage to Victoria to mark the state's centenary in 1934. After Victoria's man in London, Sir Richard Linton, made a hasty check on the cottage's authenticity, Victoria, which includes Cook's first Australian landfall, Botany Bay, accepted Grimwade's offer.

Earlier, interest in the cottage from America had prompted the Dixons to stipulate that the cottage would not leave England. But this was now changed to the British Empire.

At the sale, auctioneer Arthur Thompson invited opening bids of £1,000. When a Middlesbrough man offered £300, Thompson commented: 'There are people who appreciate this cottage more than the people of Cleveland.' Grimwade got it for just £800. In a letter to Sir Richard Linton, Annie Dixon described the sale as a 'great transaction', which was 'already linking Australia more closely with this country in a concrete and happy way.'

Great Ayton soon witnessed evidence that it was parting with a tourist jewel. Opened to the public by the Dixons on the day before workmen began dismantling it, the cottage attracted more than 1,000 visitors.

The bricks, beams, tiles and other features were all carefully numbered before being packed. In exchange for the cottage, Great Ayton got a thirteen-foot (3.9m) high granite obelisk to mark the vacant plot. Casual visitors might suppose Capt Cook's reputation as a great nagivator is a trifle inflated. For a plaque reads:

Lieut James Cook RN, of The Endeavour, first sighted Australia near this point, which he named Point Hicks, after Lieut Zachary Hicks, who first saw the land.

A less prominent plaque explains that the obelisk is a replica of the one at Point Hicks, from which its stone was hewn.

Shunned by Great Ayton parish council, the unveiling of the obelisk took place on the same day that the reassembled cottage was opened in Melbourne. Some say the parish council's boycott stemmed less from regret at the loss of the cottage than because its site had been donated to Middlesbrough, which still maintains it - in immaculate, if too-municipal, style. Though the *Melbourne Herald's* original report described the cottage as 'where Capt Cook went in the intervals between his voyages' Australians took it to be Cook's childhood home. Dockers and hauliers gave their services free to unload the packing cases and transport them to Fitzroy Gardens. A building firm re-erected the cottage at cost.

As the true connection with Cook became better known, interest in the cottage waned. Neglected by the authorities, its condition caused the knighted Grimwade to complain: 'The cottage disgusts me every time I see it. Its only purpose now is as a monument to the base ingratitude of Melbourne City Council. Heaven knows why I paid all that money to bring it here.'

But the cottage gradually regained esteem. In 1978 it was painstakingly restored to mark the 250th anniversary of Capt Cook's birth, with structural changes made after Cook's time rectified. The tiny garden, too, was replanted to create a cottage garden of the period. The cottage today is therefore as close as possible to its appearance when Cook knew it. Whether it then had its covering of ivy is unknown. But today's plant was grown from 'slips' shipped out on the SS *Dunedin* .

Despite its limited link with Cook, the cottage is a potent reminder of his humble origins - the more so for having been built by his father. Meeting his father there Cook would speak of his great voyages and of personal and family matters. The author of the first guidebook to the cottage got it right when he wrote: 'We are certain something of Cook lives and lingers in the walls of this cottage today...Its threshold felt Cook's heel as he entered. Its walls heard his voice and the voices of his parents.'

Apart from the obelisk and Airyholme Farm, Great Ayton has further reminders of Cook: his (twice-rebuilt) schoolroom with his reputed desk; the graves of his mother and five of his brothers and sisters, with headstones carved by Cook Senior; a splendid bronze figure of the young Cook facing seawards; and the 51ft (15.5m) tall Capt Cook's Monument up on Easby Hill.

But the cottage would have surpassed all these as a reminder of Great Ayton's finest son and one of Britain's outstanding historical figures. What folly to have let it go.

Forests - Blessing or Blight?

Wandering across what he called 'the windswept watershed solitudes' of Allerston Moor, between Pickering and Scarborough, W. Ridley-Makepeace came across an unfamiliar feature - a conifer plantation. Carefully describing how it was fenced, with a gated roadway, he greeted it in his 1931 book *Walks and Talks on the North York Moors*, in glowing terms:

> This plantation will be a prominent feature of the landscape in future. We are in the midst of a portion of the great work of the Forestry Commission - one of the most far-reaching schemes of His Majesty's Government, in order that we may ultimately grow our own softwood timber instead of importing such large quantitues from Scandinavia...We now see on these Allerston and Dalby Warren Moors the creation of what will be known as the 'Allerston Forest', and the planting which has begun on the Sutherland Lodge and Keldy Castle Estates will be a portion of the 'Rosedale Forest.

Ridley-Makepeace added almost two pages of statistics on the new forests. But whether he would have been as enthusiastic twenty or thirty years later is open to doubt. By then his 'windswept solitudes' would have disappeared. So too would the cotton grass whose 'white silky tufts waving in the wind' he also admired on the same walk. 'Nowhere nearer from Whitby and Goathland can such an abundance of this moorland plant be found,' he observed.

Allerston's 'windswept solitudes' were only a fragment of the much greater loss of moorland. Dozens of small dales along the southern edge of the North York Moors were smothered by dense plantations. The names of these dales - Bee Dale, Rosekirk Dale, Heck Dale, to name but three - still appear on maps, but the dales themselves are submerged in a dark green sea.

Yet they may live again. For Forest Enterprise, as the Forestry Commission is today known, recognises the error of its former ways. And as the plantations of Ridley-Makepeace's time mature, they are being carefully 'restructured', to look better and support more wildlife. If not yet banished, the Gothic-horror forest is in retreat.

Its original unchecked advance was welcomed because the First World War had exposed a serious shortage of home-grown timber. Set up to rectify this worrying deficiency, the Forestry Commission staged special ceremonies to inaugurate its first plantings - in Devon and Morayshire in 1919. The programme reached the North York Moors in 1921, when plantations of Scots Pine, Sitka Spruce and Douglas Fir were established at Dalby. Some of the original trees still stand, retained now for both historic and aesthetic reasons.

But for about half a century the massed ranks of the conifers marched grimly across much of the Moors. Vistas of open moor and chequered dale gave way to the vast, block-like plantations. Absorbed like ink on blotting paper by the uniform deep-green canopy, patterns of light and shade vanished. The interiors of the forests soon became a tangle of dead lower branches - dark, chilling and lifeless.

Covering 46,000 acres (18,650ha) the commercial forests in the Moors today account for 20pc of the national park. The ambitious remodelling now underway therefore amounts to a change in the landscape almost as great as when the forests arrived. A fifth of the national park is slowly undergoing a radical change in character.

The revamping is part of a nationwide programme. But one of its chief architects is a forester with considerable experience of the North York Moors. Now retired and living at Kilburn, Tony Spencer was the Forestry Commission's York-based Conservator of Forests for North England. In 1995 his innovative work on forest design earned him Europe's top forestry award, the Wilhelm-Leopold-Pfeil Prize. On receiving this, he told an audience of fellow foresters his ideas had evolved.

Admitting that 'local people and others concerned with the countryside had always resented the abrupt change of land use from sheep grazing on the open hill to dense evergreen plantations,' he said that while this unpopular transformation had been justified because it created a 'sustainable asset' that supported jobs, physical problems began to develop with the forests themselves.

At 40-50 years of age, the uniform stands of trees became very vulnerable to gale damage. The Forestry Commission's first response - to clear large areas before the trees reached the critical age - produced more problems. Criticised as unsightly, the tree stumps were an obstacle to replanting, which was also made difficult by the compacted earth.

Devised by Mr Spencer, today's alternative strategy centres on replacing large, uniform plantations with a patchwork of smaller blocks of trees, of varying age and species. This is achieved by selectively clearing only parts of plantations before maturity while allowing others to survive beyond their normal economic span.

Defined with respect for contours and natural features, cleared areas in the valleys are limited in size to between two-and-a-half and twelve acres (1ha-5ha). On the moor tops no more than 63 acres (25ha) are usually cleared as a single block. The straight boundaries of old are being abandoned for more flowing, natural lines. Forest roads have wider borders, which allow in more sunlight, helpful to plants and wildlife.

Though it still accounts for less than ten per cent of the total forest area in the North York Moors, the proportion of broadleaved trees has also been increased. No longer deployed merely to provide colour at the edges of the plantations the broadleaved trees are used to define streams as they do in the 'natural' countryside. Sometimes even a forest gutter is given this treatment, to mimic a stream where non exists. The result is what Mr Spencer described to his audience as 'a more visually acceptable mosaic of coupes [blocks of trees] and belts in scale with the landscape.'

In the Moors, the changes are most advanced in Dalby Forest, where they have already brought at least one outstanding wildlife success. The insect-rich new forest glades are a perfect feeding ground for the nightjar, which hunts at dusk. Usually identified by the male's 'churring' call, likened to a two-stroke engine, the bird is an uncommon and elusive summer visitor to Britain. Regarded as indicating the number of breeding pairs, only four males were recorded at Dalby in 1980. But by 1995 the number had risen to 43. Guided walks by forest rangers to the nightjars' Dalby hunting glades are so popular that pre-booking is necessary. And with nightjar numbers also rising in other moorland forests, the national park has become a major UK stronghold of the bird, whose total British population is only 3,000 pairs.

Other uncommon birds that do well in the forests include goshawk, sparrowhawk, crossbill and siskin - a breed of finch. Bird-life is now varied enough to sustain a North Yorkshire Forest Bird Study Group, whose members carry out the nightjar count and do other invaluable monitoring.

The shelter of the forests has also boosted populations of deer, all three British species of which - red, fallow and the more common roe - dwell there. Seven species of bat exist within the forests, which are also home to about 200 pairs of badgers. Increasingly rare throughout Britain, the water the water vole thrives in forest ponds near Sneaton. And numerous meadow flowers that have virtually vanished from farmland enjoy a pesticide-free refuge along the forest rides.

Though Dalby is the showpiece, the new face of the moorland forests is also emerging at Cropton, Wkyeham, Broxa and Harwood Dale. More recently, work has started on the Silton, Boltby, and Guisborough forests. Soon, every forest will have its own plan, to be updated every five years, which will show it is expected to look 20-50 years hence.

Meanwhile, Forest Enterprise and English Nature are carefully protecting the fifteen sites of special scientific interest within the forests - like May Moss, a bog that supports the rare cloudberry. A similar partnership with English Heritage is expected to restore to view archaeological features now covered with trees. Ranging from prehistoric earthworks and medieval deer park boundaries to jet and ironstone workings and the remains of commercial rabbit warrens, the best of these might be linked in a forest archaeological trail.

But with about twelve million trees harvested so far, the primary purpose remains timber production. Now yielding about about 110,000 tons a year, worth about £2.2m, this is set to level off at a sustainable 160,000 tons a year by about 2015. This means the number of mature trees felled will rise from the present 87,500 to 210,000. In addition, about 340,000 immature trees, or 'thinnings', will be removed each year.

About a million tourists visit the forests each year, a quarter to Dalby. A network of drives and trails draws motorists, walkers, mountain bikers, wildlife enthusiasts and horse-riders. Some stay overnight, or longer, in camp sites, caravan parks or the Keldy Castle holiday village near Cropton. As tourist pressure on the entire national park mounts, the capacity of the forests to absorb large numbers of people is an increasing asset. At last shedding their alien and sinister image, they can perhaps now be regarded as adding welcome diversity to the national park.

Thankfully, plenty of heather moor still remains.

Maintaining the Moors

Infra-red photographs from space show the heather moorland of the North York Moors as a broad splash of bottle green amid the orange-red of cultivated land. In reality a carpet of subtle browns and greys for most of the year, the moors are transformed in late summer into a cloak of imperial purple, which billows across the 40 upland miles from the Vale of York to the North Sea.

The most extensive unbroken tract of heather moor in England and Wales, this is what gives the national park its special character. Though the heather moor occupies only a third of the park's 553-square miles, it is the single most dominant feature. Creating a glorious feeling of space and freedom, it is the great vistas of heather that earned the Moors their national park status. And it is those vistas that visitors especially expect to see.

But in the 25 years after the national park was designated in 1952, the heather moor shrank by 65 square miles - a quarter of the original total. Most - 50 square miles - was lost to forestry, with agricultural reclamation claiming the rest. The loss was particularly acute in the triangle formed by Whitby, Pickering and Scarborough, in which half the open moor vanished. In a single reclamation scheme in Harwood Dale, 1,280 acres (505ha) of open moor was converted to grassland, divided by ten miles of fences. Fifty acres of moor in Troutsdale also vanished under the plough. And it was only by buying moorland adjoining the Hole of Horcum that the national park authority prevented this highly-scenic and popular feature of the Moors being set amid potato fields.

National park authorities still lack adequate power to stop forestry or reclamation. But though heather moor is still very occasionally ploughed up - 30 acres (12.14ha) were reclaimed on Allerston High Moor in 1996 - this threat has diminished through the need to reduce the over-production that created the notorious grain mountains, milk lakes etc. And foresters, too, with more lowland available, no longer covet the uplands as much as previously.

Yet the moors remain surprisingly vulnerable. Not quite the robust wilderness they seem, they are a delicate, even fragile ecosystem. And their beauty depends almost as much on human skill as any well-packed field of wheat or productive dairy herd.

As explained in my *Inside the North York Moors*, the once tree-clad heather moors emerged through misuse by man - burning, felling and over-grazing - over many centuries. But maintaining them today demands a fine balance between two linked yet sometimes conflicting commercial activities: grouse shooting and sheep farming.

The only bird unique to Britain, the red grouse, the chief denizen of the moors, requires heather of different ages within its territory. Controlled burning creates the necessary mosaic. It provides seedling heather as food, young heather in which birds can bask, more mature heather for shelter and nesting, and overgrown heather, an emergency larder in winter, when some of its leggy stems, containing precious seed, will protrude above snow.

But since 1948, the number of moorland gamekeepers who carry out the controlled burning, between December and early April, has dwindled from 54 to a mere dozen. The burning programme has fallen behind, allowing too much moor to be covered by old leggy heather. When this dies bracken tends to take over.

Some heather, usually on level moorland close to a road, is now cut by a tractor pulling a strengthened grass mower. In the form of bales, most of this is exported to Europe, especially Holland, where it is used to neutralise odours in sewage works and food processing plants. The smells vanish when filtered through layers of the heather. If British food manufacturers and water companies are aware of this, they make very little use of it.

But despite the rotational cutting and burning, too much heather is still in poor condition. And though sheep-grazing can also assist regeneration there are problems here too. The economic as well as physical struggle of hill-farming has led to the withdrawal of about 30 flocks from the North York Moors in the last 40 years. In 1996 it was noted at Danby parish council that so few sheep were now grazing in the village that householders were having to mow verges. The following year, fears that the same thing would happen in Hutton-le-Hole following the sale of a 300-strong local flock prompted an urgent bid to the EC

Heather and forestry confront each other near Hawnby lake. Is there a rightful place for both in the national park?

Heather-baling at Fylingdales. Harvesting heather - for factories not farms - makes a little-known contribution to the moorland economy.

for help towards installing a cattle grid. In fact, a village 'grid appeal', coupled with cash from the local Spaunton estate and national park's Moorland Management Scheme raised enough for three grids, installed in 2000 to prevent Hutton's reduced flock of about 50 sheep from wandering out of the village.

Ten years before these local crises, the national park authority calculated that 60 per cent of the park's heather was over aged. Advancing by 300 acres (121.4ha) a year, bracken covered 28 per cent of the open moorland.

Though not entirely unwelcome - in spring its unfurling fronds spread a welcome flush of bright green across the dark moor, and its autumn tints bring richness and warmth - bracken harbours a blood-sucking tick that is a serious source of disease in sheep. Also poisonous, it can cause cancer and blindness. Eating bracken is the commonest cause of premature death among mature ewes on the moors.

Hard pressed on all these fronts, the heather suffered a further setback in the long hot summer of 1976 when fires destroyed eight square miles - four per cent of the national park's total. The example of a major pre-war fire on Urra Moor, where the burned area still resembles a lunar landscape, seemed to indicate that the scarred moorland, mostly between Glaisdale and Wheeldale, would never recover.

But an iniative by the national park authority promises an impressive comeback. In partnership with six universities it launched 30 research projects on the fire-ravaged moors. A key discovery is that in eroded areas, a light scattering of gravel checks further slippage. In stable parts, some fertility returns if the baked surface is slightly loosened. Cotton grass moves in, albeit thinly. But sown oats will also sometimes grow, and provide primary cover for traditional moorland vegetation. The heather will often seed itself if sprigs of the plant, cut at maximum fertility in early autumn, are laid on the moor surface. Germinating from their fallen seeds, the young plants are protected as they grow by the layer of sprigs.

By these measures the damaged moors, though still a long way from their former majestic selves, are slowly but steadily recovering. The programme has won international recognition for its major contribution to knowledge on restoring blighted moorland.

At Lockton, near Pickering, the park authority is also carrying out the world's first experiments in converting reclaimed moorland back to heather moor. Using sulphur, to neutralise the heavy dosages of lime applied when the moor was turned into farmland, this work is slow and labour intensive. Heather seeds are sown by hand, and clumps of bilberry, which is less easy to establish from seed, are transplanted from the open moorland. Though the results so far suggest that this heather-and-bilberry cover will be more broken and interspersed with grasses and mosses than on 'classic' heather moorland, the national park nevertheless hopes to demonstrate that restoring former moorland is not only practical but could be a sound economic proposition - perhaps to attract a grouse shoot.

In 1990 the park also launched an offensive on that bracken. Grants are offered for aerial spraying, the only effective treatment. By 1995 the bracken-infested area had been almost halved to fifteen per cent of the park's moorland, and the aim is to reduce this to ten per cent by 2000. In several places - the head of Westerdale for instance - bilberry, the first plant to replace the zapped bracken, has already returned vigorously, and heather is beginning to follow. The benefits are enjoyed not only by sheep farmers and grouse shooters but walkers, who are no longer hampered by the plant.

In 1995 all this endeavour received a boost from the European Community. A grant of £1.9m was given to support bracken control, heather burning and cutting, sheep-tick treatment, renewal of sheep dips and the installation of cattle grids. Backed by nineteen estates and 101 farmers, who between them control about 90 per cent of the moorland, the five-year scheme was expected to restore 1,550 acres (626ha) of heather, improve a further 23,000 acres (9,289ha), raise the stocking rate of sheep, and reduce the death rate of sheep and grouse.

Figures submitted with the bid for this grant revealed that about 20,000 grouse are shot on the moors each year. The 170 or so shooting days are estimated to provide work for around 3,800 people - beaters, 'pickers-up' and other helpers. Jobs in hotels and shops are also created or sustained by the 2,000 'bed nights' spent by the grouse-shooters in the region each year. These numbers are expected to rise once the death toll of grouse by the disease strongylosis, which currently claims about 13,500 birds a year, has been reduced. Contracted from a worm that breeds in the heather, the disease attacks the central nervous system. The EC package funds antidotes like the dosing of young birds, done by scattering medicated grit, which aids the birds' digestion.

The final piece of this jig-saw is in the valleys. Spectacular sweeps of heather moor would mean little if the intervening dales looked run-down. And that was the picture that began to emerge in the 1980s. As hill-farming incomes declined, 50 miles of stone walls collapsed, about 123 miles of hedges became badly overgrown, and many farm buildings fell into decay.

To reverse this neglect, the park authority launched its Farm Scheme in 1990. Pioneered in Upper Farndale, where it was supported by eight of the nine resident farmers, this provides grants for restoring buildings and walls, planting trees and hedges, and retaining wildlife habitats. Regarded by the national park as its 'flagship' scheme, the project now involves more than 120 farmers, in Rosedale, Danby Dale, Bilsdale and Westerdale. If extended throughout the national park as intended, the visual improvement will be enormous.

But though all these strands were pulled together in 1998 as the North York Moors Farm and Rural Community Scheme, grandly relaunched by Prince Charles, the cash underpinning the various initiatives is not secure forever. Announced a year later, the designation of the entire 170 square miles of heather moorland as a Site of Special Scientific Interest provides only token protection, since SSSI law is notoriously weak. The moors remain a prey to old threats, which could return, and new ones, currently typified by off-road driving, whose physical damage and intrusive noise go against the spirit of national parks.

In 2000 the heather moorland became a Special Protection Area, a European designation based on birdlife, here particularly the important populations of merlin and golden plover. Potentially of greater benefit - as well as more imaginative - is a concept of the Moorland Association, a nationwide alliance of moor owners. It suggests that all existing heather moor, and any bracken-infested moor capable of being restored, should be declared a Purple Belt, enjoying the same near-inviolate protection as the urban Green Belt. Though the urgency behind this has slackened since the idea was conceived in 1987, that very fact might be the strongest reason for creating Purple Belts now. For it is when our wild places become a target of commercial greed that defending them is most difficult.

Symbolised by this Bransdale grouse butt, grouse shooting is the *raison d'etre* of the heather moors.

CHAPTER 11

A MOORS MISCELLANY

Rabbits - The Forgotten Industry

Concealed in the extensive forests between Pickering and Scarborough are the remnants of a once-considerable industry. Though now completely forgotten it was active until the 1950s.

The myxomatosis epidemic ushered in with that decade drove the final nail into the coffin of 'warrening', the commercial farming of rabbits. Most warrens had already long been abandoned, as a passage in W. Ridley-Makepeace's book *Walks and Talks in the North York Moors*, published in 1931, reveals.

Intrigued by the frequent occurrence of the phrase 'old rabbit tipes' on the six-inch Ordnance Survey map of the Pickering moors, he observes:

> The spelling confused me, and referring to Murray's Dictionary, the word 'tipe' is given as a kind of trap or device for catching rabbits. It is a 'pit covered with a wooden floor, having a nicely balanced trap door near the centre, into which the rabbits fall.' I have to confess that in all my walks over these moors I never came across a rabbit 'tipe.'

But the pits of more than 100 'tipes', now usually spelt 'types', still exist in the Pickering-district forests. Together with associated boundary walls and warreners' tracks they form easily the best surviving complex of rabbit warrens in the North of England and probably in Britain. Though many of the types have been filled with stone as a safety measure, at least one will probably be restored and displayed to the public.

Introduced to commercial rabbit warrens in the eighteenth century, the types pushed an industry started by the Normans to its technological peak. Credited with introducing the rabbit to Britain, the Normans reared the animals in enclosures, and sent in ferrets to drive them into nets. The rabbits were an important source of skin, fur and meat.

Warrening became more sophisticated with the creation of artificial mounds. Easier for the rabbits to burrow into than the harder level ground of the former enclosures, they encouraged breeding. Once regarded as prehistoric earthworks, these artificial burrows are now officially called pillow mounds from their elongated shape. At least two groups exist in the North York Moors - on Hutton Nab at Hutton-le-Hole, and Levisham Moor. In medieval days, snaring and shooting joined netting as a means of catching the rabbits.

Whether the type, or trap, was a sudden, brilliant invention or evolved gradually isn't known. But it revolutionised warrening. The idea was to catch the rabbits in a pit immediately inside a small walled enclosure, which the rabbits entered by a small wooden tunnel at the foot of the wall. The tunnel's floor extended over the pit, where it took the form of a tilting trapdoor, which could be pegged level.

To catch the rabbits, food was placed in the enclosure. After a day or two, when the rabbits were accustomed to coming and going, the trap-door peg was removed. Incoming rabbits dropped into the stone-lined pit, which was corbelled at the top to prevent them leaping out when the warrener arrived to collect them. Poachers were deterred by a padlocked board over the pit, which was about one yard (0.9m) in diameter and depth.

As a profitable way of using the poorest land on a farm, warrening was once widespread throughout Britain. As agriculture improved, however, most lowland warrens gave way to arable fields or pasture. But the moors around Pickering, with their thin sandy soil, remained a rare warrening stronghold.

Between 1987 and 1989 the late Don Spratt, a leading amateur archaeologist from York, and Alan Harris, a retired geographer from Hull University, identified the remains of seventeen warrens in the Pickering forests. The largest, at High Dalby, covered 1,800 acres (730ha). Its numerous enclosures and types had probably yielded 16,000 rabbits a year.

Other major warrens were at Allerston (1,200 acres, 486ha), Low Dalby (1,100 acres, 445ha), Scamridge (700 acres, 283ha), Troutsdale (400 acres, 162ha), and Cockmoor Hall (300 acres, 121ha). Added to the 500 acres (202ha) of three smaller warrens at Langdale End, this amounts to 6,000 acres (2,430ha) formerly devoted to the humble rabbit. No wonder a warrener ranked higher in the rural pecking order in this corner of the North York Moors than a shepherd or gamekeeper.

Not all the captured rabbits were killed. A few does were released for breeding. Sometimes, so many rabbits were caught that they suffocated in the pit, which spoilt their meat. But the meat was always less valuable than the skins and fur, prized for making hats, gloves and capes. The moorland warrens supported a mini industry of hatters and furriers in Malton, Scarborough, Whitby, Pickering and York. Skins also went to Lancashire, and some were shipped from Scarborough to London.

Before the advent of the turnip in the eighteenth century, the main food used to lure the rabbits was the stripped bark of hazel and ash. These were often planted and coppiced specially for the warrening trade, and right up to the 1920s, when the Forestry Commission arrived, the tenanacy agreements of farms at High and Low Dalby included the right to cut hazel as winter rabbit feed. In return, the tenants were required to leave a breeding stock of rabbits for their successors.

Still surrounded by a few open fields within the forest, Dalby's High Rigg Farm is thought to have been the last to operate a warren, probably until

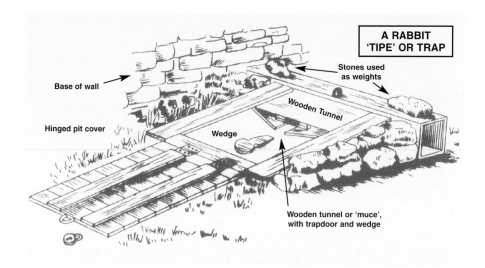

A RABBIT 'TIPE' OR TRAP

Base of wall

Hinged pit cover

Stones used as weights

Wooden Tunnel

Wedge

Wooden tunnel or 'muce', with trapdoor and wedge

Rabbits beware! Thousands were caught in warreners' 'tipes', or traps, like the one illustrated here.

Kildale's Warren Moor mine - an ill-fated enterprise.

myxomatosis gripped North Yorkshire in 1954. A decayed type on the farm still has its wooden tunnel, known as a *muce* .

In partnership with English Heritage and the national park, Forest Enterprise hopes to fully restore one of the types. If a suggested archaeological trail in the forests is also developed, the restored type, unique in Britain, would be its highlight.

Warren Moor - The Mine That Failed

Descending Sleddale Bank, between Commondale and Kildale, a sharp-eyed motorist might glimpse a tall chimney tucked into a fold of hills. Walkers can obtain a much better view. For the footpath between Little Kildale and Baysdale passes the square chimney, a nicely-proportioned structure which tapers gently to an elegantly-flared top.

Built chiefly of brick, but with plinth, crown, and banding of sandstone, the chimney stands on a grass hillside among a few scanty, fenced-off ruins. Overlooking the infant river Leven these are the remains of the Warren Moor Ironstone Mine. Conceived with high hopes by a London speculator named John Watson, it had a short but eventful history. Over a period of eight years, two attempts to work the mine profitably ended in dismal failure. A deep pit that the chimney was intended to ventilate was never even fully sunk. The local estate manager, George Pierson, assessed the venture accurately at the outset when he said: 'I cannot but think that Watson's plan savours a good deal of the visionary.'

But Watson wasn't the only person excited by the prospect of mining at Warren Moor, where a seam of ironstone outcrops on the north bank of the Leven. The first enthusiast was Pierson's employer, Mrs Edmund Turton, of Kildale Hall. As ironstone fever swept the Cleveland district of the North York Moors in 1850s she spent £1,000 promoting a Parliamentary Bill to nullify covenants against mining in the will of a previous owner.

Approval of the Bill in 1855 brought the Middlesbrough ironmaking firm of Bell Brothers, later the mighty Dorman Long, on to the scene. Their withdrawal after sinking trial boreholes on Warren Moor should have been a warning. But in 1864 Watson turned up. Though he lived in London and his main business interest was in coal mining in the Forest of Dean, he had already pioneered trade in Cleveland iron ore, collected from beaches. He might have hailed from Cleveland originally, and perhaps was related to Thomas Watson, a prominent ironstone manager and engineer, chiefly in the Esk Valley.

In his diary for 1865, when he was directing shaft-sinking operations at a mine in Commondale, Thomas Watson records several visits to nearby Warren Moor. The diary reveals that a trial bore in May struck the main bed of Cleveland ore at a depth of about 230ft (94.2m).

This was the signal for John Watson to seek partners in developing a mine, and in September he wrote to George Peirson: 'Mr Murray, of the firm of Branson and Murray, Contractors, Birmingham, and Government Contractors for the Plymouth fortifications, and others of his friends, have joined me in taking the lease of the Warren Moor Royalty.'

Thomas Watson had already pegged out sites for workmen's timber cottages, about 20 of which were built. The positions of shafts, kilns and a reservoir were also fixed. So confident was Watson that he pressed for a lease of 99 years rather than the 60 offered at first. Strangely, the agreed period was 42 years. The rent for Watson's 1,500 acres (607ha) was set at £500 in the first year, 1866, rising in stages to a ceiling of £1,500 from the fourth year onwards. The company also agreed to pay a royalty of fivepence (2p) on each ton of extracted ore.

While the shafts were being sunk, ore was extracted from drift mines in the hillside. To minimise the royalties, the ore was roasted, or *calcined*, on fires in the open air. A kiln planned for this process, which reduces the moisture content and hence weight of the ore, was never built, and a pile of the crudely-baked ore from the open fires still lies at the mine.

The overall picture didn't impress the already-sceptical George Peirson. When no rent had been paid by February, 1867, he wrote to Watson demanding payment. To guard against the possible removal of the mine's assets, including its three horses, Peirson set up a spying operation. The estate foreman, a man named West, was ordered to visit the mine at least twice day - 'or leave a man working in sight.'

Pierson's suspicions seemed well-founded when West reported: 'I have been to the Warren Moor Works tonight. The portable engine is all taken to pieces...The men are stoped [sic] ...There is nothing as yet taken from the place.'

Though the company soon paid off the rent arrears, Peirson urged the estate to seek settlement of other debts, such as for the fencing supplied by the estate. Writing to the estate solicitor, he declared: 'I consider they deserve no forbearance...These parties keep no plans of their mines, and have never completed their fencing or paid the tenants for damage to their crops.'

In July, 1867, West noticed equipment being moved from the mine. Watson's vehement denial of knowledge of this carries the ring of truth. Perhaps the mine manager, realising that the end was in sight, was selling the equipment off his own bat, possibly in lieu of unpaid wages.

The mine entrance was on the Kildale-Westerdale road, at the sharp bend between the railway bridge and West House farm. Buildings there included the mine's 'Tommy Shop,' where the miners were required to buy candles and other materials for their work at prices set by the company. Nearby was a cottage occupied by John Brooks, a mine employee who collected or received the rents for the mine cottages, which stood a little further up the valley.

On 13 February 1868, Thomas Sowerby, the estate's solicitor, turned up at Brook's cottage to serve a demand for payment of debts totalling £427 10s (50p). The intention was to repossess the mine if the debt was unpaid. Brooks refused to accept the demand, on the back of which Sowerby wrote down what happened:

> Brooks said he was not authorised to pay, so I demanded possession, which he said he was not prepared to give. I then demanded payment

at the door of the office of the company and at the mouth of the shaft. Not receiving any answer, after an interval I demanded possession of the premises at both places...John Brooks being present the whole time...

Watson later told the estate that the venture had cost him £3,000 more than he and his partners had invested. Unmoved, the estate decided to sue the company for £2,000. But a hearing fixed for July at York Assizes in 1868 was withdrawn when Watson's solicitor wrote: 'I believe Watson to be hopelessly ruined. I cannot get myself a single farthing from him.' Probably deciding to cut its losses, the estate allowed 17 months to elapse and then sold the equipment as its own property, fetching £1,381.

The mine's failure was due mainly to the poor quality of the ironstone. With Kildale known to be on the edge of the main ironstone field, the low grade ore from the drift-mined top seam made the operators realise that the expense of opening-up the much deeper main seam was very unlikely to be justified.

But the high prices for iron in 1872 persuaded three more London speculators to re-open the Warren Moor mine. Renamed Leven Vale, it initially did so well that in December, 1873, the directors contemplated adding to a row of stone cottages they had already built for their miners. But in 1874 the price of iron collapsed and the company went bankrupt. Although two further London hopefuls, described as 'merchants', took out a prospecting licence in 1875, the Warren Moor mine was finished.

In the valley between the mine and the road, traces of the enterprise include not only the pile of calcined ore, but fragments of brick fireplaces from the timber cottages, and foundations of the stone cottages and workshops, whose stone was used in 1929 to build Kildale's village hall. Though all the remains are on private land, where permission is needed to explore, a right of way between the former mine entrance and Kildale's East Green Beck farm crosses the low embankment of a tramway that linked the mine to the Esk Valley railway.

Consolidated a few years ago by the national park in partnership with the Kildale estate, the buildings clustered round the 65ft (19.8m) high chimney include the vaulted head of a ventilation shaft, beds for pumps and a winding engine, and part of the boiler house. Bricked up oval openings at the base of the chimney are its former flues. Of the four only that from the boiler house is thought to have been used. A second was probably intended to ventilate a long drift, and a third would have served the main mine if it had been developed. Sunk to an estimated depth of 150ft (45.7m) before being abandoned, its shaft was still about 70ft (21.3m) short of the main seam.

Warren Moor wasn't the only mining failure in Kildale. Other unsuccessful mines were at Lonsdale (1866-68) and Coate Moor (1872-74). But neither has the colourful history of Warren Moor, or such a prominent landmark as the chimney to remind us of it. At the lonely, silent ruins today, it is easy to picture West posting his hillside spy, and solicitor Sowerby, probably cloaked against the February weather, bawling his demand for possession down the mine shaft.

Sandsend Cement

Once, workmen repairing the sea wall at Sandsend didn't need to go far for cement. Just a minute's walk from the shore, a mill produced cement that would set in water. Applied to the wall between tides, it was also prized for patching up wooden ships holed at sea. Had it been available to Capt Cook, many of whose Whitby successors routinely carried it in the 19th century, he would have had much less trouble when *Endeavour* struck the Great Barrier Reef.

Tucked into the hillside at Sandsend's Eastrow, where it is unnoticed even by most users of the nearby car park serving the beach and Mulgrave Woods, the cement kiln still survives. The more prominent building alongside, originally a corn mill, housed the remainder of the works.

Their surprising location, a pretty seaside village, isn't the only unusual feature of this virtually-unknown industrial venture. Quick-setting as well as water-repellant when still wet, the cement was manufactured to a 'Roman' formula. Much sought after largely for its pleasing creamy colour, production began at Sandsend in about 1820 as a spin off from the massive clifftop alum works. Reshaping the headland through the extraction of the alum shale and dumping of the sterile waste, these operated for 252 years - easily the longest-enduring industrial enterprise in the Moors.

The cement bonus was the brainchild of William Atkinson, a London architect who remodelled Mulgrave Castle for the Marquis of Normanby in the late 18th century. Like many in the building world he had been excited in 1791 by the success of a long series of experiments by Isle of Sheppey man James Parker to discover the composition of Roman cement. The basic material proved to be dogger stone, a Jurassic mudstone often found as nodules on beaches. Sandsend had more than most, as dogger often turned up in the alum shale.

Lord Normanby took up Atkinson's suggestion to exploit the hitherto-discarded dogger. It was now turned to cement powder by being burned in the specially-built conical kiln. So plentiful was the supply that, in return for an annual rent of £40 and royalty of 8s (40p) per ton, the Marquis allowed a Hull cement manufacturer to take an unlimited amount from his shore, from Staithes to Sandsend. But the local works were also fed with dogger collected south of Whitby, mainly Saltwick Nab, by local fishermen, for whom it was a new 'catch.' Even children gathered 'small dogger', exchanged for pocket money. What a pity if their stone turned out to be 'Cheese Dogger', a worthless low-grade type, which smelt of cheese when split.

The prized character and quality of Sandsend's 'Roman' cement is mirrored in a clause in a contract to supply a Wandsworth builders' merchant with 12,000 bushells a year, stipulating that the works would not supply 'any other house in London or within 30 miles thereof.' The restriction didn't impede a trade that was so brisk that a cooper's shop was erected at the works to make the barrels in which the cement was sold. Powered by the old mill wheel, a sawmill was also opened.

When the alum works closed in 1871 it was considered worthwhile opening drift mines in the back of the old alum quarries to maintain a supply of

Sandsend cement works. Kiln on right.

Sandsend cement kiln, with loading steps on the right.

dogger. In an early example of flexible working, the half dozen or cement workers acted as miners from Tuesday to Thursday. On the other days they broke up the dogger at the works and stacked it in the sandstone kiln. Lit on Friday, this smouldered away over the weekend. Mothers sometimes took children up the stone steps at the side, provided for stacking, to inhale the fumes, which were believed to cure whooping cough.

Competition from major companies led to the mill's 1933 closure. In 1998 the Rural Buildings Preservation Trust applied to restore the mill and re-introduce 'traditional cement production', presumably as a tourist attraction. Though fears about noise, dust and smell stifled this idea, the Trust was given permission to adapt the building for small-scale crafts or industry. Whether its obscure yet fascinating history as a cement works comes to the fore remains to be seen.

Moor Sheep

In his 1848 *The History and Antiquities of Cleveland* John Walker Ord observes: 'A hardy breed of sheep possesses the heaths and moorlands, which they seem to enjoy as their peculiar right and domain.' True long before Ord's time, that remains true today. Whether foraging in deep heather, grazing by a moorland stream or sheltering by a dry stone wall, the moor sheep are as much part of the moors as the heather itself.

Indeed, without the sheep, the moors wouldn't exist. It is their extensive grazing, especially since the monasteries established their great sheep runs in medieval times, that has prevented the invasion of scrub on to the moors. Helping to keep the heather in good heart, their nibbling also maintains the moorland turf and checks the spread of bracken. The late Dick Bell, a forester and gamekeeper who became the first full-time warden of the Moors national park, aptly dubbed the sheep the 'park keepers.'

Introduced by the New Stone Age nomads who were the region's first settlers in about 3000BC, sheep have played a part in creating the landscape for as long as man. But their crucial contribution came with that monastic age in the twelfth century. With the double aim of taming the wildernesses that made up their estates, and developing a sustainable economy, the monks turned to sheep. Grazing cleared land, these fed and clothed the monks, and earned income through the sale of their wool. The sheepskin was used as parchment.

The largest monastic flock was Rievaulx's, whose 14,000 sheep were of two breeds. The larger, which supplied milk as well as meat and wool, is believed to have been an ancestor of today's Wensleydale, a breed not now kept in the Moors. The smaller, a blackfaced sheep, was almost certainly a forerunner of both the Scottish Blackface, the 'traditional' sheep of the Moors, and its now-more-numerous companion, the Swaledale.

The latter has been recognised as a separate breed only since 1920. The next year, Jack Calvert, of Keld, Swaledale, moved to Langdale End, Hackness, bringing some Swaledales with him. In 1922 Estill Peacock, of New Gill Farm,

'Hardy denizens of the moors.' Swaledales wintering near Commondale.

Going to the sale. Sid Garbutt, of Huthwaite Green, Scugdale, driving his lambs in 1960 to the since-defunct Swainby sheep sale.

Farndale, bought a Swaledale ram and two lambs from Jack Hodgson of Askrigg, Wensleydale, to form the nucleus of the first indigenous Swaledale flock in the North York Moors.

To the layman, the only difference between a Swaledale and a Blackface is the white patch, or 'badge', across the Swaledale's snout and mouth. But the Blackface is stockier and heavier than the Swaledale. Its fleece is also thicker, and it provides more meat, on a carcass that is better suited for butchering. Today accounting for about a quarter of the moor sheep in the North York Moors, the Blackface is found chiefly in Eskdale, especially Commondale, and at Hutton-le-Hole.

The greater popularity of the Swaledale rests on key practical and economic advantages. Willing to range further for natural food the Swaledale is therefore less dependent on costly supplementary feed, like hay and vitamin blocks. This in turn means less labour. Retired Eskdale farmer Jim Muir, former long-serving secretary and chairman of the Blackfaced Sheepbreeders' Association of North East Yorkshire, says: 'To get the best out of Blackface you need to shepherd them more.'

The less demanding Swaledale has also proved ideal for the complex crossbreeding at the heart of sheep farming. When its days on the moor are over a Swaledale ewe is crossed with a Bluefaced Leicester. Termed a Mule, the offspring of this union is crossed with a Suffolk or Texel to create top quality fat lambs.

Dating back to 1820, when it was founded by farmers around Goathland, Saltersgate and Levisham to prosecute sheep stealers, the Blackfaced Breeders' Association now represents moor sheep farmers generally. Alas, they are a diminishing band. Between 1976 and 1996 membership of the BSA declined from 130 to 97. Over a longer period, the reduction in moorland flocks has been more dramatic - from 406 in 1954 to about 140 today. Though the average flock size has increased from about 100 breeding ewes in the 1950s to about 300 today, the overall number of sheep, now estimated at between 50,000 and 60,000, is thought to have declined by half in the same period.

Partly due to diminishing returns of hill farming everywhere, the withdrawal of moorland flocks has been hastened by road deaths. These reached crisis level in 1979 when about 600 sheep in flocks alongside the Whitby-Guisborough and Whitby-Pickering roads - about ten per cent of the total - were killed. Thirty years of wrangling about fencing these highways, which was resisted by the national park through fear the fences would impair the moorland vistas, ended with the fencing of the Whitby-Guisborough road in 1982-3, followed by Whitby-Pickering five years later. The completion of the second scheme merited a visit by the Minister of Agriculture, who unveiled a plaque at Sleights.

But the fences came too late for many farmers. Along the Whitby-Guisborough road, where 3,256 sheep grazed in 1977, it is now quite an event to spot a sheep. The scenic loss is considerable, with thistles and rough grass replacing the cropped roadside turf, and a kind of heathland - at best a mixture of birch, pine and leggy old heather, at worst a wilderness of gorse and coarse grass - ousting the broader panorama of heather.

The carnage on several secondary roads is now reaching the scale that compelled action on the main roads. Two hundred and sixty two sheep died on the Lockwood Beck to Hutton-le-Hole road in 1994. Among ideas seriously considered by the national park authority as alternatives to fences has been clothing lambs in luminous jackets!

All that is needed, however, is greater care by drivers. Despite their ignorance of kerb drill, sheep very rarely walk suddenly into the road. Their 'attitude' at the roadside generally hints at their intentions. A ewe gazing over the road to its lamb, for example, might well be about to cross. Anticipation by drivers would cut out most sheep deaths. And to any motorist who complains that sheep shouldn't be allowed to wander on the road, the answer is that the sheep were there long before the cars or the roads.

But more pressure on the sheep farmer is imposed by rustling. In 1995, 2,535 sheep, worth £117,650, were rustled from moor flocks. To stem such losses, farmers now run Operation Sheepwatch, with night-time vehicle patrols, two-way radios, and a phone-and-fax information network. In 1996 losses dropped to just 250.

The rustling itself isn't always as sophisticated as the Operation Sheepwatch counter-measures suggest. A spate of thefts in the Stokesley area turned out to be the work not of a well-organised gang but a moorland farmer. Aided by his dog and sometimes a couple of accomplices, he simply walked the stolen sheep back to his farm, often over a distance of five or six miles, and once an astonishing twelve miles. In nineteen night-time raids he rustled 884 sheep. Jailed in 1988 for three years he was detected when Osmotherley's local 'bobby', PC Norman Barningham, tracked a rustled flock across six miles of farmland and moorland to the farmer's barn.

Whatever causes the withdrawal of a moorland flock, its removal threatens others. For moor flocks are 'heeafed' - meaning they remain instinctively on their own stretch of moor. But without a neighbouring flock that is similarly 'heeafed' they lose this territorial sense. As Jim Muir neatly puts it: 'The best boundary for one flock is another.' Remove the middle one of three flocks, and those on either side stray in, creating much extra work for their shepherds. Following the retirement of a Hutton-le-Hole shepherd in 1996, and the sale of his 300-strong flock, it has required three new cattle grids, installed on adjoining roads in 2000, to prevent the sheep that graze the village greens wandering far away. A similar problem at Danby has not been resolved.

Shepherding involves much more movement of flocks than many people suppose. At the start of the shepherding cycle, in October-November, the ewes are fetched down from the moor to join the tups (rams) in enclosed fields. After three weeks, the now pregnant ewes are returned to the open moor, where they spend the winter. The shepherd regularly checks them and puts out feed.

In April he brings the sheep down again for lambing. Until fairly recently this took place on the open moor. Farmers believed that the sooner a lamb got accustomed to its hard environment the better sheep it would make. But since a shortage of labour forced the shepherds to carry out lambing in the fields, this traditional wisdom has been turned on its head. 'Inby' lambing, as it is called, has raised the survival rate of lambs from about 85 per cent to 95 per cent.

After lambing, at the end of April, the flock is driven back to the moor. But it is brought down yet again for the ewes to be clipped in late June or July. And a further round-up takes place in August when the 'draught ewes', adults too old to face another moorland winter, are brought off to be sold for the breeding programme. This usuallly occurs when the ewe is six years old and has lambed four times, generally producing a single lamb each time. She will spend a further two years on a lowland farm.

Together with the draught ewes, 'wether lambs', castrated males, are also sold in late summer. Still great moorland occasions, sheep sales take place at Goathland, Glaisdale, Castleton, and the Lion, Blakey. Four more - at Kildale, Swainby, and two at Ingleby Greenhow - have disappeared with the contraction of sheep farming.

The bulk of the farmer's income comes from the sale of the draught ewes and wether lambs. The fleeces rarely bring more than enough to cover the cost of clipping - and sometimes not even that. Tough and wiry, the wool of both Blackface and Swaledale is used chiefly in carpets. Some Blackface wool goes to Italy as stuffing for mattresses. Though greatly reduced in recent years this trade is a direct link with Rievaulx Abbey's sheep days, for much Rievaulx wool was bought by Italian merchants. They stayed in guest accommodation at the abbey's great woolhouse at Laskill.

The many sheep-inspired farm names in Bilsdale - Ewe Cote, Woolhouse Cote, Wether Cote, High Ewe Cote and more - testifies to the former dominance of Rievaulx's sheep farming. Other names mirroring the strong link between sheep and the moors are Sheepwash, near Osmotherley, now a popular picnic place, the Sheep's Pool, another former dipping place, in Harwood Dale, and the Rudstone, identifying a bed of iron-rich clay on Urra Moor, which shepherds used to make reddle for marking their sheep.

Best of all is the continuing presence of the sheep themselves. They give life and character to any moorland scene, none of which is complete without them. Long may the upland of the North York Moors be their 'peculiar domain.'

The Bridestones

To mark the centenary of the National Trust in 1995, its Yorkshire region buried a time capsule. Candidates for the burial site included the York Minister's Treasurer's House, at the very heart of the county, and Fountains Abbey, the most popular National Trust property nationwide. But the capsule rests at the Bridestones, on the moors north of Pickering.

Among the capsule's contents is an oak plaque fashioned from a fallen tree near the Bridestones. Engraved on it is a list of events that occurred during the Trust's first century, such as the first powered flight, the two world wars, the 1963 assassination of President Kennedy, and England's 1966 World Cup soccer victory.

It is because the Bridestones go back much further than any of these that they were regarded as the most appropriate place to leave a message for posterity.

Bilsdale Foxhunt Inscription - commemorating a notable chase?

The 'Planning Row' Stone, Saltersgate.

212

For these strange sandstone outcrops, weathered into fantastic shapes, stretch back into the mists of time. Solitary amid 400 or so acres of heather, they have the same potent affinity with the moors that made the Flyingdales 'Golf Balls' such celebrated landmarks before they were swept away in 1994. But the strange harmony here is nature's not man's.

It was in the Jurassic period, between about 135 million and 200 million years ago, that the rocks of which the Bridestones are composed were laid down. A vast sea advanced and retreated several times across what is now the North York Moors. Sometimes a silty, shallow delta, and at others a clear blue coral sea. Material washed into the former by rivers, and deposited in the latter in the form of dead sea creatures, was compressed into a series of rocks, chiefly sandstones.

In the next geological period - the Cretaceous, which ended about 65 million years ago - these deposits were topped by a layer of chalk, estimated to have been 1,800ft (548m) thick.

About 26 million years ago the entire mass began to rise from the sea, gradually forming the dome of the Moors. The chalk and other soft deposits were subsequently washed away by rain. At the Bridestones, the particular tilt of the land also encouraged the relatively rapid wearing away of the underlying softer sandstones. But harder parts resisted this erosion. They formed caps which, as the erosion continued all round, protected the various bands of rock directly beneath.

The Bridestones thus emerged. The variable erosion rate of the layers of rock that make up each stone has aided wind, rain and frost to sculpt them into their present fantastic, often top-heavy shapes. Like Brimham Rocks in the Dales they are a Yorkshire version of the granite tors of Cornwall.

Divided by the steep narrow valley of Bridestone Griff, the stones, about fourteen in all, stand in two groups - Low Bridestones and High Bridestones. Of uncertain origin, the name has inevitably inspired legends about brides. One tells of a couple who, after their wedding at nearby Lockton, set off across the moor to walk to their new home. Caught in a storm they spent the night huddled under one of the mushroom-shaped stones - henceforth a 'bridestone.' It is also said that Lockton lads used to race the four miles to and from the Bridestones during a wedding for the prize of the bride's garter. But no-one today remembers the race taking place.

Some authorities suggest the name comes from the ancient British goddess Brigantia, who was also known as Brigid or Bridget. But most believe it stems from a Norse word meaning 'brink', or 'edge'. For the stones are poised above not only Bridestone Griff but Dovedale Griff a little further west. The location of a different set of 'Bridestones' in the Moors - a much-ruined circle of small standing stones on Bilsdale's narrow Nab Ridge, supports the 'brink' theory. But as two similar circles of 'Bridestones' stand on the more rolling Sleights Moor, doubt still exists.

The natural Bridestones vary considerably in size. The largest four or five are about 25ft (7.6m) high and about 80ft (24m) wide. They belong to the 'Low' group, so called because it is lower down on the moor than the 'High' group. Nicknamed Saltpot and Pepperpot - though which is which, and whether either resembles the objects in question, are matters for debate - are also part of the Low group. The Ryedale writer Dorothy Cowlin sees in one stone a resemblance to Samuel Johnson's biographer James Boswell - 'a suggestion of a pert little nose and jaunty lawyer's wig.'

A National Trust property since 1944, Bridestones Moor is also a nature reserve, cared for by the NT and Yorkshire Wildlife Trust. With Dalby Forest close by, the setting of the stones is not quite as impressive as when the entire area was open moor. But from a car park off the Dalby Forest Drive, which is the only road access to the stones, an attractive one-and-a-half mile trail leads visitors around the stones and also through old woodland alongside Staindale Beck, where the kingfisher is sometimes seen.

The site of the time capsule is marked by five oak saplings. But worth watching for is a much greater rarity - a plant called chickweed wintergreen. A bit like wood sorrell, with tiny white flowers from mid-June to early July, this plant originally colonised glades in the forests which spread across the moors after the Ice Age 10,000 years ago. As the trees were gradually cleared, the wintergreen cleverly adapted to open moor. But in the last century or so most of it has been killed off by the controlled heather-burning on grouse moors. The unburned Bridestones Moor is a precious refuge, and one clump blossoms almost at the base of one of the largest stones.

Stories in Stone - 2

[Of the 55 pieces in my Inside the North York Moors, the one that stirred the biggest response was Stories in Stone. More than 20 years later, I still receive inquiries prompted by this account of moorland stones with a tale to tell.

I introduced the topic by relating how I stumbled upon a seat hewn from a large boulder on a hillside near Ingleby Greenhow. After explaining its probable origin I drew attention to a little-known carving on the nearby Ingleby Incline _ a man wearing a stovepipe hat, perhaps the work of a railway navvy.

A year or two ago my son Stephen came across yet another virtually unknown engraved stone in the same area. Where better, then, to start this second selection of Stories in Stone?]

Just below the crest of the hillside between the rough moorland road of Rudland Rigg and the Ingleby Incline on the Rosedale Railway runs a line of crags. Rarely visited, they contain a small natural cave. Crudely carved inside is the word: FOXHUNTERS.

The first six letters are on one face of a jutting rock, the remaining four on the other. Also engraved is the date 1775 and seven sets of initials. Ending in either W, C, or G, these are probably of members of the Wood, Cook and Garbutt families, long-established in nearby Bilsdale.

Founded in 1688 by Helmsley's Duke of Buckingham the Bilsdale Hunt is among the two or three that claim to be the oldest hunt in England. Perhaps the inscription in the cave marks the conclusion of a particularly long hunt back in

1775. The initials could be those of the huntsmen present, perhaps witnessing a kill in the cave. The inscription is certainly too long to have been carved during a hunt, whose followers were unlikely to be equipped with hammer and chisel anyway. So whoever carved it must have gone there specially. And what other reason could there be than to commemorate an outstanding run?

A desire to address posterity on stone seems to run deep in the North York Moors. Exactly two centuries after those Bilsdale huntsmen left their mark, a farmer at Saltersgate did much the same thing for a very different reason. Angry at the national park's refusal to allow him to erect a large barn, he planted a conifer wood, which didn't require permission. And at the brow of Saltersgate bank he erected an engraved slab which reads: 'W. Lorne Wilkinson planted this viewpoint in protest against planning official intrigue. 1975.' Less contentiously, he marked the entrance to his farm road with a fine stone carving of ram's head, set into the turf and engraved: LORNE'S LOT. At the opposite side a small standing stone bears the words: MARYLAND 1965. WLW.

Likely to be among the most enduring Millennium monuments are two new markers in the Moors. Moved from Spaunton Moor, where it had lain for 10,000 years after the Ice Age, a natural A-shaped moorland boulder now stands 8ft (2.5m) tall on Danby High Moor. Resembling the most ancient moorland monoliths, but engraved with a cross, in whose angles appear the letters A D M M, the stone crowns the highest point (about 1,000ft -304m) in the central moors, close to the Lyke Wake Walk and Coast to Coast Walk. Discreetly chiselled near its base are the initials of the North Yorkshire Moors Association, which conceived and carried out the project through public subscription. Meanwhile, just a few miles to the south, Lastingham gave a similar idea its own appropriate twist. Set up on the edge of the moor overlooking the village, a large boulder bears a most beautiful carving of a Saxon crosshead, with the dates AD 654, when a monastery was founded at Lastingham, and 2000. The work of sculptor Jennifer Tetlow, who lives in the village, this recognises Lastingham's role as a cradle of Christianity - origin of the Millennia concept.

More obscure but equally long-lasting should be an unusual reminder of the Queen's Silver Jubilee at Appleton-le-Moors - an old gatepost on the common, neatly carved with the letters and figures EIIR/1952/1977. Close by, among larches, a stone chiselled with the logo of the Council for the Protection of Rural England salutes Catherine McDougall (1890-1950), first secretary of the Ryedale branch of CPRE.

Separated by 40 miles, a pair of standing stones now identifies the start and finish of the Lyke Wake Walk, whose name they display. The walk's founder is honoured by a simple inscription on a small but shapely boulder by the path in Clain Wood, Scugdale: 'Bill Cowley 1915-1994.'

Another recent memorial is a tablet in a stone wall at Rosedale Intake, Danby. Inscribed 'In Memory of Danny Bowes, Dry Stone Waller' it commemorates a popular Danby man - cricketer as well as waller - who died, aged 25, when his car was swept into the swollen Esk off a flooded concrete causeway alongside Danby's Duck Bridge on the night of May 23, 1994. The tragedy led to a barrier being installed downstream from the causeway, which

The Bridestones - most freakish landmarks of the moors. (The figure is unknown.)

had been built only a short time before the accident to protect the picturesque hump-backed bridge from vehicle damage.

A tragedy of almost a century earlier is poignantly recalled by a small stone at Water Ark waterfall, Goathland, engraved: 'In memory of Sydney Porritt, who was accidentally drowned June 24th 1908, aged 16.' A Whitby lad on a Sunday school outing he is thought to have died either jumping the beck or falling in when unable to stop himself as he ran down the steep hillside. Since the eight-year-old son of a Beckhole farmer was drowned at the same spot in 1829 when returning home from Goathland school, local children had been forbidden from using the Water Ark path as a short cut.

The Goathland district is particularly rich in memorial stones. A metal plate on a substantial pillar a few yards up the track to Birchwood Farm, is inscribed: 'On this spot John Calvert of Goathland fell asleep 18 June, 1907, aged 77 years.' A roadman who, on that perhaps-hot day, had been breaking and spreading whinstone on the Whitby-Pickering road, Calvert collapsed and died on his way home, probably while sitting down to rest. His body wasn't found until next morning, and his memorial stone was erected by friends at Goathland Golf Club, where he had lovingly tended the greens. A popular Goathland 'character', he once considered taking on the tenancy of the Cross Pipes Inn - the former inn near the church, whose licence was eventually transferred to the Mallyan Hotel. Advised that trade was slack and he could be left with unsold ale he replied cheerily: 'Whya, what ah can't sell ah can sup.'

Twenty-nine years before his own sad death Calvert no doubt shared Goathland's grief at the fate of another popular village figure - George Baker. Sexton and gravedigger, Baker was also a tailor, who tramped round outlying farms repairing clothes.

While on his round on 5 December 1878, he was needed to a dig a grave. Francis Calvert, a villager who knew his route, went to fetch him. He found him at a cottage on the Scarborough road, about twelve miles from Goathland, and the pair set off back at about 5pm.

About halfway home, they rested at an inn at Littlebeck, since closed. As they resumed, snow began to fall. According to one version of events Baker, 68, soon decided to turn back, while his younger companion pressed on. Another version claims the men disagreed on the route and parted, Baker forking left.

The younger man reached home safely that evening. There was consternation next morning when Baker was missing. Intensive searches over the next few days failed to find him. To prolong the search a £3 reward was offered for finding the body, but seven weeks of searching still drew a blank.

The discovery of his body on 26 January caused what the *Whitby Gazette* called a 'sensation'. For Baker had died high on Fylingdales Moor, far Littlebeck or Goathland. Having lost his bearings in the blizzard, the elderly tailor had battled for almost five miles across the wildest part of the district before collapsing with cold and exhaustion. As with Calvert, his snow-covered corpse lay close to a track - here the old road from Saltersgate to the coast over Lilla Howe. Many people had passed within 100 yards (91.4m) of the body.

With the snow still too deep and soft for a horse, villagers carried the tailor's body home on a bier - a melancholy sight graphically reported in the *Whitby Gazette*:

> A company of about fifty collected together for the purpose. The ling (heather) was set on fire to give light and furnish signals along the route. The gloomy errand, the red glare of which lit up all the hills, and the slow silent torch-lit procession carrying the bier, will not soon be forgotten by those who saw it. The body was in a remarkably good state of preservation considering the length of time it had been under the snow.

A fund was set up for Baker's widow, and a rough stone was erected where his body had been found. Deep in long heather within the Fylingdales Early Warning Station, it is engraved on one side: G. BAKER AGED 68 YEARS. The inscription on two other sides, also in capitals, summarises the story thus: 'In Mem of GB who was lost on the 5 of Decem 1878 and was found hear [sic] on the 26 Janua 1879.' (The final digit, 9, has been accidentally chipped off.)

Another winter death on the moors is recorded on a stone on the little-visited moor north of Danby Beacon, which states: 'H. Coling perished here January 27 1848.' Some say Coling was an estate worker who died when controlled heather-burning got out of hand. Others claim the 'H' stands for Hannah, a local woman who got lost in a snowstorm while walking from Ugthorpe to Lealholm.

No speculation is needed at a well-dressed stone on Wheeldale Moor. Its plaque records: 'In memory of John Booth who died on this spot September 5, 1853, aged 84. He was gamekeeper to Richard Hill Esq, of Thornton, for 56 years.' Miraculously, the plaque survived bullets that scarred the stone when the moor was used for military training during the Second World War.

Dated 1835, a large square stone which overlooks Westerdale from just outside Castleton is reputedly the site of a gibbet. Another was once thought to have stood near the top of Bilsdale's Newgate Bank, where a large flat stone with a post hole still survives. But the stone's name, Beacon Stone, supports a theory that the stone was a link in a beacon chain. A farm halfway up the valley is called Beacon Guest, and the first Ordnance Survey 6-inch map, 1857, gives the name Beacon Stoop to a since-vanished stone on Cringle Moor, one of the hills that divides Bilsdale from Cleveland. Receiving its signal from Roseberry Topping the Cringle beacon would pass it into Bilsdale, through which it would reach Ryedale.

Among other stones with a practical role is a grooved slab under an oak tree at Mountain Ash Farm, Glaisdale. A rare 'verjuice' stone, this was used for crushing elderberries and sloes, the fruit of blackthorn.

Known as the 'Rokan Ston' a tilted boulder by the Lealholm-Rosedale road, near Fryup Head, was a rendezvous point for local women who gathered loose wool. Also linked to a vanished moorland activity are ten standing stones on Bilsdale West Side. Spaced out over about a mile of moor, they mark the

A tragic tailor - the George Baker Stone on Fylingdales Moor.

The bullet-scarred John Booth Stone, Wheeldale Moor.

boundary of an area within neighbouring Snilesworth parish where the nearby Bilsdale farmers were allowed to cut turves, the top layer of twiggy heather, used as fuel. This concession made up for lack of sufficient open moor available to the farmers within Bilsdale parish itself. The stones are engraved with a T, and the former cart road that linked them can still be traced.

South of these Turf Stones is an anvil-shaped boulder engraved 'WT 1761'. The carver was almost certainly William Tyreman, shown in parish registers as occupying nearby Birk Wood Farm in 1765. The registers also record the death of Tyreman's wife, Ann, aged 77, in 1780. Hers is very probably the initial 'A' engraved in a corner of the stone, with a weathered mark, possibly a + sign, that could symbolise their marriage. And is it unreasonable to suppose that a 'JT' on another corner was their child? Of course we will never know. But it is nice to think of Tyreman chiselling away at his stone in the heather, perhaps choosing the spot for its sweeping view.

More sombrely, two moorland stones mark suicides. Dated 1835 and engraved with a cross, a stone by the Lockwood Beck road about a mile north of Castleton, is said to commemorate a servant girl. Less easy to find, a boulder in Ravengill beck, Commondale, identifies the pool where George Watson, an employee at the village's former brickworks, drowned himself in 1876. Sometimes washed over by the stream, the boulder is inscribed with Watson's now faint name and the Latin phrases 'Felo de Se' and 'Hominis Est Errare.' Translated as 'a felon (i.e. criminal) to himself,' the first phrase reflects the then legal view of suicide as a crime - which it remained until 1961. But that harsh view is softened by the stone's second phrase - 'It is man's nature to err'. The carver evidently possessed some humanity.

A better known Commondale memorial is the handsomely-tooled stone beside the moorland path to Guisborough. Carved with the exploding-hand-grenade emblem of the Grenadier Guards, which symbolises a French grenade collected by the Grenadiers' at the Battle of Waterloo, it is inscribed: 'For Remembrance. Guardsmen. Bobbie Leggott, killed in action 1916, Alf Cockerill, died of wounds 1920. Duty 1914.'

Leggott and Cockerill were shepherd lads who signed up together for the First World War, and whose deaths stirred particularly deep local feeling. Leggott is believed to have perished on the Somme, and Cockerill, a victim of gas poisoning, suffered a lingering death after the war. At the unveiling of Commondale's official war memorial, a cross in the village centre, Lord Gisborough, owner of the local estate, commented: 'I won't mention names, but you will know of one gallant lad who walked miles across the moors to tell one of his pals that he felt he must go as his country called him. That is the spirit that has made England great.'

Locals believe the 'gallant lad' was probably Cockerill, of Maddy House Farm, Commondale. His friend Alf, also Commondale-born, had moved with his family to Round Close Farm, Guisborough. Erected by Lord Gisborough shortly after he unveiled the official memorial in 1921, their memorial stone is said by some to mark the point on the moors where the lads, both believed to have been younger than the official recruiting age of seventeen-and-a-half, jointly agreed to

A Bilsdale 'turve' stone, one of line defining a turve-cutting strip.

The Tyreman stone - a family record by a Snilesworth farmer.

221

A tragic brickmaker - the George Watson suicide stone, with, below, its inscription.

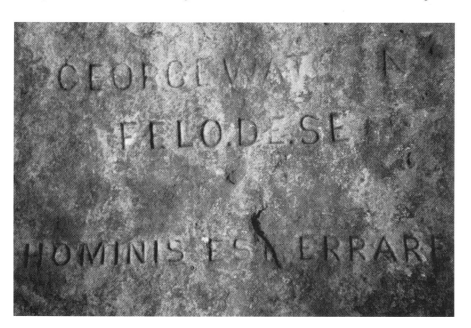

enlist. Others say the stone stands where the lads often met when tending their neighbouring flocks. From 1985 to 1996 veterans of the Northumbria Branch of the Grenadier Guards' Association made an annual summertime pilgrimage to the stone, where they stood in silent homage and laid poppies. With the trek now too demanding for the veterans, it would be gratifying if a younger generation of ex Guardsmen, perhaps with a contingent of serving soldiers, revived this admirable recent custom.

But probably the most puzzling engraved stone rests in Snotterdale. A small gill off Scugdale, this is jokingly said to have gained its unpleasant name when an Ordnance Survey man asked a farmer what the dale was called, and was told: 'It's not a dale.'

Near its head is an old jet mine, safe to enter with care. Further down, near the foot of some crags, lies a sandstone slab whose whose top side bears the following runic-like lines:

A further hieroglyphic on a side of the stone appears like this:

ESTOMⅡUF
Ⅱii

Someone once suggested to me that the inscription begins: 'Thomas in-ye-ling'. But a more credible reading of the main inscription is: 'Thomas Meynell Aedit [guarded this place] 1581'. Snotterdale was probably part of the hunting estate of the Meynell family, based at nearby Whorlton Castle. Perhaps some challenge to their ownership, or persistent poaching, led them to erect the stone - a medieval No Trespassing sign.

The firmer style of the other inscription suggests it was carved by a different hand. The words could be: 'Est Omnus Nil' - 'All Is Nothing.' If so, this presumably meant that whatever the stone had symbolised in the past - most probably the wealth and power of the Meynells - had come to naught. Like the carver of the FOXHUNTERS stone, whoever engraved this message had to go well off the beaten track to do so. Proof yet again of the extraordinary urge of moorland folk to 'say it in stone.'

Commondale Shepherds' Stone.

INDEX